ABOUT
PSYCHOLOGY

SUNY series,

ALTERNATIVES IN PSYCHOLOGY

Michael A. Wallach

Editor

ABOUT PSYCHOLOGY

Essays at the Crossroads of
History, Theory, and Philosophy

DARRYL B. HILL

MICHAEL J. KRAL

Editors

STATE UNIVERSITY OF NEW YORK PRESS

Published by
State University of New York Press
Albany

© 2003 State University of New York

For information, address
State University of New York Press
90 State Street, Suite 700, Albany, NY 12207

Production, Laurie Searl
Marketing, Jennifer Giovani-Giovani

Library of Congress Cataloging-in-Publication Data

About psychology : essays at the crossroads of history, theory, and philosophy / Darryl
B. Hill and Michael J. Kral, editors.
    p. cm. — (SUNY series, alternatives in psychology)
    Includes bibliographical references and index.
    ISBN 0-7914-5703-6 (alk. paper) — ISBN 0-7914-5704-4 (pbk. : alk. paper)
    1. Psychology—Philosophy.   I. Hill, Darryl B., 1963– II. Kral, Michael J.,
1956– III. Series.

BF38.A28 2003
150'.1—dc21   2002075879

10 9 8 7 6 5 4 3 2 1

CONTENTS

Acknowledgments

It is because their definitions are less than clear and increasingly overlapping that bringing history, philosophy, and psychology to a common ground becomes timely and important. Their differences become even less apparent when in critical dialogue. The inspiration for this book came from our experience as past editors of the *History and Philosophy of Psychology Bulletin*, the journal/newsletter of the Section on History and Philosophy of Psychology of the Canadian Psychological Association (CPA). We produced a special issue of the *Bulletin* in 1996 on the convergence of history and philosophy in psychology, in part to explore the rationale behind the name of that publication. We have now invited a larger group of authors to join these reflections on convergence. We are grateful to our colleagues in the History and Philosophy Section of the CPA for creating and continuing the forum for the exchange of ideas about psychology at annual meetings and in the *Bulletin*. The discipline of psychology has been undergoing a self-examination, looking at its relationship to other disciplines and to the currents of theory flowing through the social and human sciences, over the past several decades. It is vital to continue to place this thinking in print. We are privileged to locate this volume in State University of New York Press's Alternatives in Psychology series, and we thank Senior Editor Jane Bunker for guidance.

Michael Kral would like to acknowledge the Department of Anthropology at Yale University for providing him with the opportunity as a research affiliate to complete this book in an environment *sin qua non* for the pursuit of knowledge. Kral was also supported by the Bicentennial Professorship Fund of the Canadian Studies Committee, Yale Center for International and Area Studies.

Darryl Hill would like to thank his colleagues and students at Hobart and William Smith Colleges and Concordia University.

We both gratefully acknowledge our student and faculty colleagues at the Department of Psychology, University of Windsor.

CHAPTER ONE

CONVERGENCE AND CONJUNCTION AT THE CROSSROADS

Darryl B. Hill and Michael J. Kral

THE SOCIAL AND HUMAN SCIENCES are undergoing a conceptual transformation. While some of this change is taking place in the method and focus of research, at this time most of it is located in the realm of ideas concerning the theory, history, and philosophy of the human condition. There has been a shifting over the last century, and especially during the latter half of the 20th century, from a classical science approach to a more hermeneutic mode of thinking about the study and understanding of people. Rabinow and Sullivan (1979) describe this interpretive turn in the social sciences as refocusing attention onto "the concrete varieties of cultural meaning, in their particularity and complex texture," where cultural meaning is "intersubjective and irreducibly fundamental to understanding" (p. 5). Modeling themselves after the hard sciences, the social sciences have reached a limit to understanding. By looking across disciplines and into other epistemologies, a rethinking has swept the social sciences. "Re-thinking is the order of the day" (p. xvii), according to Goodman and Fisher (1995), who point out that the overarching problem is one of knowledge: its meaning, values, methods of inquiry, and applications.

Toulmin (1988, 1995) argues that Western epistemology has remained largely unchanged since Descartes's influence in the mid-17th century. He shows how the Cartesian program of modern Enlightenment has been based on three assumptions: the locus of knowledge is personal and individual, not public or collective; knowledge must accommodate itself to the knower's physiological mechanisms, to the "inner theater" of the brain; and the building blocks of knowledge must take the form of a demonstrably certain deductive method (e.g., classical geometry). This belief remained unchanged up until the second half of the 20th century. Toulmin maintains that we are returning to a pre-Enlightenment practical philosophy with less emphasis on written, universal, general, and timeless values and an increased focus on the oral, particular, local, and timely. Ritzer and Smart (2001) describe social theory as "almost constantly in flux . . . characterized by transformation and uncertainty" (p. 4). They argue that the most prevalent themes in current social theory include innovation, retrieval/rediscovery, translation, reinterpretation, and changing intellectual priorities and social conditions. Perhaps we are in the midst of Alexander's (1995) "epistemological dilemma," trying to separate the knower from the known, or Nagel's (1986) "view from nowhere," trying to reconcile subjectivity and objectivity. This shifting toward practical philosophy has taken place across the social sciences, upsetting much of their territorial spaces and resulting in debate, polarization, sometimes ridicule, and, more recently, dialogue.

Psychology, too, has begun to feel this movement. Some, like Smith, Harré, and Van Langenhove (1995), believe that psychology is similarly "in a state of flux" (p. 1), and they refer to a new psychology, a new paradigm encompassing such ideas as subjectivity, meaning, interpretation, language and discourse, holism, context, and particularities. While such stirrings are certainly taking place, we would argue that they are still highly marginalized within academic psychology. Most of the authors in Tolman's (1992) collection find that positivism is still strong in the discipline, a situation that seems not to have abated. Hatfield (1995) indicates that psychology was remade into a natural science (natural philosophy) from the beginning of the 18th century in a historical narrative that defines scientific psychology as quantitative and experimental. This narrative continues, as Manicas (1987) argues that most psychology is "fully committed to the autonomy of the cognitive life" (p. 315) rather than to a more socially conceived approach to the mind.

There has been some cost to psychology's insularity. For example, psychology is often not included among the social sciences. In Mazlish's (1998) philosophical history of the human sciences, which includes the social sciences, psychology is given "uneasy entrance" as it "teeters" (p. 11) between the natural and human sciences. Manicas (1987) mentions psychology in passing when he discusses the social sciences, as if to remind readers that it might have a place there. Recent books on the historic turn in the human sciences have largely ignored psychology (e.g., Ankersmit and Kellner, 1995; Cohen and Roth, 1995; Goodman and Fisher, 1995; McDonald, 1996). Likewise, works in the philosophy of psychology are typically centered within the discipline of philosophy rather than psychology, and they rarely draw on contemporary psychological discourse (e.g., MacDonald and MacDonald, 1995; O'Donohue and Kitchener, 1996a). What we hope to accomplish with the current chapter, as well as with the contributions that follow, is to restate a form of psychology, rethought as a social science, sensitive to historical, philosophical, and theoretical turns. Giddens (1990) notes that, at this historical moment, the social sciences are called to respond to the moving of modernity. In this book we argue for psychology to join in this response.

HISTORICAL TURNS

It is apparent to many that the social sciences are experiencing a resurgence in historical interests. Areas of study such as the new historicism, history of philosophy, ethnohistory, and historical sociology have ascended in recent years. The new history, however, is not a social sciences (i.e., Cartesian) program but approaches the past from multiple perspectives (see Jenkins, 1991). Ross (1998) describes "a succession of 'new histories'" during the 20th century and the "newest" new history as "the diffusion of historicism across disciplinary boundaries into the humanities and social sciences," forming a "new alliance between history and theory" (p. 100). Typical of this perspective, Cohen (1997) distinguishes between event, experience, and myth in the analysis of historical subjects. The discipline of history is experiencing conceptual, political, methodological, and practical crises of representation (Kral and Hill, 1996). Some of this "essential tension" comes from the meeting of history, theory, and philosophy, and the subsequent problems of objectivity, evidence, truth, context, teleology, concepts/categories, method, and interpretation (Stanford, 1998).

As a result of history's incursion into these other realms, some interesting questions arise. New historians shun historical truths, instead looking for historical rewrites and making the historian's "lens" itself more visible. Some, for instance Kellner (1995), are beginning to contemplate a new vision for history:

> It is that history can be redescribed as a discourse that is fundamentally rhetorical, and that representing the past takes place through the creation of powerful, persuasive images which can be best understood as created objects, models, metaphors or proposals about reality. (p. 2)

Encouraging a new cultural history, Hunt (1989) argues that "[d]ocuments describing past symbolic actions are not innocent, transparent texts; they were written by authors with various intentions and strategies, and historians of culture must devise their own strategies for reading them" (p. 14). She more recently calls for historical study to consider the interplay of intersubjectivity, aesthetics, cognition, and politics (Hunt, 1998). Some of this echoes Ware (1940), who called, some time ago, for interdisciplinary convergence and for new intellectual tools and historical methods.

Many of psychology's historians have been inspired by Foucault's (1971/1977) genealogical approach to history. As Kral and Hill (1996) argue, Foucault's genealogy identifies discursive discontinuity and dispersion, tries to undo the view of history as continuous, and emphasizes the material conditions of discourse—such as institutions, political events, economic practices, and the operations of power—as they affect the body, knowledge, and subjectivity. His historical project shows how power impinges upon historical subjects, documents events without finality, and opposes the search for the "timeless and essential secret" (Foucault, 1971/1977, p. 146). If this is the case, Hamilton (1996) is correct: "[w]e should therefore expect the process of understanding the past to be as unending as is the future" (p. 18). Historical work in psychology has already joined in this critical perspective, as Harris (1997) and others argue for knowledge of critical historical methods and thinking within psychology, lest it promote its own simplistic histories.

These and other conceptual, political, methodological, and practical crises have, borrowing from Berkhofer (1995), placed Clio, the muse of history, at a crossroads. In this sense, history becomes a hermeneutic enterprise, entering into and borrowing from the humanities, anthropology, and cultural studies (e.g., Hamilton, 1996). This blurring of disciplinary boundaries is moving many from the mere "history of" a discipline, written primarily from within, to "history and," converging disciplines with history and historiography (see Cohen and Roth, 1995).

THEORETICAL AND PHILOSOPHICAL TURNS

There is nothing new about theory and philosophy in psychology. Is it not an old story that psychology was once simply natural philosophy and its founders eminent philosophers? For a long time now, theory has been something logical positivists have used to explain observations after the fact, while avoiding the more speculative. That is, if theory in psychology was ever allowed a place at the table. Philosophy was the domain of philosophers, eagerly shunned by empiricists wishing to get on with the description of observed reality. Yet there has probably always been an undercurrent of interest in theoretical and philosophical issues in psychology. For instance, *Philosophy of Psychology* is the title of books appearing throughout the last 25 years (e.g., Block, 1981; Brown, 1974; Bunge and Ardila, 1987; Margolis, 1984; Robinson, 1985), a tradition that continues (MacDonald and MacDonald, 1995; O'Donohue and Kitchener, 1996a).

So how can we claim that there is currently a theoretical and philosophical turn in psychology? Many point to the recent rise in journals (e.g., *Theory & Psychology*) and books (e.g., Kukla, 2001) as well as doctoral psychology programs dedicated to theoretical psychology. One line of reasoning is that psychologists have only returned to theory and philosophy after a period of absence during the heyday of behaviorism and logical positivism in the first half, and especially the middle, of the 20th century (O'Donohue and Kitchener, 1996b). During this period, the philosophy of psychology was relegated to a marginal position within psychology and studied mostly by philosophers, a pattern that continues to this day (see O'Donohue and Kitchener, 1996a). A key to our argument about psychology taking a theoretical and philosophical turn is recognizing just what kind of theory and philosophy is currently being used and how. The theories that psychologists are turning to are not embedded in specific domains of inquiry (e.g., attribution theory) but more general and broad perspectives (i.e., cognitive theory, as constructed by Bem and de Jong, 1997). In this sense, psychology has been turning to grander meta-theories such as feminism, poststructuralism, social constructionism, and postmodernism (Smith, Harré, and Van Langenhove, 1995). The influx of postmodernism into psychology (e.g., Kvale, 1992) should be understood as part of a more recent general interest with postmodernism in the social and human sciences in the early 1990s (e.g., Doherty, Graham, and Malek, 1992; Hollinger, 1994; Rosenau, 1992). This philosophical and theoretical turn has led to a concern and critique of the epistemological, ontological, and moral/ethical assumptions underlying modern psychology.

THE CROSSROADS AND BEYOND

Like the other human and social sciences, psychology is "turning" increasingly to history, theory, and philosophy as serious endeavors unto themselves while scholars reflect on psychology's current identity and location among the disciplines. Yet few books on psychology explicitly address these three areas together. The newer calls for a theoretical psychology, while grounded in philosophy, have yet to address the place of history within its frame (e.g., Bem and de Jong, 1997; Faulconer and Williams, 1990; Kvale, 1992). However, an increasing number of psychologists are relying on developments from history, theory, and philosophy in their work. We believe that this calls for a consideration of their confluence in psychology.

Admittedly, many in academic psychology do not see the point. The general avoidance of theory, history, and philosophy in the writing and practice of psychology has long been evident. The teaching of the "philosophy of" or "history of" psychology in psychology departments is usually relegated to the fourth year of undergraduate work, if it is taught at all, and is often lost in graduate programs. Many academics shy away from theory in their work. Most "theories" in psychology are relevant to only a specific domain or content issue and should be best called frameworks or models, not theories (Slife and Williams, 1997). The history of psychology is also usually packaged in self-contained courses for the senior psychology under- graduate or graduate student but otherwise avoided. There are even explicit institutional sources of discouragement. One such example is the *Publication Manual of the American Psychological Association* (American Psychological As- sociation, 2001). It instructs authors to review theoretical implications and previous work "in a paragraph or two" (p. 16). As far as the history of a concept, it offers this advice: "Discuss the literature, but do not include an exhaustive historical review" (p. 16). It suggests that one should provide "an appropriate history" but avoid works of "general significance" (p. 16). These are clear signs that psychology's positivist approach eschews history, theory, and certainly philosophy.

Thus for many in our discipline, historical explorations of Joseph Breuer's psychology or philosophical explorations of Immanuel Kant's phi- losophy may be intellectually useful but practically useless. Those who in- tegrate philosophy, theory, and history within psychology have the opposite opinion. By and large, it is purpose and function that drive many to what we call "the crossroads" and beyond. What we see happening with psychology's turn to history, theory, and philosophy is not just intellectual play. Such efforts are not practically useless but practical history, theory, and philosophy.

As we contemplate the crossing of history, theory, and philosophy in contemporary Western psychology, in this era of interdisciplinary commu- nication and blurring of academic genres, we focus on several basic ques- tions. What forces are at work in pulling these areas together or keeping them disparate within psychology? How are the borders between these interests maintained and transgressed? What are some potentials and perils of crossing these boundaries? The convergences and divergences on these issues form an agenda for future psychologists working at the intersection of history, philoso- phy, and theory and developing an interdisciplinary psychology.

Considering current thoughts on the uses of history, theory, and phi- losophy in psychology, along with the chapters that follow, we have iden- tified what we think are three key arenas of convergence being studied by those working in these endeavors: a reexamination of context in modern psychology, broad considerations of the morality, values, and politics of cur- rent psychology, and integrating theory, history, and philosophy in psycho- logical practice.

CONSIDERING CONTEXT

One of the central themes in current writing is contextualization. What is context, why is it so crucial, and is it crucial for all? We see context as the events pertaining to a person or persons. This broadly encapsulates such immediate effects as interpersonal behaviors and more general structures such as roles, race, history, and culture. When psychology considers its topics, conducts its research, and publishes its findings, how much is context a factor? If context is important, as few would deny, what do we do with it, and how do we account for it? Moreover, if context is important, then how generalizable are the things we construct and study?

The emerging field of cultural studies represents one way in which the humanities are refocusing on context. Cultural studies, however, has all but ignored psychology. A brief purview of some main reviews of cultural studies (e.g., Culler, 1999; During, 1993; Grossberg, Nelson, and Treichler, 1992) reveals very few chapters on psychological topics and none written by psychologists. But there are exceptions. There are many references to Chodorow, Irigaray, and Lacan, such as Penley's (1992) analysis of homoerotic imagery in Star Trek fanzines based on Chodorow's psychoanalytic theory. However, these are marginal figures in contemporary North American academic psychology. At first glance, the *Culture and Psychology Reader* (Goldberger and Veroff, 1995) offers hope, but it is more accurately described as cross-cultural, cultural, or multicultural psychology, not cultural studies. The key difference is that the Goldberger and Veroff (1995) collection looks for the "role of culture" (culture as an independent variable) in various psychological constructs, whereas cultural studies is "committed to the study of the entire range of a society's arts, beliefs, institutions, and communicative practices" (Nelson, Treichler, and Grossberg, 1992, p. 4) or "the study of contemporary culture" (During, 1993, p. 1). This is the new context for psychology.

Two books appearing in 1990—one by Bruner (1990) and the other an edited volume by Stigler, Shweder, and Herdt (1990)—serve as catalysts for North American psychology to ask questions from a very different angle, with historical antecedents in writers such as Vico, Dilthey, and Wundt with his "Volkerpsychologie" (Shweder, Goodnow, Hatano, LeVine, Markus, and Miller, 1998). Shweder and colleagues (1998) define cultural psychology as "the investigation of both the psychological foundations of cultural communities and the cultural foundations of mind" (p. 867), such that "the study of the way culture, community, and psyche become coordinated and make each other possible" (p. 868). In the first prominent appearance of an article on this subject in the *Annual Review of Psychology*, cultural psychology is viewed as a "project designed to reassess the uniformitarian principle of psychic unity (which its authors associate with cross-cultural psychology) and aimed at the development of a credible theory of psychological pluralism" (Shweder and Sullivan, 1993, p. 498). The units of analysis for a cultural psychology include conscious and unconscious "mentalities, folk models, practices, situated cognitions, and ways of life" (Shweder et al., 1998, p. 872). Borrowing from Vygotsky, cultural psychology sets out to account for the psychic internalization of culture. Theoretical work is currently examining both innate and sociocultural constraints on the mind, and the field of cultural psychology is viewed as interdisciplinary rather than merely a subarea of psychology (see Shweder, 1999).

Particulars and Universals

Many psychologists might take the side of "the particulars," that the specifics of any given context shape and influence the phenomenon observed, so that the focus is on certain populations, or even individuals, rather than pan-human universals. Sure, these psychologists admit, general principles may eventually be derived from the particulars, but we are nowhere near figuring out what these universals are or how they operate contextually. Moreover, if we ever hope to come up with theories and models that work well in specific contexts, we need models and theories that are sophisticated enough to account for variations in circumstance. For example, Danziger's chapter reflects on the state of history in psychology and urges us to consider how the meaning of psychological objects is created within specific historical contexts.

Seeley is no doubt a proponent of looking for particulars. Her chapter on cultural turns in psychology leaves the reader with the sense that the universal truths psychology seeks cannot be found because of cultural variations in human experience. That is, human concerns are grounded in local and particular circumstances. She identifies the reasoning underlying psychology's search for universals as ethnocentric logic. As such, psychology's ethnocentric logics "compromise [psychology's] ability to speak with authority and impartiality about human behavior." Clearly, Seeley questions universalizing claims, wondering who these claims address.

Kimball's chapter is also primarily concerned with the particulars, the historical and political circumstances that contribute to conceptions of gender. Moreover, she argues that critiques of these gender models arise out of particular historical circumstances, both inside and outside the academy. She also cautions us that each critique has strengths and limitations in its own particular contexts. Thus, at least for gender, such highly contextualized limits make generalizability a distant possibility.

While a focus on particulars dominates work in history and theory, the authors in this book who are more philosophical seem inclined to work with universals. These theorists admit local context is important, but this does not dissuade them from speculating about the generalities that we may all share, or at least from lamenting the loss of universalism. So some, such as Tolman, remain optimistic about the attainment of a common good, a social consensus on what is "good," while Martin and Sugarman try to articulate what is essential, fundamental, and universal to the self. The sense is that, yes, we need to understand context, yet we also need to be looking at generalities. The search for a middle ground is a current theme in the human and social sciences. A challenge for psychology is the development of knowledge concerning a meeting ground for psychic unity, human plurality, and the varieties of contextualization. A number of scholars argue that the post–postmodern period will be one of reconciliation between classical science and hermeneutic epistemologies, with a serious reconsideration of the former (e.g., Alexander, 1995; Hunt, 1998; Mazlish, 1998; McDonald, 1993).

MORALITY/POLITICS/VALUES

The second key convergence that we have identified in historical, theoretical, and philosophical psychology is a concern with the morality, politics, and values underlying psychology. By morality, we mean a general concern for "good" along with the agency to choose what we believe is "good." Tolman's chapter contends that psychology is a moral enterprise, since "no human endeavor can be free of moral liability." Indeed, moral judgement is at the heart of our most valued scholarly practices. Reflections on the moral vision of psychology question what exactly is it that contemporary psychology is trying to achieve?

Early writers on this topic, such as Sullivan (1984), explicitly note that there had been very little critical reflection on the aims of psychology, but that this had changed substantially since the 1960s. That said, many of the early criticisms came from outside psychology. For example, philosopher Charles Taylor (1989) inspired many psychologists seeking to connect morality to the study of the self. Taylor highlights the interconnection between notions of selfhood, identity, and goodness. His comments such as "To know who I am is a species of knowing where I stand" (p. 27), and "In order to have a sense of who we are, we have to have a notion of how we have become, and of where we are going" (p. 47) rang true with many psychologists. Moreover, Taylor's clear explication of the need for agency, and therefore moral choice, in accounts of "the self" was a wake-up call that could not be ignored by those inside (theoretical or philosophical) psychology. Indeed, self theorists (at least philosophically minded ones) have been debating the moral self ever since.

Critics within psychology have also developed a wide-ranging agenda for a new critical psychology. Drawing on European concerns with "bourgeois psychology"—and its focus on prediction and control—critics accuse psychology of absolving commitments to challenge oppressive societal arrangements in psychological practices (Tolman, 1991; Tolman and Maiers, 1991). Certainly as a largely positivist science, psychology is predicated on the search for truth, but without any contemplation on the role of "vested-interests" in the creation of that truth or how some might be oppressed by such "truths" (Maiers, 1991). By the mid-1990s, Prilleltensky (1994) leveled a damning challenge to practices throughout psychology's sub-disciplines. Prilleltensky characterizes psychology as perpetuating inherently conservative, and even regressive, tendencies by upholding a status quo that exploits vulnerable groups in Western culture. Moreover, by claiming a neutral, apolitical, and anti-ideological stance, psychology unwittingly supports the existing social order, which continues to oppress and marginalize those without power.

These impulses, a relatively new endeavor in psychology, are gathering momentum and may perhaps reach "critical mass," despite their own marginalized position within psychology. Those psychologists contributing to a moral/critical turn are just beginning to establish an agenda for the revisioning of psychology. Fox and Prilleltensky (1997) explicitly direct psychologists to work on the "welfare of oppressed and vulnerable individuals and groups" (p. 1) by challenging disempowering theories and practices of psychologists. A recent collection of writings by critical psychologists shows that psychology's contributions to a just society may be starting to take on a wider appeal (Sloan, 2001). However, questions about this recent program remain. If psychology is not value-neutral, what values does it hold? Are there universal moral principles to which we can ascribe, or is morality inherently positioned? How can psychology, with its overtly individualistic focus, account for power and social factors (Mather, 2000)? A critical turn, as well as broader reflections on the morality of psychological theories and practices, is definitely underway, but many issues have yet to be resolved.

In addition to moral discourse, political concerns are being addressed in many areas of psychology, most notably in feminist psychology. Many of the themes discussed thus far in this introduction are complemented by feminist turns in psychology. Feminist criticisms of psychology begin with the premise that psychology has been gender-biased (Sherif, 1994; Wilkinson, 1997). Critics argue that mainstream psychology often has neglected the study of women and women's activities in favor of men's lives (Nicholson, 1995). Thus feminist criticisms challenge not only the content of knowledge but the way in which psychological knowledge is understood, produced, and ordered (Nicholson, 1995).

Feminist theories, like critical psychology, reinforce the claim that psychological research can be an instrument of oppression. Psychology's methods, largely positivistic and empirical, have failed their emancipatory potential, subordinating women (Lather, 1991). In other words, psychology functions to maintain power structures and practices that often exclude and oppress women (Burman, 1990). For many feminists, the most contentious issue is the claim that science is objective and neutral. Some feminist critiques of science contend that scientific epistemology is governed by an androcentric ideology hiding its interests behind objectivity (Burt and Code, 1995; Harding, 1986). Within psychology, in particular, Nicholson (1995) identifies three ways in which the assumption of objectivity manifests. First, experimental psychology focuses on the behavior of the research participant rather than people in their social, subjective, and cultural contexts. This stripping of context creates artificially autonomous entities. Second, experiments are often conducted by male researchers who interact with mostly male participants. Thus psychological research takes place in a context that disadvantages women. Third, psychological science is constructed and reproduced in a culture that subordinates women.

In response to these criticisms, feminist psychologists propose a variety of resolutions. Some seek remedial solutions, hoping to make science less gender-biased, but others seek more transformative gender-fair methods (Morawski, 1997). Transformative methods are situated and embedded in context, relational (in terms of a place in a social order), and sensitive to moral implications, personal awareness, and social context, especially in terms of how power relations such as gender contribute to subjectivity (Morawski, 1997).

Insides and Outsides
For many in this book, discussions of the morals, politics, and values of psychology involve talk of insides and outsides. This discourse debates where morals reside and values are enacted: interior or exterior to the individual, in the personal or social realms, within value systems or outside value systems? Consider Tolman for a moment. In an analysis of the "moral enterprise" that we call psychology, he contends that we must be able to deduce some sense of good. Tolman grounds his moral foundation, the essence of morality, in social action. Yet when he considers the different kinds of "goods" that exist, he proposes that the relationship between universal and individual goods is logical—one can be deduced from the other. In this sense, morals are shaped in the outside world, in social action, but we must deduce them from our interior logic.

Insides and outsides also infuse Martin and Sugarman's chapter on self theory. They find that sociocultural considerations in the nature of self and personhood have unnecessarily ignored more "ontologically prior" elements of personhood. These ontologically prior components include an identifiable, agentic, embodied human being. This is a conception of personhood with morality at its heart, consistent with Taylor, based on an essentially agentic moral being, able to choose a direction in life. But these moral elements, for Martin and Sugarman, are ontologically prior to the self, perhaps existing in the society and then internalized into the person, an outside becoming an inside.

In contrast to Martin and Sugarman's quest for self essences, Greer's genealogical analysis of the self asserts that some of the foundational bases of selfhood—agency, intentionality, and moral choice—have been abandoned by contemporary self psychology. Indeed, the self, as it is constructed in psychology, does not have a person inside, largely because it was stripped away by positivistic methods (see Smythe, 1998).

Lastly, inside/outside organizes the debate reviewed by Slife, Fisher Smith, and Burchfield in their chapter on values in psychotherapy. Are values an intrinsic aspect (inside) of psychotherapy, or can psychologists "step outside" values in their practice? Starting from the allegation that clinical, counseling, and applied psychologists may be "crypto-missionaries," converting their clients to their own values, Slife and colleagues explore different philosophical assumptions underlying values in psychotherapy and historically important theoretical developments in research on values in psychotherapy. Given several problems in the basic assumptions of each approach, Slife and colleagues arrive at the conclusion that it is impossible for psychotherapy to be value-free. If therapy cannot surpass values, if the "talking cure" is really the "talking mission," then what are we to do? They arrive at the philosophy of hermeneutics as a solution. From their perspective, values are inside us, so dialogue—externalizing values—may be one possible way of interrelating values.

DOING PHILOSOPHY, THEORY, AND HISTORY IN PSYCHOLOGY

The last convergence pertains to those who build conjunctions between history, theory, and philosophy in psychology. They use this interdisciplinary inquiry toward a particular goal. Moreover, they face barriers and obstacles integrating insights from this study into their work.

Uses

At first glance it may seen obvious how to use theory, philosophy, and history in psychology. Simply review the theory that pertains to your concept, perhaps see what philosophers have to say about it (or connect it to relevant ideas), and try to conceptualize the history of the topic, including the historical context in which it emerges. According to Danziger, we must consider history, since theory alone fails to account for the "biography of objects." Historical forces—including material and nondiscursive—are central to the construction of a concept. His is a call to examine the historical nature of psychological objects and how "institutionalized practices or discursive traditions" influence this history, while emphasizing the mutability and incoherence of objects.

Other considerations are also involved. Many authors in this book use history, theory, or philosophy to develop and articulate a critical challenge to mainstream psychology. Slife and colleagues are probably the most explicit in their uses of theory, philosophy, and history. In their hands, history provides "perspective illumination," theory examines underlying assumptions and tensions, and philosophy reveals the meta-frameworks of positions. Ultimately—at least for Slife and colleagues—philosophy, in the form of hermeneutics, is a solution for understanding values in psychotherapy, but one also could easily envision other dimensions playing a crucial role.

Kimball's chapter on how political challenges to conceptions of gender have influenced the theory of gender in psychology, and how these theories have been resisted by events in historical contexts, is also instructive. Her work can be, consistent with Danziger, a biography of the psychological object we call "gender." Although Kimball's analysis is optimistic that further radical critiques of gender are now possible, since these critics do not use the concepts and language of the majority, they have less impact. Moreover, we take the lesson from cultural psychology such as that reviewed by Seeley: if we do not consider context, which ultimately circumscribes generality, we are missing the point.

The critical perspective certainly becomes clear with Stam's analysis of the two histories of the 1970s' crisis in social psychology. Traditional historical accounts partition the crisis into one isolated point in time, lay to rest the contestations of the day, and have a minimal impact on theory in psychology. Critical histories, however, assert that these issues have always been with us, question boundaries between social psychology and sociology, and show how basic social psychological theories are historical. Thus while traditional histories often substantiate disciplinary boundaries and theoretical stasis, critical histories point to the historical nature of theory and the illusory nature of disciplinary boundaries.

Barriers and Obstacles
Recent work on the history, theory, and philosophy of psychology encounters many barriers and obstacles. If the above arguments are accurate, then, as Tolman asserts in his chapter, unless psychology comprehends the moral dimensions of its theories and alters its concepts to account for human needs and interests, it will distort and mislead us about human experience. This is most certainly the argument of self theorists, as Greer and Martin and Sugarman illustrate in this book. But others urge caution in this quest for the moral dimensions of humanity. In the very least, cultural psychologists (e.g., Seeley) warn against any hegemonic or universalizing claims to moral knowledge. However, it is likely this quest for human interests is incompatible with the methods of mainstream psychological research (e.g., Greer).

Kimball's chapter is more explicit than most about the barriers and obstacles that theoretical innovators face when they consider gender. A major barrier is that theoretical articulations are often so critical of dominant ideology or practices that they are rejected by the majority of the discipline. Critiques cannot be incorporated into the existing theoretical framework, a framework in which many have much invested. Moreover, politically driven critiques often challenge even the most basic of assumptions—such as the naturality of gender—so they are rejected without question. Or, as Stam so eloquently summarizes: there are those who wish to perpetuate the status quo, and they will resist critical histories that question boundaries, both disciplinary and theoretical.

The relationship between theory and practice becomes a crucial item in the future agenda of psychologists working at the crossroads of these inquiries. Some believe that making theory is a social practice. In their chapters both Tolman and Danziger write about "social practices" that are inherently moral, theoretical, and historical. For Tolman, social practices—socially cooperative efforts—are necessarily moral, because they are fundamentally human enterprises, as is psychology. Thus it may be through practice that we ultimately understand a common good (see Bourdieu 1977). Greer's chapter is blunt about this: disciplinary practices—power/knowledge relations among researchers, practitioners, and the consumers of psychological knowledge—create theoretical concepts in both their methodological and investigative forms. Thus the self, like other constructs in psychology, is the product of social practices. However, often it is the case that such theoretical conceptions are at odds with the methods used to study them, as is the case in self research. So another challenge is making disciplinary practices consistent with theoretical assertions. Yet there are reasons to be pessimistic: for example, cultural psychology has had only a limited impact on psychological concepts and practices (e.g., Seeley).

CONCLUSION

While psychologists have always worked with history, theory, and philosophy, currently something different is going on. At this point in time, psychology is undergoing a radical reconsideration. Returning to Toulmin (1995), we are reminded of the Kuhnian paradigm shift:

> At the end of the century, we have the same tasks that faced European thinkers in the 1650s: to rebuild not merely our intellectual account of "knowledge," but also a social and political order within which epistemology will be free of the excess individualism of the Cartesian tradition. (p. xv)

The intellectual times certainly are changing, and we believe that psychology must examine closely its own epistemology, language, categories, methodologies, and the multiple turns that continue to raise questions about its own "psyche." To know psychology's frames of mind is to make explicit its options. We strongly urge psychologists to turn, actively, to these newer messages and to examine their own work and thought. It is the best of times for psychology to now passionately join forces with history, theory, and philosophy, and to see what evolves. It may not be an easy fit, but it is a necessary one. Psychology *and* history *and* theory *and* philosophy. As Geertz (1995) aptly states, "take care of the conjunctions and the nouns will take care of themselves" (p. 261).

REFERENCES

Alexander, J. C. (1995). *Fin de siècle social theory: Relativism, reduction, and the problem of reason*. London, UK: Verso.

American Psychological Association. (2001). *Publication manual of the American Psychological Association (5th Ed.)*. Washington, D.C.: Author.

Ankersmit, F. & Kellner, H. (Eds.). (1995). *A new philosophy of history*. Chicago, IL: The University of Chicago Press.

Bem, S., & de Jong, H. (1997). *Theoretical issues in psychology: An introduction*. Thousand Oaks, CA: Sage.

Berkhofer, R. F. (1995). *Beyond the great story: History as text and discourse*. Cambridge, MA: Harvard University Press.

Block, N. (Ed.). (1981). *Readings in philosophy of psychology* (Vol. 2). Cambridge, MA: Harvard University Press.

Bourdieu, P. (1977). *Outline of a theory of practice*. Cambridge, MA: Cambridge University Press.

Brown, S. C. (Ed.). (1974). *Philosophy of psychology*. New York, NY: Barnes & Noble.

Bruner, J. (1990). *Acts of meaning*. Cambridge, MA: Harvard University Press.

Bunge, M. A., & Ardila, R. (1987). *Philosophy of psychology*. New York, NY: Springer Verlag.

Burman, E. (1990). *Feminists and psychological practice*. London, UK: Sage.

Burt, S., & Code, L. (Eds.). (1995). *Changing methods: Feminists transforming practice*. Peterborough, ON: Broadview Press.

Cohen, P. A. (1997). *History in three keys: The Boxers as event, experience, and myth*. New York, NY: Columbia University Press.

Cohen, R., & Roth, M. S. (1995). *History and . . . : Histories within the human sciences*. Charlottesville, VA: University Press of Virginia.

Culler, J. (1999). What is cultural studies? In M. Bal (Ed.), *The practice of cultural analysis: Exposing interdisciplinary interpretation* (pp. 335–347). Stanford, CA: Stanford University Press.

Doherty, J., Graham, E., & Malek, M. (Eds.). (1992). *Postmodernism and the social sciences*. New York, NY: St. Martin's Press.

During, S. (Ed.) (1993). *The cultural studies reader*. New York, NY: Routledge.

Faulconer, J. E., & Williams, R. N. (Eds.). (1990). *Reconsidering psychology: Perspectives from continental philosophy*. Pittsburgh, PA: Duquesne University Press.

Foucault, M. (1977). Nietzsche, genealogy, history. In D. F. Bouchard (Ed. & Trans.) & S. Simon (Trans.), *Language, counter-memory, and practice* (pp. 139–164). Ithaca, NY: Cornell University Press. (Original work published 1971)

Fox, D., & Prilleltensky, I. (Eds.). (1997). *Critical psychology: An introduction*. Thousand Oaks, CA: Sage.

Geertz, C. (1995). History and anthropology. In R. Cohen & M. S. Roth (Eds.), *Histories and . . . : Histories within the human sciences* (pp. 248–262). Charlottesville, VA: University Press of Virginia.

Giddens, A. (1990). *The consequences of modernity*. Stanford, CA: Stanford University Press.

Goldberger, N. R., & Veroff, J. B. (Eds.). (1995). *The culture and psychology reader*. New York, NY: New York University Press.

Goodman, R. F., & Fisher, W. R. (Eds.). (1995). *Rethinking knowledge: Reflections across the disciplines*. Albany, NY: State University of New York Press.

Grossberg, L., Nelson, C., & Treichler, P. A. (Eds.). (1992). *Cultural studies*. New York, NY: Routledge.

Hamilton, P. (1996). *Historicism*. New York, NY: Routledge.

Harding, S. (1986). *The science question in feminism*. Ithaca, NY: Cornell University Press.

Harris, B. (1997). Repoliticizing the history of psychology. In D. Fox & I. Prilleltensky (Eds.), *Critical psychology: An introduction*. Thousand Oaks, CA: Sage.

Hatfield, G. (1995). Remaking the science of the mind: Psychology as a natural science. In C. Fox, R. Porter, & R. Wokler (Eds.), *Inventing human science: Eighteenth-century domains* (pp. 184–231). Berkeley, CA: University of California Press.

Hollinger, R. (1994). *Postmodernism and the social sciences*. Beverly Hills, CA: Sage.

Hunt, L. (1989). Introduction: History, culture, and text. In L. Hunt (Ed.), *The new cultural history* (pp. 1–22). Berkeley, CA: University of California Press.

Hunt, L. (1998). Postscript. In E. Domanska (Ed.), *Encounters: Philosophy of history after postmodernism* (pp. 272–276). Charlottesville, VA: University Press of Virginia.

Jenkins, K. (1991). *Re-thinking history*. London, UK: Routledge.

Kellner, H. (1995). Introduction: Describing redescriptions. In F. Ankersmit & H. Kellner (Eds.), *A new philosophy of history* (pp. 1–18). Chicago, IL: University of Chicago Press.

Kral, M. J., & Hill, D. B. (1996). Convergent trends, conjunctive turns. *History and Philosophy of Psychology Bulletin, 8*(2), 4–6.

Kukla, A. (2001). *Methods of theoretical psychology*. Cambridge, MA: Massachusetts Institute of Technology Press.

Kvale, S. (Ed.). (1992). *Psychology and postmodernism*. Newbury Park, CA: Sage.

Lather, P. (1991). *Getting smart: Feminist research and pedagogy with/in the postmodern*. New York, NY: Routledge.

MacDonald, C., & MacDonald, G. (Ed.). (1995). *Philosophy of Psychology: Debates on psychological explanation*. Cambridge, UK: Blackwell.

Maiers, W. (1991). Critical psychology: Historical background and task. In C. W. Tolman & W. Maiers (Eds.), *Critical psychology: Contributions to an historical science of the subject* (pp. 23–49). New York, NY: Cambridge University Press.

Manicas, P. T. (1987). *A history and philosophy of the social sciences*. Oxford, UK: Basil Blackwell.

Margolis, J. (1984). *Philosophy of psychology*. Englewood Cliffs, NJ: Prentice Hall.

Mather, R. (2000). The foundations of critical psychology. *History of the Human Sciences, 13*, 85–100.

Mazlish, B. (1998). *The uncertain sciences*. New Haven, CT: Yale University Press.

McDonald, L. (1993). *The early origins of the social sciences*. Montreal, Kingston, ON: McGill-Queen's University Press.

McDonald, T. J. (1996). Introduction. In T. J. McDonald (Ed.), *The historic turn in the human sciences* (pp. 1–14). Ann Arbor, MI: University of Michigan Press.

Morawski, J. (1997). The science behind feminist research methods. *Journal of Social Issues, 53*, 667–681.

Nagel, T. (1986). *The view from nowhere*. Oxford, UK: Oxford University Press.

Nelson, C., Treichler, P. A., & Grossberg, L. (1992). Cultural studies: An introduction. In L. Grossberg, C. Nelson, & P. Treichler (Eds.), *Cultural studies* (pp. 1–22). New York, NY: Routledge.

Nicholson, P. (1995). Feminism and psychology. In J. Smith, R. Harré, & L. Van Langenhove (Eds.), *Rethinking psychology* (pp. 122–142). Thousand Oaks, CA: Sage.

O'Donohue, W., & Kitchener, R. F. (Eds.). (1996a). *The philosophy of psychology*. Thousand Oaks, CA: Sage.

O'Donohue, W., & Kitchener, R. F. (1996b). Introduction. In W. O'Donohue & R. Kitchener (Eds.), *The philosophy of psychology* (pp. xiii–xix). Thousand Oaks, CA: Sage.

Penley, C. (1992). Feminism, psychoanalysis, and the study of popular culture. In L. Grossberg, C. Nelson, & P. Treichler (eds.), *Cultural studies* (pp. 479–493). New York, NY: Routledge.

Prilleltensky, I. (1994). *The moral and politics of psychology: Psychological discourse and the status quo.* Albany, NY: State University of New York Press.

Rabinow, P., & Sullivan, W. M. (1979). The interpretive turn: Emergence of an approach. In P. Rabinow & W. M. Sullivan (Eds.), *Interpretive social science: A reader* (pp. 1–21). Berkeley, CA: University of California Press.

Ritzer, G., & Smart, B. (2001). Introduction: Theorists, theories and theorizing. In G. Ritzer & B. Smart (Eds.), *Handbook of social theory* (pp. 1–9). Thousand Oaks, CA: Sage.

Robinson, D. (1985). *Philosophy of psychology.* New York, NY: Columbia University Press.

Rorty, R. (1982). *Consequences of pragmatism (Essays: 1972–1980).* Minneapolis, MN: University of Minnesota Press.

Rosenau, P. M. (1992). *Postmodernism and the social sciences.* Princeton, NJ: Princeton University Press.

Ross, D. (1998). The new and newer histories: Social theory and historiography in an American key. In Molho, A., & Wood, G. S. (Eds.), *Imagined histories: American historians interpret the past* (pp. 85–106). Princeton, NJ: Princeton University Press.

Sherif, C. W. (1994). Bias in psychology. In A. C. Herrmann & A. J. Stewart (Eds.), *Theorizing feminism: Parallel trends in the humanities and social sciences* (pp. 117–135). Boulder, CO: Westview Press.

Shweder, R. A. (1999). Why cultural psychology? *Ethos, 27,* 62–73.

Shweder, R. A., & Sullivan, M. A. (1993). Cultural psychology: Who needs it? *Annual Review of Psychology, 44,* 497–523.

Shweder, R. A., Goodnow, J., Hatano, G., LeVine, R. A., Markus, H., & Miller, P. (1998). The cultural psychology of development: One mind, many mentalities. In W. Damon & R. M. Lerner (Eds.), *Handbook of child psychology, Vol. 1: Theoretical models of human development* (5th ed.) (pp. 865–937). New York, NY: Wiley.

Slife, B. D., & Williams, R. N. (1997). Toward a theoretical psychology: Should a subdiscipline be formally recognized? *American Psychologist, 52,* 117–129.

Sloan, T. (Ed.). (2001). *Critical psychology: Voices for change.* New York, NY: St. Martin's Press.

Smith, J. A., Harré, R., & Van Langenhove, L. (1995). Introduction. In J. Smith, R. Harré, & L. Van Langenhove (Eds.), *Rethinking psychology* (pp. 1–9). Thousand Oaks, CA: Sage.

Smythe, W. E. (Ed.). (1998). *Toward a psychology of persons.* Mahwah, NJ: Laurence Erlbaum.

Stanford, M. (1998). *An introduction to the philosophy of history.* Malden, MA: Blackwell.

Stigler, J. W., Shweder, R. A., & Herdt, G. (Eds.). (1990). *Cultural psychology: Essays on comparative human development.* New York, NY: Cambridge University Press.

Sullivan, E. V. (1984). *A critical psychology: Interpretation of the personality world.* New York, NY: Plenum.

Taylor, C. (1989). *Sources of the self: The making of the modern identity.* Cambridge: Harvard University Press.

Tolman, C. W. (1991). Critical psychology: An overview. In C. W. Tolman & W. Maiers (Eds.), *Critical psychology: Contributions to an historical science of the subject* (pp. 1–22). New York, NY: Cambridge University Press.

Tolman, C. W. (Ed.). (1992). *Positivism in psychology: Historical and contemporary problems.* New York, NY: Springer-Verlag.

Tolman, C. W., & Maiers, W. (Eds.). (1991). *Critical psychology: Contributions to an historical science of the subject.* New York, NY: Cambridge University Press.

Toulmin, S. (1988). The recovery of practical philosophy. *The American Scholar, 57,* 337–352.

Toulmin, S. (1995). Forward. In R. F. Goodman & W. R. Fisher. (Eds.), *Rethinking knowledge: Reflections across the disciplines* (pp. ix–xv). Albany, NY: State University of New York Press.

Ware, C. F. (Ed.). (1940). *The cultural approach to history.* New York, NY: Columbia University Press.

Wilkinson, S. (1997). Still seeking transformation: Feminist challenges to psychology. In L. Stanley (Ed.), *Knowing Feminisms: On Academic Borders, Territories, and Tribes* (pp. 97–108). Thousand Oaks, CA: Sage.

CHAPTER TWO

WHERE HISTORY, THEORY, AND PHILOSOPHY MEET

THE BIOGRAPHY OF PSYCHOLOGICAL OBJECTS

Kurt Danziger

A RECENT VOLUME of contributions to the history of science appeared under the somewhat unusual title, *The Biographies of Scientific Objects* (Daston, 2000). The papers collected in this volume dealt with the historical trajectory of such "scientific objects" as cytoplasmic particles, the ether, culture, and economic value; in other words, objects from both the natural and the social sciences. Two of the contributions (Kaufmann, 2000; Goldstein, 2000) dealt with objects that have ended up in the domain of psychology, namely, dreams and the self. One might consider them examples of "psychological objects."

The imputation of biographies to "scientific objects" immediately raises two questions: what are scientific objects, and in what sense do they have biographies? To answer the second question first, the use of "biography" here is metaphorical. The familiar genre of biography traces the historical trajectory of individuals (Fancher, 1996). One might also trace the historical trajectory of a group of individuals, for example, humanistic psychologists or neobehaviorists. Furthermore, one can explore the historical trajectory of particular investigative practices, for example, introspection (Danziger, 1980; Lyons, 1986), psychological statistics (Danziger, 1987; Gigerenzer, 1993), experimentation (Danziger, 1990; Dehue, 1997, 2001), or forms of instrumentation (Benschop and Draaisma, 2000). Another kind of diachronic study, to which more attention has been paid recently, traces the historical trajectory of objects in the human sciences. Michel Foucault's genealogical studies (1977a, 1977b) are relatively early, though controversial, examples of this genre that had some notable echoes in the history of psychology (Rose, 1996; Smith, 1992). More recently there have been other examples, such as the one mentioned at the beginning of this chapter, that really owe little or nothing to the influence of Foucault.

What is meant by the "biography" of scientific objects is the historical study of how domains of phenomena come to be constituted as such, and how they are transformed into objects of scientific scrutiny and manipulation, how they grow and gain in saliency, and how they change with age and are eventually supplanted or given a new identity. In some cases, of course, the time of their demise has not yet arrived, so that one is describing the past of an object that is still very much with us. That applies, for example, to the two psychological objects mentioned above, dreams and the self. These are with us now, and taken for granted now, but that does not mean that they do not have a past that can be investigated.

One reason it seems odd to speak of objects, scientific or otherwise, having biographies is that our histories have been so preoccupied with the acts of individual persons that the material at which these acts were directed has been degraded to the status of mere *manipulanda*. Individual historical actors may well see them as such, and it is quite proper for their biographers to follow them. But from the broader perspective of the historian, it is clear that the objects at which individual persons direct their efforts are more than just *manipulanda*. They may be that, as far as the individual working on them is concerned, but they also exist independently of any individual's efforts. Moreover, they exist historically, that is, they change over time; the scientific object I encounter today is not the same object I would have encountered fifty years ago. The history of these changes is something quite different from the history of any one individual's contribution to these changes, no matter how significant they were.

WHAT ARE SCIENTIFIC OBJECTS?

When one speaks of "scientific objects," one makes use of the root meaning of "object" in several European languages. The meaning is one of putting against or throwing before (Daston, 2000, p.2). So scientific objects are the things that scientists confront as material to be explored, worked on, manipulated, and understood. They may believe these objects to be part of "nature," the ultimate scientific object, but historically one only encounters these objects through the medium of texts, records, and instruments. Those encountered in texts, such as scientific articles or books, are appropriately referred to as "discursive objects." They would include the gamut of scientific concepts, theories, and hypotheses. But because records, even if they are quantitative, are ultimately uninterpretable and meaningless without recourse to texts, they are usually also regarded as discursive objects. A similar argument can be made about instruments. Discursive objects have an independent existence in a discursive domain shared by numerous subjects. As such, they have a history of their own that is quite different from the history of any individual author who may have played a part in their history. A particular author's text on the ether, economic value, culture, dreams, intelligence, or emotion may be part of that author's intellectual biography, but it is also part of the history of a certain discursive object that began before this author's intervention and continued after it. This second history is a history of objects, not a history of subjects.

In the rather naively positivist older histories of psychology, the targets of psychological investigation and speculation did of course warrant a considerable amount of attention. But the model for these historical accounts was the scientific literature review. In this genre, a sharp distinction between empirical data and theoretical hypotheses or interpretations was generally maintained. That is quite justified in the context of ongoing laboratory research, where a great deal has to be kept out of view in order to make some progress on a few heavily circumscribed aspects. But for historical studies, this distinction is not productive. On the contrary, it destroys much of the value of historical studies that lies in the possibility of gaining a broader perspective on scientific work than is possible or desirable within the walls of the laboratory. From this broader perspective, it is quite apparent that there have never been any purely empirical data untainted by any theoretical framework or presupposition. There is no empirical observation that does not require some discursive interpretation to give it a communicable form, and data are not raw "findings" but careful constructions in accordance with explicit and implicit rules. While engaged in empirical work, it is usually best not to brood on these matters, or one would never get anything done. But historical studies offer an opportunity to step outside these limitations and to see the contents of science as the amalgam of theory and data that they are (Danziger, 1993). This too is implied in talk about scientific objects, for they represent a fusion of the theoretical and the empirical. Discursive, theoretical construction goes into the making of these objects, but they are always instantiated in empirical exemplars. Intelligence, for example, is a psychological object that requires a certain understanding of what is meant by the term and procedures that produce instantiations of the object in the form of test scores. Both the accepted meaning of the object and the procedures by which it is made manifest are subject to historical change. When one studies this change, one has a unique opportunity to gain insight into the intimate connection between the theoretical, procedural, and empirical elements that together constitute an object such as test intelligence.

Insofar as the older historiography of psychology was concerned with objects at all, it treated them not as discursive objects but as natural objects. It was taken for granted that the constructed categories within which psychologists conducted their research, categories such as motivation, intelligence, and personality, corresponded to objective divisions in the natural world. The historically contingent character of such divisions was not recognized. Therefore, the history of psychology could never include the history of its objects; these were timeless, though their appearance was covered by a veil. This meant that history became an account of the discoveries and errors made by individuals as they sought to unveil the true essence of the natural objects that were the focus of their investigations.

The counterpart to this naive naturalism is provided by historians who treat all scientific objects as discursive objects. When these two extremes meet, "science wars" are the likely result (Ross, 1996). However, discourse reductionism is no less problematical than the kind of naturalism that renders discourse invisible. To point out that many of the phenomena we look at in the history of the human sciences are discursive in nature is one thing; to claim that all is discourse is another. Such a claim may be all that one needs if one's historical account is to be purely descriptive, but if one wants to suggest causal interconnections, one has to go outside discourse if there is not to be a relapse into a new kind of idealism, discourse idealism. Whether this represents an advance over more traditional kinds of historical idealism is a moot point.

The tendency to absorb everything into discourse becomes particularly questionable in the case of social practices. There is little justification for doing so, except for the argument that practices can only be known in terms of some discursive description, such as "measuring," or "testing," and this anchors them firmly in the realm of discourse. But this ignores the fact that social practices are also known by their extradiscursive effects; psychological practices, for example, can affect such things as body weight, somatic functioning, pain, and an individual's physical location. These things may enter discourse, of course, but even when they do not, they are still there to be affected by various social practices. That implies an extradiscursive, material status for crucial aspects of these practices.

Both discursive and nondiscursive practices are involved in the construction of scientific objects. The use of particular verbal descriptions, or the decision to apply a particular set of mathematical symbols or visual representations, will result in a particular construction of an object. But the extradiscursive aspects of laboratory procedures also contribute to the construction of objects in one way rather than another. All social practices cannot simply be assimilated to the category of "discourse." That should be reflected in one's terminology. Referring to all scientific objects generically as "discursive objects" would imply that "all is discourse." I therefore prefer the generic term *epistemic objects* (Rheinberger, 1997), which does not commit one to an elision of the difference between discourse and practice.

Epistemic objects come in various kinds. One way of differentiating them is in terms of the kind of construction to which they owe their existence: some, such as theoretical inventions, might be the product of purely discursive practices; in others, material practices that impinge on bodies, human and nonhuman, might play the crucial role. But in most cases both kinds of practice will be involved, and what makes for distinctions among epistemic objects are the differences between different kinds of discursive and material practices. Differences in both discursive and material practices found in laboratory and clinical settings, for example, make for differences in the epistemic objects characteristic of these settings. One can also distinguish among these objects by referring to particular groups of specialists to whose investigative practices these objects owe their existence.

Among the kinds of things that contribute to the history of epistemic objects, three are particularly important. They are people, social practices, and instruments. Without people, with their interests, projects, preferences, resistances, and so on, there obviously would be no epistemic objects. However, this is not a one-way relationship. People cannot construct epistemic objects without engaging in some form of action. In the case of scientific objects, these actions take the form of particular social practices, such as experimentation, communication, engaging in theoretical discourse, and so on. They also rely on tools and instruments whose history is closely related to that of epistemic practices but is not identical to it.

THE BIOGRAPHY OF PSYCHOLOGICAL OBJECTS

What sorts of questions arise when one adopts the framework of a biography of epistemic objects? One set of questions addresses the *emergence* of such objects. We can trace the birth of the object from a time when it did not exist, or existed in a completely different form, or as something without any significance, to a time when it has become highly salient, broadly recognized and targeted in discourse and practice. The psychological object, "behavior," provides a good example of such emergence (Danziger, 1997). Right up to the late 19th century, it did not exist at all; the word "behavior" was part of a moral discourse that was the exact antithesis of the morally neutral discourse of which 20th century "behavior" was such a crucial component. One can easily follow the course of this birth that took place over just a few years at the very end of the 19th and the beginning of the 20th century. One can then inquire into the circumstances of this birth, what projects and interests propelled it onward, and what practices endowed certain interpretations of phenomena with the status of objective truths.

A second and related set of questions pertains to the critical transformations that scientific objects sometimes undergo in the course of their historical existence. To revert to the biographical analogy, like William James, we can distinguish between the once born and the twice born. Some people go through a crisis at some point in their lives from which they emerge a changed person. Occasionally, this might even happen more than once in a lifetime. Similarly, there are psychological objects that seem to have been born more than once. They can even do something people cannot do—they can have a rebirth after death. Dreams might be a good example. They were always known, of course, and endowed with all sorts of meaning, but their emergence as specifically psychological objects cannot be definitely established until the second half of the 18th century. But this baby soon sickened and, for a time, seemed to be dead. However, dreams reemerged as significant psychological objects in the discourse and practice of psychoanalysis.

But this kind of rebirth is not so common. More common is the case where an object undergoes a critical transformation without an interim period of complete oblivion. The exceptionally long biography of the object "memory" could provide several examples, but I will just mention one, very briefly. For centuries, memory was defined as an object of the inner life, intimately tied to the conscious experience of recollection. (The fact that there was also a long tradition of speculating about the physical basis of memory did not affect this definition any more than speculation about the physical basis of perception affected the status of perception as a psychological object.) Then, during roughly the last quarter of the 19th century, memory was reinvented as a biological object. A highly visible step in this transformation was an address by Hering, the eminent physiologist, to the Imperial Academy of Sciences in Vienna on the topic of *Memory As a Universal Function of Organized Matter* (Hering, 1870/1902). Essentially, what Hering proposed was an enormous expansion in the meaning of "memory," so that it could cover everything from visual recall to the inheritance of acquired characteristics, instinct, habit, and even the effects of exercising a muscle. This was not some strange, idiosyncratic notion without effect on the biography of memory. On the contrary, it was apparently a perceptive reading of current trends, for it continued to be widely echoed for many years (see, e.g., Butler, 1880). It was very much in line with the post–Darwinian wave of transforming all psychological functions into biological functions. In the case of memory, this transformation was also fostered by early medical studies of memory defects associated with brain lesions. In the late 19th century, memory as a biological object had its own name. It often was referred to as "organic memory." Quite soon, however, the implied distinction between memory as a psychological and biological object was dropped, and the biological object captured the unqualified term "memory" for itself.

The birth or rebirth of an epistemic object never takes place in a vacuum but is always embedded in a broader historical context. In the late 19th century transformation of memory, certain well-documented historical changes seem to have played a role. In key regions there was at that time a very noticeable preoccupation with a past that was rapidly being swept away by massive industrial development, urbanization, and technological development (Shore, 2001; Terdiman, 1993). This preoccupation helped establish memory as a target for scholarly and medical-scientific interest (Roth, 1989). But not everyone was preoccupied with the past in the same way. Social conservatives tended to romanticize the past as such, while those who put their faith in science and progress, being skeptical of such adumbrations, were more likely to emphasize the difference between the past as it really was and *memory* for the past that was prone to error. This fostered a special interest in memory as an object of medical-scientific inquiry. The biologizing of memory had placed it within the province of science, and henceforth it could be deployed in the campaign that those on the side of science and progress waged against the defenders of tradition (Hacking, 1995b).

These developments created the conditions under which memory could become an object for experimental psychology. That it might become such an object was by no means obvious in the late 19th century. Wilhelm Wundt, a key figure in the establishment of experimental psychology, thought that memory was a category of folk psychology that had no place in a scientific treatment of psychological problems. He considered it "analogous to a large number of other forms of mental work, such, for example, as reading, writing, counting, and using numbers for complex processes of calculation" (Wundt, 1896/1907, p. 282). For him, memory was not a fundamental psychological process but a complex effect produced by other psychological processes. He wasted little time on it. In this, he was following in the footsteps of his influential predecessor, J. F. Herbart, whose elaborate design for a scientific psychology had no place for memory which was dismissed as "an empty name" (Danziger, 2001).

However, as I have suggested, conditions at the end of the 19th century favored the emergence of memory as a scientific object. It took shape in the work of Ebbinghaus and G. É. Müller. However, their well-known technique of testing for the reproduction of memorized lists could only be regarded as a technique for investigating "memory," if memory was given a very particular meaning. Ebbinghaus (1983) explicitly considered the traditional phenomena of memory, conscious remembering, unsuitable for scientific study. But if one redefined memory as simple retention, one had an entity that *was* susceptible to objective testing without any reference to conscious experience. This redefinition of memory was eminently compatible with what Hering had proposed some years before. The conception of memory as simple retention converged nicely with the notion of memory as a biological object. Without the popularity of the latter, the Ebbinghaus version would hardly have been accepted as capturing the essence of memory. Indeed, someone like Wundt, for whom memory was not a biological object, could never regard the Ebbinghaus version as adequate.

This historical example shows an interesting interaction between a scientific object, memory, and various scientist subjects, Hering, Wundt, and Ebbinghaus (and many others I have not singled out for special mention). First of all, there were certain things everyone agreed on without question, namely, (1) that there was something objective out there that they were all writing about; (2) that this object was distinct from other objects out there; and (3) that its name was "memory." The reason they were able to take all this for granted—which people from another time and another place might not—is that they were recipients of a common discursive tradition in which memory had already featured as an independent object for many centuries. One might even go so far as to say that they were more than recipients, that they were the instruments, of this discursive tradition. But they were not entirely passive instruments. They were able to advance their own interpretation of the nature of this object they all agreed existed out there, and in doing that, they contributed something to the discursive history of this object.

These observations lead to an important generalization: although the conceptual categories, the theoretical and empirical entities, of a science such as psychology usually present themselves as quasi objects that seem to reflect an underlying reality independent of any subjects, one cannot ignore the relationship of these objects to the subjects for whom they are objects. How objects present themselves depends on the way people act in regard to them. In other words, there is an intimate relationship between social practices and the way the world is conceptualized.

DISCURSIVE OBJECTS AND THE NATURAL WORLD

Psychologists work in a world that is already divided into different kinds of objects, memories, dreams, perceptions, sensations, and selves, to mention a few. But the distinctions among these objects depend on a net of categories that enables us to identify examples of each kind of object. Without such a net the world would resemble William James's "blooming buzzing confusion." But where do these categories come from? All we can say for sure is that they are discursive categories. We use them unreflectively because of the cultural-linguistic community in which we participate. However, there are differences among such communities in the way they divide up psychological phenomena, and there are certainly historical differences in the divisions that existed at one time or another. Yet each group of language users during any historical period seems to have been convinced that its particular network of categories accurately reflected the objective organization of the world in which they lived. The problem is that if all the different networks are considered reflections of one common natural world, they cannot all be accurate reflections. Some of them must be quite wrong, others perhaps less wrong, and yet others, hopefully, correct. How do we separate the wheat from the chaff?

This is where science comes in. It is supposed to provide the categories that are as close to a correct reflection of nature as possible at any particular time. Science develops its own categories and, hence, its own objects, based on experimental procedures. Ultimately, such procedures enable us to make the link between discursive scientific objects and natural objects because of the undeniable resistance that our discursively planned interventions meet when they are imposed on the natural world (Pickering, 1995). That may work well enough in the natural sciences, but it does not work too well in most areas of psychology. The reason is that the subject matter in most psychological investigations is pliable in a way that the subject matter of the natural sciences is not. This pliability results from the fact that psychological experimenters and subjects are usually members of the same cultural-linguistic community, while the conditions of experimentation prevent the reciprocity normally found in such communities. Subjects in most psychological investigations accept a role that virtually eliminates their normal capacity for answering back. The circumscribed responses that they are allowed to make become the property of the psychologist who is free to choose or even to invent the categories in which they are to be classified. Accepting the psychologist's authority in these matters, subjects may also take over the psychologist's categories and interpret their own experience and conduct in these terms. That deprives the psychologist of the benefit that the natural scientist derives from the natural world's total indifference to the scientist's discursive world.

People construct epistemic objects, but epistemic objects also shape people. That is of particular significance for the history of psychology, a discipline that is heavily engaged in classifying people and attaching its own labels to their behavior. But when people find themselves and their actions characterized in a particular way, their self-perception and their behavior can be greatly affected. This effect has been explored by Hacking (1995a), who refers to it as the "looping effect of human kinds." Categories such as "homosexuality," "multiple personality disorder," or "post-traumatic stress syndrome" were not made up by those on whom they were bestowed as labels. They were professional constructions whose historical origins have been identified with some precision (Hacking, 1995b; Young, 1995). But once the label is accepted, it affects the way individuals make sense of their life and experience and therefore leads to new courses of action.

The pliability of its subject matter also makes it more difficult for psychology to emulate one of the crucial achievements of modern natural science, namely, the replacement of categories that are arbitrary with respect to the natural world by categories that better reflect its organization. For example, in Aristotelian physics there was a category of superlunary objects, that is, objects beyond the orbit of the moon. Such objects do exist, and theories about superlunary objects were proposed, but it turned out that the distinction between superlunary and sublunary objects had not captured any fundamental characteristic of the physical world and therefore was a hindrance rather than a help in the development of scientific physics. In modern psychology, the risk of drowning in arbitrary categories is enhanced by the ease with which artifactual phenomena can be experimentally constructed. At least the Aristotelian physicists had to take the world as they found it; the experimental psychologist can easily generate a whole domain of phenomena that is held together by nothing more than the procedures used to generate them. Take memory for lists, for example. This is a well-defined research domain, now more than 100 years old, with ever-new theories (e.g., Brown, Preece, and Hulme, 2000) dedicated to the explanation of precisely the phenomena generated within this domain. Yet it is less certain than ever that list learning is anything other than an arbitrary category quite analogous to the superlunary objects of Aristotelian physics.

The coming and going of such categories is not the story of "a mirror to nature" that yields ever-more accurate reflections but a much more mundane story of social interests, everyday practices, and human preoccupations. Categories that are formed in this way have been dubbed "relevant kinds" to distinguish them from the "natural kinds" aspired to in the natural sciences (Goodman, 1978; Hacking, 1999). This distinction is not one that yields mutually exclusive sets, however. Any given kind may turn out to be both relevant and natural. This may be true of some psychological kinds, but others, I suspect, have a "natural" basis only in the trivial sense that they presuppose biologically intact human individuals. The important thing is not to prejudge the issue, as has happened so often in the past, when both researchers and clinicians would introduce their latest pragmatic invention as though it constituted a real slice of nature that existed always and everywhere, quite independently of psychologists' professional and scientific interventions. To such claims one's response ought to be: show me. The possibility that there are such universal psychological objects should not be dismissed a priori. But, on the other hand, neither can their existence be established a priori, as has been customary in the past. To plausibly establish the existence of such objects a great deal of historical and cross-cultural work is required. Until this work is done, there should be no pretense that any psychological object has anything other than a local and temporary relevance. An established tradition of assuming the opposite simply makes it unlikely that the required work will ever be done. In the interests of a less parochial, more truly scientific psychology, the onus of the proof should be placed squarely on those who would claim the status of a truth of nature for their favorite psychological objects.

Whether psychologists' categories mirror the way the world is made up is not a question that is hugely popular in the psychological literature.

Insofar as the question surfaces at all, it does so under the heading "external validity." But this represents a disciplinary domestication of the issue, reducing it to questions that are answerable by the standard empirical and statistical techniques in vogue within the discipline of psychology. This bootstrap operation implies a very strong authority claim, namely, that the discipline has the means to adjudicate the question of whether its own cognitive products represent a reliable and true reflection of an objective reality outside the discipline. Although such a claim may serve a useful defensive function in policing the boundaries of the discipline, it is vulnerable to various criticisms.

The source of this vulnerability lies in the way disciplinary autonomy has become defined in terms of methodology. Here it is important to avoid the circularity of testing the validity of one's assumptions by employing methods that embody those very assumptions. It sometimes seems as though psychologists feel most safe from unwarranted outside intrusion when they can wrap themselves in the mantle of methodologies peculiarly their own. The trouble is that these methodologies are not particularly appropriate for throwing light on the kinds of questions that have been raised here. They are severely limited in their suitability for studying long-range effects that involve complex and unique causal systems. For the study of such effects, there is still no substitute for historical methods, including cross-cultural ones.

As an example, consider the highly significant question of investigating the effects of psychologists' interventions on their subject matter. Certainly such effects can and should be investigated in the micro-world of the psychological laboratory, and for that purpose the traditional methods of the discipline are useful, as indicated by the literature on "the social psychology of the psychological experiment." But for investigating this kind of effect in the big wide world outside the laboratory, where the effects may take the form of unique, though highly significant, events that are entangled with a multiplicity of circumstances and extend over long periods, it is still necessary to have recourse to a historical approach. Nowhere does this apply more strongly than in the study of the constructive activities, cognitive and practical, which produce the psychological objects that form the subject matter of the discipline.

PSYCHOLOGY AND ITS HISTORY

Approaching the history of psychology in terms of the biography of psychological objects has significant implications for the relationship between the discipline and its history. Traditionally, practitioners of the discipline have too often made use of a historical perspective to create two essentially false impressions, namely, that the field of psychology represents some kind of unity, and that, in spite of some ups and downs, history is a story of progress.

The very title of many texts used for pedagogical purposes conveys the impression that there is indeed a relatively coherent and unified topic known as the history of psychology, and by implication, that the field whose history this is manifests a similar coherence and unity. But how does one decide what properly belongs in a history of psychology and what does not? Potentially, the history of psychology is as broad as a history of human subjectivity in general (Richards, 1987; Smith, 1988). It might include large parts of the history of art, literature, and religion, as well as much else. If history of psychology texts tried to do justice to this potential richness, they would either lack coherence or else convey a kind of coherence that is foreign to the kind projected by a science of psychology. So the content of texts is selected in accordance with implicit criteria that enhance the appearance of coherence and historical continuity. Assumptions that currently enjoy widespread acceptance in the discipline and issues that are currently salient shape these criteria, and this easily generates an overall sense of progressive development toward the present.

There are various ways of presenting the history of psychology that help avoid these dubious effects. One way is to embed this history in the much broader history of the human sciences (Smith, 1997), but more often, constriction rather than expansion of subject matter has been the preferred route. This can be accomplished in different ways, for example, by restricting oneself to one limited period and maintaining a relatively narrow cultural focus (Reed, 1997). The use of the biographical method opens up other ways of avoiding the mirage of coherence and progress (Fancher, 1996). Yet another approach is the one suggested here. If one treats the history of psychology in terms of the history of psychological objects, one need claim no more coherence for the field than is implied by an assembly of such objects. Although, for the psychologist historian, the choice of objects is likely to be determined by their recent salience within the discipline, the emphasis on their fundamental historicity works against any unjustified narrative of progress.

In one respect, a history of scientific objects reduces the gap between science and the history of science. It does so by recognizing the phenomenal objectivity of the topics on which scientists work. These topics present themselves as things out there that have nothing to do with the subjective life of the scientist. That sense of objectivity has to be respected by the historian. Certainly the targets of the scientist's activity are objects, but that does not mean that they are necessarily natural objects that have no history. Insofar as they do have a history, they are also a target for the investigations of the historian, though it took some time for that to be recognized. Taking their cue from sociologist R. K. Merton (1957), an earlier generation of historians of science was inclined to accept a split between the study of scientific objects, which is the domain of science itself, and the study of scientists, which is the domain of the history and sociology of science. Scientists were part of history, and the objects that science investigates were not, a position that was also implicit in the work of a number of historians of psychology.

With the growing recognition that objectivity and historicity are not incompatible, however, that position was widely rejected. It became clear that while scientific objects may be independent of the subjectivity of individual scientists, this does not mean that they cannot be historically contextualized. Their phenomenal existence depends on specific cultural conditions, investigative practices, institutional arrangements, and so on, which are all historically variable (Latour, 2000). The history of science is very much concerned with the content of science. Especially in psychology, there are no ahistorical objects that exist in some timeless space beyond human activity.

Although the same objects, memory or motivation for example, are targets for the investigations of both scientists and historians, there is a division of labor between them. The latter investigate scientific objects as historical objects, whereas the former treat them as natural objects. But because of a culturally reinforced tradition of taking for granted the status of psychological objects as natural objects, their history as discursive objects has been relatively neglected. It is too easily assumed that psychological objects have essential qualities forever fixed by nature. Moreover, it is unfortunately the case that there are strong professional interests bound up with the belief in the rock-solid permanence of certain psychological objects. The political implications of different constructions of the object "memory," for example, have been painfully evident during the last two decades.

That leaves historians with a twofold critical task. On the one hand, they need to investigate what lies behind the historical persistence of some psychological objects, the contribution of institutionalized practices or discursive traditions, for instance. On the other hand, they need to question the tendency to credit psychological objects with much greater historical persistence than they in fact possess and to make visible the extraordinary historical mutability of these objects. Inevitably, that will not make their work popular among those with vested interests in the status quo, but significant sections of the discipline will not be threatened by critical historical investigations and may even be encouraged by them (Danziger, 1994). Ultimately, historical studies are about historicity. The demand for a priori limits on historicity would subject historical investigation to a kind of censorship, producing a muzzled history that threatens no one. I believe that the historiography of psychology can make a more significant contribution to the discipline than that.

REFERENCES

Benschop, R., & Draaisma, D. (2000). In pursuit of precision: The calibration of minds and machines in late nineteenth-century psychology. *Annals of Science, 57*, 1–25.

Brown, G. D. A., Preece, T., & Hulme, C. (2000). Oscillator-based memory for serial order. *Psychological Review, 107*, 127–181.

Butler, S. (1880). *Unconscious memory*. London: D. Bogue.

Danziger, K. (1980). The history of introspection reconsidered. *Journal of the History of the Behavioral Sciences, 16*, 240–262.

Danziger, K. (1987). Statistical method and the historical development of research practice in American psychology. In L. Krüger, G. Gigerenzer, & M. S. Morgan (Eds.), *The probabilistic revolution* (Vol. 2, pp. 35–47). Cambridge, MA: Massachusetts Institute of Technology Press.

Danziger, K. (1990). *Constructing the subject: Historical origins of psychological research.* New York, NY: Cambridge University Press.

Danziger, K. (1993). Psychological objects, practice, and history. *Annals of Theoretical Psychology, 8*, 15–47.

Danziger, K. (1994). Does the history of psychology have a future? *Theory & Psychology, 4*, 467–484.

Danziger, K. (1997). *Naming the mind: How psychology found its language.* London, UK: Sage.

Danziger, K. (2001). Sealing off the discipline: Wundt and the psychology of memory. In C. D. Green, M. Shore, & T. Teo (Eds.), *The transformation of psychology: Influences of 19th century philosophy, technology, and natural science* (pp. 45–62). Washington, DC: American Psychological Association.

Daston, L. (Ed.). (2000). *Biographies of scientific objects.* Chicago, IL: University of Chicago Press.

Dehue, T. (1997). Deception, efficiency, and random groups: Psychology and the gradual origination of random groups. *Isis, 88*, 653–673.

Dehue, T. (2001). Establishing the experimenting society: The historical origin of social experimentation according to the randomized control group design. *American Journal of Psychology, 114*, 283–302.

Ebbinghaus, H. (1983). *Urmanuskript über das Gedächtnis 1880.* Passau: Passavia.

Fancher, R. (1996). *Pioneers of psychology* (3rd ed). New York, NY: Norton.

Foucault, M. (1977a). Nietzsche, genealogy, history. In D. F. Bouchard (Ed.) *Language, counter-memory, practice: Selected essays and interviews by Michel Foucault* (pp. 139–164). Ithaca, NY: Cornell University Press.

Foucault, M. (1977b). *Discipline and punish: The birth of the prison.* New York, NY: Pantheon.

Gigerenzer, G. (1993). The superego, the ego, and the id in statistical reasoning. In G. Keren & C. Lewis (Eds.) *A handbook for data analysis in the behavioral sciences: Methodological issues* (pp. 311–339). Hillsdale, NJ: Erlbaum.

Goldstein, J. (2000). Mutations of the self in old regime and post-revolutionary France. In L. Daston (Ed.), *Biographies of scientific objects* (pp. 86–116). Chicago, IL: University of Chicago Press.

Goodman, N. (1978). *Ways of worldmaking.* Indianapolis, IN: Hackett.

Hacking, I. (1995a). The looping effects of human kinds. In D. Sperber, D. Premack, & A. J. Premack (Eds.), *Causal cognition: A multi-disciplinary approach* (pp. 351–382). Oxford, UK: Clarendon.

Hacking, I. (1995b). *Rewriting the soul: Multiple personality and the sciences of memory.* Princeton, NJ: Princeton University Press.

Hacking, I. (1999). *The social construction of what?* Cambridge, MA: Harvard University Press.

Hering, E. (1902). *On memory*. Chicago, IL: Open Court. (Original work published 1870)

Kaufmann, D. (2000). Dreams and self-consciousness. In L. Daston (Ed.), *Biographies of scientific objects* (pp. 67–85). Chicago, IL: University of Chicago Press.

Latour, B. (2000). On the partial existence of existing and nonexisting objects. In L. Daston (Ed.), *Biographies of scientific objects* (pp. 247–269). Chicago, IL: University of Chicago Press.

Lyons, W. (1986). *The disappearance of introspection*. Cambridge, MA: Massachusetts Institute of Technology Press.

Merton, R. K. (1957). *Social theory and social structure*. New York, NY: Free Press.

Pickering, A. (1995). *The mangle of practice: Time, agency, and science*. Chicago, IL: University of Chicago Press.

Reed, E. S. (1997). *From soul to mind*. New Haven, CT: Yale University Press.

Rheinberger, H. J. (1997). *Toward a history of epistemic things: Synthesizing proteins in the test tube*. Stanford, CA: Stanford University Press.

Richards, G. (1987). Of what is history of psychology a history? *British Journal for the History of Science, 20*, 201–211.

Rose, N. (1996). *Inventing our selves: Psychology, power and personhood*. Cambridge, UK: Cambridge University Press.

Ross, A. (1996). *Science wars*. Durham, NC: Duke University Press.

Roth, M. S. (1989). Remembering forgetting: Maladies de la memoire in nineteenth century France. *Representations, 26*, 49–68.

Shore, M. (2001). Psychology and memory in the midst of change: The social concerns of late 19th-century North American psychologists. In C. D. Green, M. Shore, & T. Teo (Eds.), *The transformation of psychology: Influences of 19th century philosophy, technology, and natural science* (pp. 63–86). Washington, DC: American Psychological Association.

Smith, R. (1988). Does the history of psychology have a subject? *History of the Human Sciences, 1*, 147–177.

Smith, R. (1992). *Inhibition: History and meaning in the sciences of mind and brain*. Cambridge, UK: Cambridge University Press.

Smith, R. (1997). *The Fontana history of the human sciences*. London, UK: Fontana.

Terdiman, R. (1993). *Present past: Modernity and the memory crisis*. Ithaca, NY: Cornell University Press.

Wundt, W. (1907). *Outlines of psychology*. London, UK: Williams & Norgate. (Original work published 1896)

Young, A. (1995). *The harmony of illusions: Inventing post-traumatic stress disorder*. Princeton, NJ: Princeton University Press.

CHAPTER THREE

THE MORAL DIMENSION OF PSYCHOLOGICAL PRACTICE, THEORY, AND SUBJECT MATTER

Charles W. Tolman

NOT LONG AGO it was commonly held that the subject matter of psychology and its scientific study were morally neutral, an understanding expressed in the phrase "value-free science." We have come a long way in the last half century, and few will be found among us today who defend this view. But fewer still, it appears, are willing to embrace the consequences of moral engagement, let alone attempt to spell out just how theory and practice in our discipline are moral, that is, not value-free. No introductory textbook that I know of—if such books can be taken as the wind vanes of the discipline—invites its readers to take seriously the notion that psychology may be a necessarily moral science.

What I propose here is this: psychology is unavoidably a moral science in every respect, and that to ignore this fact results in a great disservice to the discipline, to all of those who serve it, and to those who are served by it. I shall begin with what is relatively easy to show, namely, that our professional practice is necessarily governed by moral considerations. But though agreement on this claim is at first easy to attain, it will be evident that the claim is not at all straightforward. Those who agree may understand what they are agreeing on differently. We will have to examine how this is so. Having done that, I shall proceed to show that our theories about the subject matter on which we practice are also subject to moral judgement. That is, a theory is not just examinable with respect to its truth, but it can also be assessed for moral rectitude. Nazi theories about race, for instance, were not just false, they were morally vicious. Finally, psychological practice and theory have moral involvements just because their subject matter is moral in nature. I will argue that morality is in fact just what makes us human and distinguishes us from other animals. Thus no human endeavor can be free of moral liability.

PSYCHOLOGICAL PRACTICE

Recently, a colleague, whose opinion I had grown to trust, surprised me with the claim that psychologists, particularly those who work in the history of the discipline, seemed to him inappropriately preoccupied with moral judgement and seemed determined to use professional journals and conferences as launchpads for revolution. It appeared to me that the allegations were related: if practices or ideas current in psychology are judged to be morally vicious, then attempts to overthrow them in favor of more virtuous ones ought to be expected. Most would be disappointed if such corrective attempts were not made.

The objections seemed to me particularly curious, given academe's often well-advertised commitment to codes of ethical practice. The *University of Victoria Faculty Handbook*, for instance, contains an eight-page "Policy on Scholarly Integrity" that calls for intellectual honesty in all scholarly activities, whether in dealing with students or in research practice. With regard to the latter, it specifically lists examples of misconduct that all right-minded researchers abhor. These include plagiarism, falsification of research data, failure to give appropriate recognition to intellectual contributions made by colleagues, using others' unpublished work without permission, and so on. Assuming that public pronouncements of this sort merely put in writing understandings that are commonly held in academe, I was puzzled by my colleague's particular assertion that moral judgments were far more likely to topple otherwise laudable scholarship than they were to enhance it. What could possibly be laudable about scholarship that detaches itself from such moral judgements? Is it not precisely the observance of the moral standards of scholarship that makes the work laudable?

The "Tenure Document" (TD) in the *University of Victoria Faculty Handbook* contains two pages on academic freedom and professional ethics. These are interesting because they go beyond the appearance of an externally imposed set of rules regarding professional conduct. The implied internal relation between freedom and duty is distinctly moral. Academic freedom "involves the right of a faculty member, free from the threat of institutional reprisals and without regard to outside influence, to teach, investigate, publish, and speculate without deference to prescribed doctrine, to participate in the formulation of academic policies, and to criticize the University" (TD, 1.1.2). But this freedom of university professors entails the obligation to "seek and state the truth as they see it" (TD, 2.2.1). The moral tenets that we accept as governing our activities thus make it a duty to seek and state the truth and to criticize authority in light of truth. Would the recalcitrance of authority warrant our going as far as rebellion and revolution? It seems a reasonable deduction that it would.

With regard to psychology in particular, Canadian psychologists are specifically governed by a *Code of Ethics* authored by a committee of the Canadian Psychological Association (1991). This document confirms the general views expressed in the University of Victoria documents. As might be expected, it offers greater detail in matters having to do with nonresearch practice, stressing the need to respect the dignity of individuals, to engage in responsible caring, and to maintain integrity in relationships. Under the principle of "responsibility to society" we are enjoined to contribute to "society's understanding of itself and human beings generally, through a free pursuit and sharing of knowledge" (IV.1). Moreover, we should act "to change those aspects of the discipline of psychology which detract from beneficial societal changes" (IV.17) and to "speak out and/or act, in a manner consistent with the four principles of this Code" (IV.26). I take this to mean just what the University of Victoria document means, namely, that we exercise our freedom as scholars and practitioners under an obligation to conduct ourselves with honesty and dignity, in the interest of the individual and common good, and to criticize and resist openly all impairments or obstacles to the achievement of such good.

I think all this adds up to moral judgement lying essentially and necessarily at the core of the best scholarly practice in all academic areas. Moreover, we are obliged by these moral codes to speak out and criticize in ways that vested interests might very well understand as revolutionary.

SOME COMPLICATIONS

MORALITY VERSUS MORALIZING

Surely my esteemed colleague did not mean by his remarks that he would reject any claim that he had moral obligations under codes of professional ethics. I suspect that his target was not morality as such but moralizing. Our sense of morality, of what is moral and what is immoral, is very powerful. It is just this power that is often co-opted by those who would use it in interests that may not be our own by implying that we are being immoral when we act in ways that they themselves do not approve. We are vulnerable to this for many reasons. Our parents and teachers used this technique. When we were children, these people were the authorities on what was right and what was wrong. To err had consequences often enough for us to take moral admonishments seriously. For the most part, and for the majority of us, this proved to be a strategy that worked in our favor. It kept us out of trouble and it did instill in us a moral sense that was appropriate to the world in which we lived.

Taking such guidance from others continues to be useful to the extent that the others have our interests at heart, and if we have not yet or not fully reflected on the problem of what is moral. Of course some of us have reflected on the problem and have, as a result, established a certain degree of independence in our moral judgements: we prefer to judge a matter for ourselves rather than simply being told by others what is right and wrong. We want to be sure that the judgement is founded on principles that we consider truly moral. When others do admonish us in ways that expect us to forego our own judgement, particularly when they do so under the guise of authority, we quite properly resent it. It is an insult to our intelligence as well as to our moral sensibilities.

But making moral claims is not the same thing as moralizing. Moralizing demands unquestioning compliance; moral claims demand only conscientious examination. There may be many things moral about which most of us are quite certain: we should not murder one another; we should not steal from one another; we should promote the development of others, and so on. But there are many things that are not so clear: whether or not the destruction of a fetus constitutes murder; whether capital punishment is murder; whether the possession of marijuana should be regarded as a criminal offense, and so on. Where there is uncertainty, moral claims deserve closer examination.

It is hoped that nothing in this chapter will be seen as moralizing. I am advancing moral claims and inviting the reader to assess the arguments for himself or herself.

MORALITY VERSUS VALUES

Are values moral? Is value discourse the same as moral discourse? Much of the time the answer is yes. When one speaks of valuing life in discussions of capital punishment, abortion, or murder, the language of values is clearly congruent with the moral. But often value discourse takes a distinctly non-moral turn. This happens, for instance, when one lays claim to the right to hold values that he or she does not necessarily expect of others. For instance, while the values of a person who understands and respects morality will likely be moral, the values of a professional killer will likely not be moral. Values tend to be highly subjective, individualized, and particular—"your values versus mine!"—whereas the good of morality must be objective, social, and universal. It should also be clear that the objectifying and/or socializing of values in no way in itself guarantees morality. If this is confusing, it is because, as George Grant has pointed out, the discourse of values is a relatively new one that arose as a way of facilitating technological progress (Grant, 1998, p. 465). This discourse, according to Grant, came to replace the moral discourse of the good, with the effect that our notion of the good has been emptied of content. It is the restoration of that content with which we are here concerned.

MORALITY AND ETHICS

Ethicality and morality may be identical, but they need not be. In fact, in this and the last centuries, the two have been more typically separated. Ethics refers in the popular sense to standards of conduct, usually in restricted spheres such as medicine, banking, scientific research, and psychological practice. These standards or rules make sense because they are based on a set of agreed-upon aims in the pertinent area of practice. That is, if there is some agreement on what good medical practice is (e.g., curing patients), then any standards that are thought to promote that aim (e.g., patient confidentiality) will be seen as ethically justified.

Again, this *may* be moral. That is, a code of ethics may express a commitment to higher principles that can be regarded as the basis for its morality. But it is not necessarily moral. It could be just what it appears on the surface to be, namely, a means of more effectively achieving the technical ends of medical practice. It may also be a way of avoiding litigation, or of keeping up one's reputation as a medical doctor. In all such cases, what governs is not morality but *prudence*.

As I shall attempt to show in what follows, the subject matter of psychology is characterized by its morality. Morality must then be *constitutive*. Ethical codes, on the other hand, tend not to be constitutive of the actions they govern. They are *regulative* only. Nothing, then, is necessarily proved regarding the point of this chapter by the existence of codes of ethics governing psychological practice, either in application or in research. And the grounds on which these codes regulate are most often prudential ones, such as the avoidance of being sued, although, once again, even prudence *may* be moral.

CONCLUSION

Thus one might well agree that the practice of psychology is subject to moral-like judgements and mean simply that one feels personally that practice should be of such and such a nature, or that it is best to practice in such and such a way in order to avoid getting into trouble. When I claim that psychological (or any other kind of) practice is subject to moral judgement,

I do not mean that such judgement is based on personal preferences as values may be or on prudence as ethics may be. Thus I am saying much more than some who agree at first blush might be willing to admit. The moral cannot be personally relative or merely a matter of prudence. If it were, then the judgement would be empty (as Grant often imagined it to be, in fact). Like epistemological relativism, moral relativism is self-destructive. I cannot reasonably claim something to be true if I reject the possibility of objective truth, and I cannot reasonably claim something to be good if I reject the possibility of an objective good. There can be no good for me if there is no good as such, just as nothing can be true for me if there is no truth as such.

What, then, is good?

THE GOOD

What underlies any moral theory is a conception of the good. I shall here approach the problem of specifying the good from two directions. First, I shall examine the assumption that what is good for one is good for all, that is, that genuine goods are common or universal, not particular. Second, I shall examine the question of what it is that makes a genuine good necessarily good. Once a conception of the good is thus established, we can move on to the questions of psychological theory and subject matter.

THE COMMON GOOD

The problem of the common good is theoretically allusive. An example of this is found in an article appearing in an organ of the Harvard Divinity School, entitled "Faith, Politics, and the Common Good" (Dionne, 1998). The author speaks of the "rules" by which we "navigate through the current moral and economic crises." "Getting the rules right . . . ," he says, "is the precondition for creating a dynamic society. But getting the rules right cannot really occur unless all of us commit ourselves to achieving a more comprehensive understanding of the common good" (p. 2). And that is where his analysis stopped. What we need to know, however, is what a comprehensive understanding would be. That is seldom adequately spelled out.

On this as on other issues, politics often stands in the way of clear theorizing. The particular political problem I have in mind, and the one that is most likely to burden Dionne's otherwise correct conclusion about rules, is that the good of the dominant powers in society is invariably portrayed as the "common good." This was the basis already of Marx's observation in the 1840s, that "The ideas of the ruling class are in every epoch the ruling ideas, i.e., the class which is the ruling *material* force of society, is at the same time its ruling *intellectual* force" (Marx and Engels, 1846/1970, p. 64). The ruling class is also the ruling *moral* force, all too often with the aid of the institutional church.

The confusion of *claims to common good* with the *common good as such* has been the basis of many popular and seemingly compelling rejections of the idea of common good. Popular postmodernism, for example, rejects the notion of common good, just as it rejects as oppressive any allusion to absolutes or universals. There exists instead, postmodernists claim, only a chaotic plethora of many particular goods, each of which is determined by persons individually. The consequences of this kind of moral relativism are, however, all too obvious to most thoughtful observers. Without engaging the issue here, I will say that I cannot accept this or any other relativist stance. I can only attempt theoretically to explicate the common good if I believe that there is such a thing. Relativism may be attractive in the short run, but we cannot live with it for long. It is imperative, then, that we seek a satisfactory theoretical account of the common good and of its *universality*.

COMMON GOOD VERSUS DISTRIBUTED GOODS

A distinction must be made between the common good and goods that are better called "social" or "distributed" by virtue of the fact that they are, at least at the initial level of analysis, decomposable.[1] Decomposable here means that they are essentially individual goods that are shared by members of a group. The use of public funds to construct bicycle paths does not in any obvious way benefit those who do not now or ever will ride bicycles. This is a good that benefits bicycle riders directly and perhaps indirectly some automobile drivers who are glad to have bicycles off the roads. We may attempt here to extend the benefits to others by rationalizing, but we are not likely to reach the entire population: there will always be those for whom bicycle paths cannot be construed as any kind of good at all.

This good is decomposable in that it appears to be essentially an individual good. It becomes a social, distributed good only because there is a sufficient number of individuals affected by it. The justification for public funding for paths is an argument that invokes the utilitarian calculus of the greatest good for the greatest numbers. At some point the extent of good received by bicycle riders is judged to outweigh the cost to non-bicycle riders. Of course, this point will never be precisely calculable. Thus the politicking of advocacy groups is indispensable to the actualization of such goods.

This type of good stands in contrast to the truly common good, which is not decomposable. It is not fundamentally individual, made social by recourse to the utilitarian calculus. It is a good for the individual because it is essentially common. A relatively uncontroversial example of such a good is *language*. Language depends on our ability to follow rules and to know consciously that we are following them, but, it turns out, following a rule is incomprehensible outside of a social setting. Rule following is not something that individuals do, or can do, totally on their own. An unsocialized, isolated individual cannot follow a rule, because in order to do so, one must know that what one does under the rule at one time is the same as what one does at another time. But the meaning of "same" cannot be understood without reference to a horizon of already existing meanings—as is evident to us when we refer to a dictionary to clarify the meaning of a particular word. On his or her own, the isolated individual simply cannot get started. For less isolated individuals, the problem is solved in that the horizon of meanings exists *in society*. As individuals, we learn meanings, we learn language, *from* others. Moreover, any improvement to the language, such as the addition of vocabulary that increases its power of discrimination, necessarily benefits all users of the language. The language user will not be found for whom an improvement in language cannot be construed as any good at all.

A similar case can be made for the *culture* of which language is a part. Culture is a common good from which all benefit. Culture is not subject to the utilitarian calculus. The goods secured by commandments such as "you shall not commit murder" and "you shall not steal" are also common goods. We all benefit from security of person and property, and an offence against one is taken as a threat to all.

We might ask whether decomposable social goods and nondecomposable common goods are as mutually exclusive as I have portrayed them here. The analytic distinction is important, but it should not detract from a possible underlying identity. I suspect that the following account is correct: there is one universal common good, of which all particular common goods (such as culture, language, and security of person and property) are manifestations. Moreover, insofar as individual goods are objectively good, they are derivative of common goods. What I am proposing here is the inverse of the utilitarian "bottom-up" scheme, according to which individual goods are thought to be fundamental, with social goods (which are often then claimed to be common) being composed of individual goods through distribution. I propose instead a "top-down" scheme, in which a universal good is fundamental, with all particular goods, both social and individual, being deduced from it.

There are sound reasons for favoring the top-down scheme. Among other things, it is consistent with the commonality of goods that our language appears to presuppose. All of the diverse things that we call "good" must have had something in common before we assigned them this label. Otherwise, the word "good" would be arbitrary and meaningless, which it clearly is not. This implies that the individual goods that are taken to be the irreducible units of utilitarian theory are not absolutely exclusive of the common good: their independence is relative only, and their real connection to the common good is simply obscure. There may be a common good in bicycle paths after all!

But the plausibility of a top-down theory will hinge on our ability to specify the precise nature of the common good, so that we might demonstrate how particular social and individual goods are deduced from it. This is the task that I shall undertake in what follows.

BASIS AND NATURE OF THE COMMON GOOD

Let us deal first with that which distinguishes the human species from all others. Hegelian philosophers have called it a *concrete universal*, concrete because further distinctive characteristics can be deduced from it. It is distinguished from *abstract universals*, which are merely the most general features of a class. An example will help clarify this distinction. Physically we share all features of our bodies with at least one other species of animals, except our soft earlobes. But soft earlobes tell us absolutely nothing about our being human. More philosophically minded thinkers have preferred to describe the human species as toolmakers. This is more concrete in the Hegelian sense. While not every individual human may make tools—as opposed to having soft earlobes—it is possible to deduce from toolmaking other characteristics that we consider uniquely human, such as language and culture— we cannot do this from soft earlobes.[2]

But even toolmaking must be specified further. We may note, for example, that chimpanzees and other apes are known to use tools and even to make them in rudimentary ways. What *is* distinctive of humans is the *context* in which we make and use tools. This is a context of *social relations*. Humans, unlike the most advanced chimpanzees, make and use tools in cooperation with others. It is characteristic, for instance, that the maker of a tool and its user may be different persons. Moreover, the same tool can be shared by various users and passed on to subsequent users. What links these people is the *meaning* of the tool, which is its use in a social practice.

It has been thought puzzling by some that humans developed a vocal means of communication, since gestures appear to be more natural and are more effective at long distances. Moreover, it is now well known that while chimpanzees can learn limited means of vocal communication, they find it easier and more effective to learn sign language based on gestures. The answer to the puzzle about humans, however, is to consider the *social relations* in which human labor occurs, where labor is understood as the making and using of tools in the social production of that which satisfies our basic needs. If humans came to cooperate around the manufacture and use of tools, then gestures would interfere with those activities. Vocal communication was, under these circumstances, the more natural. It is not natural for chimpanzees, because they do not cooperate around the manufacture and use of tools.

The argument can be developed at much greater length, if needed, to support the conclusion that *practice—the cooperative provision for basic needs through production of collectively agreed-upon outcomes by the social use of mediating tools*—is the most fundamental human characteristic, the differentia of the species. It is practice that makes us, and allows us to continue to be, human. A corollary here is John Macmurray's (1961) conclusion that since practice is the most fundamental human characteristic, and practice is necessarily and essentially social, social or interpersonal relations are the most fundamental human problem. They are fundamental because we cannot become fully human outside of such relations. They are problematic because they are not natural but intentional. That is, the cooperative social relations that provide the context for our full development as human beings are the result of conscious deliberation on the part of participants. This explains why human relations so often go awry, the most common form of deviance being the abandonment of their mutually supportive form (*agapé*) for instrumental forms. The need for supportive relations is, in turn, a need for community. Community is thus an alternative label for the most fundamental human problem, and it is a problem because we can only practice in communities.

Practice is the most fundamental human characteristic; community is the most fundamental human problem. We have an ideal of communities of practice in which all members are engaged in a common effort directed at the maintenance and further development of their own humanity under mutually supportive relations. This is the *ideal* of the common good. Violation of the common good, under this view, would constitute anything that detracts from practice—the cooperative provision for basic needs—and the development of our humanity.

We are concerned about hunger in the Third World, but most of us know that the problem is not solved by sending food. That is, in a sense, the least of the problems faced by the affected people. What they need is the means by which to collectively produce the food that they need, that is, to participate in the production of that which satisfies their needs: this is what they have been deprived of, and this deprivation is what is dehumanizing them. It is not the lack of food as such. Likewise for the unemployed youth with no prospects for the future in our own society: it is not just a problem of having the means of consumption. If it were, then welfare would be an adequate solution, but we know that welfare is not the solution. What is needed by the affected people is meaningful participation in social production. It is only such participation that creates the possibility of their full development as human beings.

We cannot become fully developed as human beings by ourselves, but only in community with others. If such development is good, then it is a common good. If it is by practice that we develop in community with others, then practice is the source of the common good, and anything that restricts social practice is a violation of the common good. We can also see why language and culture should provide easy models of what we mean by "common." This is because of their intimate connection to practice. Language is its fundamental instrument. Practice would be impossible without it. Culture is the complex web of social relations and understandings within which practice occurs. Without the supportive context of culture, again, there would be no practice—and without practice, we would not be human.

I am suggesting, then, that everything we have ever thought about the common good and everything we have ever thought about living rightly, morally, ethically, and lovingly can be rethought as deductions from the nature of human practice. What is common about the common good, then, is the necessarily social, essentially human, irreducibly cooperative nature of practice and its connection to our very humanity. The imperative against racism and other social evils stems from their violation of the community upon which our humanity depends, for, as the wise John Watson of Queen's wrote many years ago, "the good of all is the true principle of human action" (Watson, 1908, p. 233).

THE HUMAN UNIVERSAL

The moral problematic emerges here as one of correspondence of particular and universal, of the particular individual action and the universal principle that it realizes. But it is surely not mere, abstract universality that makes it moral. It is because the universal is *human*—as individuals, we are but particular instances of universal humanity. In realizing ourselves, we realize humanity. My life is human life; my health is human health; my knowledge is human knowledge. The obvious essential sociality of all universal ends and of intentional action itself points to this. That which is essentially social in individual intentions, actions, and their ends signifies our humanity. An obligation to self is an obligation to others, but it reaches beyond particular others, eventually to *all* others. Individual goods, to the extent that they *are* good, are ultimately identical to the common good. Our lives do not exist in a vacuum; they are shared with others. All our universal ends are ends shared with others; they are essentially social. Human life is something in which each and every one of us participates. To want life absolutely is to want it for all who share in it. It is the same with health, good relations, and knowledge. These are goods for me, but they are also common goods. They are good for me *because* they are common goods. The moral is grounded in the identity of particular and universal goods.

THE MORAL IMPERATIVE

It is an important question as to wherein lies the compulsion behind the moral imperative. We may see at the level of rhetoric why we ought to do things, but how does this move us to appropriate action? As I have already said, it is characteristic of actions that they are not causally but logically linked to their motives, intentions, and reasons. The moral compulsion is a *logical* compulsion. We are all strongly driven to do certain things, and we are driven by reasons, not by causes. I was strongly driven to finish this chapter for the editors of this book. What drove me was a reason based on an understanding of obligation both to others and to myself. Not to have finished it, without good excuse, would have been both immoral and irrational. In finishing the chapter, there is an identity of my own individual good and the common good. Understanding this identity left me no *reasonable* option but to do what followed from it logically and morally.

THE MORAL NECESSITY OF PSYCHOLOGICAL THEORY

Knowledge, like practice, does not belong to isolated individuals. It is always constituted collectively. What I know I have either learned from others or discovered with the aid of others. And what I need to know is always more than what I have at my immediate disposal. Thus we have a division of labor that includes teachers, experts, consultants, and libraries. The needs satisfied by knowledge are not just my needs but human needs. If, as Hegel maintained, the highest development of self-consciousness is universal self-consciousness (1807/1967, p. 375), then my duty to myself is also duty to others; and since this duty cannot be fulfilled without knowledge, my duty to myself and to others becomes a *duty to know*. It can thus be argued, as Israel Scheffler (1967) does, that the motives of scientific reason are just as moral as they are intellectual. This recognition yields a

> new and enlarged vision of the moral standpoint—of responsibility in belief, embodied not only in a firm commitment to impartial principles by which one's own assertions are to be measured, but in a further commitment to making those principles ever more comprehensive and rigorous. Thus, though science has certainly provided us with new and critically important knowledge of man's surroundings and capacities, such enlightenment far from exhausts its human significance. A major aspect of such significance has been the moral import of science: its dynamic articulation of the impulse to responsible belief, and its suggestion of the hope of an increased rationality and responsibility in all realms of conduct and thought. (p. 4)

The key to the *imperative* character of theoretical knowledge lies in the priority of the practical (i.e., the moral) over the theoretical and the ultimate unity of the two. A practical action differs from an event in that its course is inherently indeterminate. It is the actualization of a *possibility* and therefore always requires a choice based on a distinction between right and wrong. A person will never knowingly violate his or her own interests: he or she will always chose what he or she considers to be the right thing to do. Of course, external constraints are in force here. The aim of any action is to make a resistant, objective world conform to the actor's needs or intentions. What is right, then, will always be that which, on appropriate reflection of both intentions and objective constraints, will achieve that aim. But this by itself does not yet constitute morality, which emerges only on reflection of the necessary interdependence of the individual and humanity-at-large. Our personal interests are essentially and ineluctably linked to the common interest; they are, as I have already suggested, the *particular* expressions of the *universal* human interest.

To act morally, however, the person must also *know* of his or her interdependence with others, must understand something of his or her own humanity, must be cognizant of the possibilities for action on any given occasion, and must be able to anticipate the practical consequences of his or her action on the basis of which its morality is judged. In order to act morally, and thus ultimately in one's own interests, one must have true knowledge, and since what is needed will not always be given in sensations, this knowledge will have to be theoretical knowledge.

Just as the distinction between right and wrong is inherent in acting, the distinction between true and false is inherent in knowing. To claim to know something is to claim that it is true. We do not believe except that we believe truly. And again, like the rightness of action, claims to truth are subject to universal constraints: objective truth expresses the harmony between particular and universal.

We must *know* because we must live rightly. The most moral life, and thus also the life most distinguished by its freedom, can only be led by those best informed about the real possibilities of action, about the actual physical and social consequences of actions and their correspondence to intentions, and about the nature of the real interrelation and interdependence of agents. Therein lies the theoretical imperative. Theoretical knowledge is a necessary instrument, a use-value, a means for the fulfilment of the moral imperative, of which the theoretical imperative is thus derivative.

Now, again, all of this would be a relatively simple matter if the required knowledge were immediately given in sensory experience, but it is not. As Heraclitus understood, nature loves to hide. It is not surprising, therefore, that in society a division of labor should develop in which some members of society are specifically charged with the expansion of human knowledge. This is a weighty charge: the common good is directly at stake. And the task is an inescapably theoretical one, which, while in the service of the practical, cannot be reduced to the practical. It is very difficult indeed to see how the obligations entailed in the theoretical imperative can adequately be met by abandoning the scientific quest for knowledge in favor of aesthetic or religious expression. These, too, inform the practical sphere of human existence in important ways, but they do not yield the theoretical knowledge about which we have been speaking. The object of aesthetics and religion is direct, not instrumental. It is valued as an end in itself and not for its use. Its discourse is expressive, not theoretical. While these modes of relating to the world are essential to the human experience—indeed, they form the ground for theoretical knowledge—they do not in themselves provide the *cognitive means* to the moral imperative that only theoretical knowledge can provide. In short, there is no substitute for theoretical knowledge, and the psychologist, like all scientists, is historically, morally bound to enlarging it. Under the present argument, to do otherwise would constitute bad science, malfeasance of duty, and an impeachable breach of public trust.

THE NECESSARY MORALITY
OF THE PSYCHOLOGICAL SUBJECT MATTER

Psychology, I think it can reasonably be said, ought to concern itself with illuminating what people do and what they think. Some observers, driven by a greater need for tidiness, may urge that thinking is in fact just a form of doing or acting, so psychology should deal really only with what we do. So let us turn first to the distinction between acting and thinking. There is a larger argument to be made, but a minimal case for their distinction is made by observing that acting always has effects on the world around us. I do not mean reflexes, of course. They just happen, and we would have to strain meanings beyond normal limits to conclude that they do anything. I mean acting in the sense of *doing something*. Doing something changes our world, however minutely.

Now it may be alleged that thoughts also have effects. And this is true, but *only* if the thinker decides to translate the thoughts into actions. What is in fact remarkable about thinking is precisely that it has no immediate effect on the world, and that is a good thing. The real value of thinking is that we can try many things, contemplate no end of possibilities, with absolutely no risk to ourselves, our fellow human beings, or our environment. A more traditional way of expressing this is to say that thinking is *theoretical*, while acting is *practical*.

But the relationship between acting and thinking is not reciprocal in this regard. That is, while we can think without acting, we cannot act without thinking. Again, we are not talking about spinal or other reflexes that clearly do not require thinking. In doing something, we always know, in however minimal a degree, what we are doing.

It is said that people sometimes act without thinking, but when we say this, we mean that they do things without due consideration. They are thinking, just not thinking enough or rightly. Thinking may occur by itself without acting, but acting is always accompanied by thinking. Thus acting is *inclusive*; thinking is *exclusive*.

I want to acknowledge that talking is situated in a kind of gray zone by this analysis of the psychological subject matter. On the one hand, it can be like thinking out loud and thus have the exclusive character of thinking. On the other hand, it may have very definite consequences, as when I shout to warn others of a fire. This does not disturb the analysis; it just means that speaking is ambiguous with regard to it.

There is another important distinction between acting and thinking. This has to do with the kinds of judgements we make about them. On the whole, thoughts take the form of propositions and are thus subject to being judged as true or false. Actions, on the other hand, are judged to be right or wrong. Right and wrong, however, come in significantly different forms. What we do may be judged right or wrong *technically*, *morally*, and/or *aesthetically*.

The problem is obviously more complex than this. For one thing, it might be objected that the action as such is not that which is immoral but its ultimate purpose or intent. Or the aesthetics of the object, no matter what was intended, is in the eye of the beholder and thus not, properly speaking, a judgement to be made of the action as such. Then there is the obvious objection that many actions tend to be regarded as both morally and aesthetically neutral.

Such objections do rightly point to the complexity of the analysis, but they do not destroy it. For one, motives and intentions are, as I shall again assert in a moment, *intrinsic* to actions. They are the necessary thought-accompaniments of action that are implied by its inclusivity. A doing without purpose is not really a doing: it is a reflex or something akin to it. And, again, as I will want to argue, the effects of my actions are also entailed in them. Thus motives, intentions, actions, and effects are intentionally related to one another in their rightness or wrongness. Actions simply cannot be parted from that which is subject to judgement.

An additional complication that should be acknowledged is that the distinction I have drawn between thought and action is not absolute. There exists a kind of equivalence between the technical rightness of action and the truth of thought. Moreover, there is a sense in which thoughts, too, may be in some sense technically right or wrong, morally right or wrong, or aesthetically right or wrong. But this is not surprising, considering that thought is necessarily part of every doing.

What we need to say, then, is that it is *typical* of thinking that it is judged true or false, that it is *typical* of acting that it is judged right or wrong, and that the latter rightness or wrongness results in three types of judgements, namely, technical, moral, and aesthetic. Moreover, it is clear that actions are not *either* technical *or* moral *or* aesthetic; they tend, rather, to be all at the same time, though one may dominate our attention in any given situation at any given moment.

What is the nature of the thought that is included in action? It is surely not simply an internal narration. The important role that thought plays in relation to action is in its motive and intention. It is in fact the intention that defines the action, making it the kind of action it is, and thus makes it subject to judgements of the three kinds. I cannot do anything well, morally, or beautifully, except that I do *something*, and that something is determined by the intention. I am not just walking; I am going somewhere.

I am not just moving my arms; I am waving to a friend, and so forth. *It is the presence of intention that defines action and distinguishes it from reflexes and other bodily reactions to stimuli.*

A number of other things can be said about human action. First, action always involves a *choice*. Whatever we do in any particular situation, we could have done something else. However conscious of the fact we may be, we always act in the way that we choose to act. A corollary of this is that we can always have refused to do what we did.

Second, action implies *agency*. This is most evident when we have urges, desires, or motives that conflict. It is sometimes claimed that it is simply a matter of the stronger desire prevailing. But what determines which is the stronger motive? When Jeremy Bentham confronted this problem, he was forced to say that what was stronger depended on the particular individual. But that only means that the *subject* determines the strength and therefore effectively decides which desire to act upon. The choice, in short, is the subject's. And that means that the subject is also an agent.

Third, choosing to act in some particular way is always directed at the anticipated consequence. Action is *teleological*. This is already implied in the labels we give to actions: sitting down, eating breakfast, taking a shower, making a gadget. And it is the goal of the action that governs judgements of technical appropriateness, but also of the moral and aesthetic appropriateness of the action.

Fourth, actions are *not caused* by external circumstances. Of course, they are governed by external circumstances. A major concern of the subject is appropriateness to these circumstances, but the circumstances do not cause the action. It is the subject/agent himself or herself who determines what action shall be performed, and that determination is made on the basis of the reason implicit in the action's motive and intention. It is only this reason that serves as a sufficient condition for action.

A sufficient condition is just what one needs for an adequate causal account. But the reason, which is the sufficient condition, cannot be a cause in the strict sense. Causes, rightly considered, are necessarily independent of their effects. But the reason is not independent of the action. It is part of the action. Without the reason—that is, apart from the thought accompaniment—the action would not be an action. The action is just the realization of the reason, an intention carried into its objective form. Another way of saying this is that the action is the deductive consequence of its reason, that is, of its motive and intention. The relationship is not causal, it is *logical*.

These characteristics of action—choice, agency, teleology, noncausality/logicality—all imply each other, forming an integral set of mutual interconnections. To exercise choice, we must have agency, which, again, would make no sense if our actions were caused by external conditions. And all of this is necessarily teleological: we choose in terms of anticipated consequences. The entire set of mutual implications is summarized in the word "intentional," which also carries with it the entailment of thought and meaningfulness.

If this picture is correct, then the three categories of rightness/wrongness—technical, moral, and aesthetic—can now be seen not merely as kinds of judgements that we make of actions after the fact; they are also the criteria by which choice is made and thus govern intentions. What we do is just that which we have decided is the right thing to do under the circumstances. (The possibility of being mistaken by our own or others' judgements later is of course not ruled out.)

Before drawing further implications from all of this, we must stop to compare what I have said with the usual textbook definition of the subject matter of psychology, namely, behavior and cognition (or some variation on this duality). Behavior is still conceived in terms of responses to stimuli. We should be able to see now that this is totally inadequate. It allows no room for the choice, agency, teleology, and noncausality/logicality that are so evident to us as actors in the real world. We ask our "subjects" to respond to stimuli, and they often do this for us, giving us the data we need to test our hypotheses. But all thoughtful subjects, including "subjects," know very well that it is not the stimulus that finally determines what they do. It is considerations of politeness and decency toward the experimenter and a consequent decision to be cooperative and to follow the experimenter's instructions. These considerations and decisions are traditionally ignored by psychologists in accounting for their experiments. Impolite or uncooperative "subjects" are simply eliminated as bad apples. But our decision to cooperate or not to cooperate is absolutely essential to our actions and to ourselves as human beings. So, behavior, understood as a function of experimentally manipulated conditions, is a very poor specification of the subject matter of psychology.

How about cognition? It would seem necessary from our analysis that cognition is an appropriate subject matter of psychology, but only if its origin and role in action are recognized. Outside that origin and role, cognition is as abstract and potentially misleading as is behavior.

So a justifiable subject matter of psychology is intentional action, and intentional action is intrinsically characterized by choice, agency, teleology, noncausality/logicality, and meaning. It is also *essentially social*. This already follows from what we have said. The choice, agency, teleology, and noncausality/logicality are all made possible because action is thoughtful and therefore meaningful. But the principal carrier of meaning in our lives is language, and there is a good case to be made, as Wittgenstein and others have argued, that language is essentially social. There is no private language, because there can be no private meanings. Meanings exist necessarily and only in a basically three-way relation between the subject, the object, and other subjects. Now if meanings are essentially social and action is essentially meaningful, then action is essentially social.

Moreover, actions, meanings, and language are essential components of what we call culture. We cannot have culture except by participating with others in social practices. We cannot have language except by participating with others in communicative activities. Likewise, we cannot have meanings except by participating in the shared experiences of others. I cannot *act* except that I act in concert with others. We are essentially cultural beings.

This becomes still more evident from the structural characteristics of action. On the one hand, actions *require* movements but are *not defined* by the particular movements made. There are many different ways of achieving the aims of any particular action. One of our technical choices is to select from among the available movements those which are the most appropriate to the particular circumstances. I can compose a letter to a friend by hand, by typewriter, or by audiotape. What I do in particular will be different in each case, but the action of composing a letter remains the same. Actions are thus made up of, or constituted by, what has been called "operations."

But if we move upward to see what actions themselves constitute, we find that they make up larger structures, sometimes called "activities" or "practices." Writing a letter makes no sense outside the need for keeping in touch with others. Giving lectures makes no sense outside the educational activities of institutions such as universities. Even taking showers makes no sense outside the sphere of the hygienic rituals of modern social life. The point is that while actions and their components are clearly identified with the acting individual, actions make sense only in the context of the broader social and cultural practices of which they are a part.

To speak of the structure of intentional action, then, is really just another way of speaking about its teleology. With a particular aim in mind, we select from among available operations for those most appropriate to our needs and the requirements of the situation. More importantly, the larger structure, activity, or practice implies that the immediate aim of every intentional action is only a means to something larger. Every intentional action points, implicitly or explicitly, to something beyond itself. Thus my eating breakfast sustains life. Taking a shower facilitates social relations in a hygiene-conscious age. Mowing the lawn creates an aesthetically more pleasing environment for oneself and one's neighbors. All the work we do contributes to the maintenance of the structures of social practice upon which our culture, and thus also our humanity, depend. The larger ends of action are all ultimately and essentially social and cultural.

Outside the social/cultural context, intentional action not only makes no sense: strictly speaking, outside the social/cultural context it could not have come into existence in the first place. And if intentional action is the defining feature of our humanity—which it clearly is!—then we are constituted as human beings only in the social/cultural context; that is, humans are *essentially* social/cultural beings—keeping in mind that, as I argued earlier, the *human* social is not equivalent to the *animal-natural* social; the *human* social is characterized by culture and thus better designated as *society*. Humans are, in short, essentially *societal beings*.

Because we are societal beings, partaking in societal existence through participation in social practices, of which actions are necessarily a part (actions are always doing something that is *socially* defined), it is evident that other people are essential to our actions and thoughts. Behind my taking a shower are all those others who make the fixtures, install them, and operate the water works, and those others with whom I expect to interact. My decision to take a shower is filled with implicit obligation to myself and many others. So just as actions are essentially characterized by choice, agency, teleology, noncausality/logicality, and meaning, they are also characterized by *obligation*. It is obvious that there will always be an implicit obligation to myself in deciding what to do; I am, after all, acting always, so far as I know, in my own best interests. But obligation to others is equally pervasive in my actions. As a fully integrated participant in societal existence, there is nothing I do that does not have repercussions, however remote, for others. Even our most personal and private acts are carried out in consideration of others. Moreover, I could not act at all without the past and present support of others. Now whatever else the *moral* may be, it certainly includes these effects upon and obligations to other people.

GENERAL CONCLUSION

The necessary conclusion is that we are essentially *moral* beings; intentional action is essentially *moral* action. And psychological theories that fail to recognize the moral dimension of the psychological subject matter, which means virtually all of those that have emerged in the 20th century, will not only fail adequately to account for human acting and thinking, they will necessarily distort and mislead. The social, moral dimension of human action is not just another variable that can be held constant. To hold it constant would be to reduce truly human action to the level of mechanical behavior—which is, of course, exactly what has been done in psychology during the last 100 years. The result has been a psychology more suited to the *control* of effectively dehumanized beings than to *generating understandings that serve genuinely human needs and interests*.

I strongly agree with what I take to be the intended imputation of the remarks made by my esteemed colleague and which I mentioned at the beginning of this chapter: there is no room in psychology or in any other science for moralizing. Indeed, moralizing is improper in science as elsewhere, just because it fails to respect the human subject as an essentially moral being. But psychology will commit an impropriety of the very same nature if it falls short of recognizing the moral nature of its subject matter. Only psychology's recognition of itself as a thoroughly moral science—in practice, theory, and subject matter—will create the conditions for realizing its full potential to generate real knowledge that can be used to promote human development.

NOTES

1. I am indebted for much of the argument and examples in this section to Taylor (1995).

2. The question of the differential from a paleontological perspective is discussed at greater length in Tolman (1987).

REFERENCES

Canadian Psychological Association. (1991). *Canadian code of ethics for psychologists*. Ottawa, ON: Author.

Dionne, E. J., Jr. (1998). Faith, politics, and the common good. *Religion & Values in Public Life, 6*(2/3), 1–3.

Grant, G. P. (1998). Faith and the multiversity. In William Christian and Sheila Grant (Eds.), *The George Grant reader* (pp. 461–482). Toronto, ON: University of Toronto Press.

Hegel, G. W. F. (1967). *The phenomenology of mind* (J. B. Baille, Trans.). New York, NY: Harper & Row. (Original work published 1807)

Macmurray, J. (1961). *Persons in relation* (Vol. 2 of the Gifford Lectures delivered in the University of Glasgow in 1953–54). London, UK: Faber & Faber.

Marx, K., & Engels, F. (1970). *The German ideology. Part I.* New York, NY: International Publishers. (Original work published 1846)

Scheffler, I. (1967). *Science and subjectivity*. Indianapolis, IN: Bobbs-Merrill.

Taylor, C. (1995). *Philosophical arguments*. Cambridge, MA: Harvard University Press.

Tolman, C. W. (1987). Human evolution and the comparative psychology of levels. In G. Greenberg & E. Tobach (Eds.), *Cognition, language, and consciousness: Integrative levels* (pp. 185–208). Hillsdale, NJ: Erlbaum.

University of Victoria. (1996). *Faculty handbook*. Victoria, BC: Author.

Watson, J. (1908). *An outline of philosophy*. Glasgow, UK: James Maclehose and Sons.

CHAPTER FOUR

PSYCHOTHERAPISTS AS CRYPTO-MISSIONARIES

AN EXEMPLAR ON THE CROSSROADS OF HISTORY, THEORY, AND PHILOSOPHY

Brent D. Slife, Amy Fisher Smith, and Colin M. Burchfield

THIS CHAPTER DESCRIBES an intriguing case of the "crossroads" of history, theory, and philosophy. As we will attempt to show, there is simply no meaningful way to understand the role of values in contemporary psychotherapy without these crossroads, and understanding this role is now sorely needed. Never has there been more tension or tumult surrounding the issue of values. For years, therapists have been taught to eliminate, suspend, or at least minimize their own values while conducting psychotherapy: psychoanalysts recommended that therapists be "blank screens" (Franklin, 1990; Freud, 1912/1963); behaviorists advised they be "objective" (Wilson, 2000); and humanists suggested they be "interpersonal mirrors" (Rogers, 1951).

Recent developments, however, make clear that therapists cannot escape or even minimize their values (Beutler and Bergan, 1991; Kelly, 1990). Therapists have long known that certain professional values were unavoidable, such as caring for and protecting their clients. Still, recent empirical and theoretical work has shown how deeply these inescapable values go—even to the level of personal moral and religious values (Tjeltveit, 1986). Researchers have shown that therapists not only *use* such personal values in therapy but also *urge their clients* to use them (Beutler, 1979; Tjeltveit, 1999). Therapists may not be completely aware of this persuasion process, but it is occurring nevertheless (Beutler, Arizmendi, Crago, Shanfield, and Hagaman, 1983; Smith and Slife, in press). In this sense, therapists may be, as Paul Meehl (1959) once feared long ago, "crypto-missionaries" (p. 257) attempting to convert their clients to their own value system.

Needless to say, this situation has put practicing therapists into a quandary. What are they to do with their values? There are clear ethical injunctions against imposing personal values on clients (American Psychological Association, 1992), but if such values are inescapable—both in using and in urging clients to use them—then what is the most effective and ethical course of action? Here we submit that this pivotal question cannot be answered without the simultaneous consideration of history, theory, and philosophy. As we will contend, the original discomfort of therapists with their values is not comprehensible without the context of *history*, indeed, a history that goes back to the Middle Ages. Recent conclusions that values are inescapable cannot be understood without the *theoretical* developments that spawned them. And finally, as we will argue, the solution to this therapy dilemma involves a dramatic change in the *philosophy* that undergirds psychotherapy. We review each of these aspects of the values issue in turn.

HISTORY: ACCOUNTING FOR
THERAPEUTIC VALUE SENSITIVITY

Why are so many therapists uncomfortable with and confused about the use of their values in therapy? Much as good scientists are assumed to be objective and value-free observers of psychological facts, good therapists are assumed to be objective and value-free observers of therapeutic facts. Indeed, if therapists do not strive for objectivity and value-freeness, they are considered unethical (Wilson, 1995). That is, if they do not value being value-free, then they are thought to violate the values of the discipline—for not being sufficiently value-free. The obvious paradoxical nature of this ethical injunction—to value being value-free—was never really questioned until relatively recently. Why? As we will see, psychotherapy was conceived in an era that reacted to perceived value abuses of the past—abuses that supposedly date back as far as the premodern era.

"Premodern" Values

The reason for the scare quotes around the term "premodern" in the section heading is that our modern, Enlightenment-based understanding of the premodern era is not necessarily the way the premodernists viewed themselves. However, this understanding is itself the issue (Bartlett, 1993; Gadamer, 1995; Jones, 1969b), because psychology—born of the modern era—has implicitly adopted a particular view of the premodern era that we should explore here—the view that premodern values were both subjective and absolute.

The terms "subjective" and "absolute" may seem contradictory. However, many premodern values are considered subjective because they were without objective foundation. That is, these values seem arbitrary and unjustified through our modern lenses, though they were certainly not arbitrary and unjustified to the people of premodern times (Jones, 1969a; Leahey, 2000). Indeed, premodernists viewed such values as universal and eternal rather than arbitrary and subjective, because such values were thought to be revealed by God. The problem from an Enlightenment or a modern perspective is that some of the religious and political leaders of the premodern era used their status and power to assert their own personal (and subjective) values rather than those of God. Hence, the modern criticism of the premodern era is that virtually anyone with power—whether religious or political—could decide what was right and good without justification, or at least without the "objective" form of justification that modernists now require.

The term "objective justification" is used here to distinguish it from the *divine* justifications of many leaders of the premodern era. That is, these political and religious leaders regularly invoked supposedly absolute truths to justify their values and actions. Actually, the power held by such leaders was itself considered absolute; kings were kings, and cardinals were cardinals by virtue of their divine origins or morality (Jones, 1969a). However, few people in the modern era would regard divine justifications as "objective," because they typically stem from a particular religious perspective, and thus are biased. Consequently, premodern values are viewed as both absolute and subjective; they supposedly originated from God, and they lacked any objective justification. For the modernist, this view is much the same as having no justification, even though divine revelation was the ultimate in justification for the premodernist. Indeed, such divine justifications seem to many modern persons as little more than excuses to validate the subjective interest of the king or religious leader, especially when horrendous oppression and tyranny was the result.

MODERN VALUES

Our modern era is, in this respect, both a reaction to and a correction of perceived premodern problems, including the premodern understanding of values. Modernists formulated two basic ways of combating the perceived abuses and tyranny of the premodern period—both strategies of neutrality. That is, both take the power out of the hands of arbitrary and subjective authorities and replace this power with supposedly nonarbitrary and neutral procedures for determining the values. Modernists view such strategies and procedures as rational and thus relatively value-free. The two strategies that dominate this attempt at value neutrality are, in some sense, the opposite of the two themes identified in the premodern era—subjectivism and absolutism; the main strategies of the modern era are objectivism and relativism.

Again, these two strategies may seem contradictory at first, but they can be seen as variations on the same theme of neutrality (Bernstein, 1983). The neutrality of objectivity is perhaps the easier to see. Objectivity supposedly disallows arbitrariness or bias (and thus subjectivity). Unlike the divine justifications of the premodern era, the justifications of the modern era are viewed as objective or free from subjective values. Recall that one of the modern criticisms of the premodern era was that some of its leaders were promoting their own subjective values through supposedly divine justifications. In order to avoid these subjective excesses, the modern era emphasizes justifications that are based on "objective" methods.

The most prominent of these methods is, of course, the scientific method. The scientific method is particularly popular, because it is the shotgun wedding of two systems of justification—empiricism and rationalism (Slife and Williams, 1995). That is, scientific validation implies justification not only in terms of rigorous reasoning (rationalism) but also in terms of cold, hard facts (empiricism). Neither rigorous reasoning nor hard facts are viewed as subjective, because neither is thought to be controlled arbitrarily by those in power. Scientific method is itself in control, itself a neutral procedure for determining the good and the effective.

Relativism may be the more difficult of the modernist strategies to view as neutral, yet it is probably the more frequently used in this capacity in psychotherapy. Instead of powerful people deciding what is right for everyone, the philosophy of relativism holds that people should decide for themselves, relative to their own unique situations. From a modernist lens, premodern religious and political leaders often dictated the values of their people. Rather than choosing their own values, premodern commoners were obedient to the supposedly divine decrees of their premodern leaders, leading to abuse and even tyranny. Relativism appeared to be the modern antidote to these abuses, because it seemed to empower individuals to make their own value choices, free from any external coercion or influence.

Robert Bellah and his colleagues call this modern, relativistic strategy *expressive individualism,* because the individual is considered to be in the best position to know what is best for him or her (Bellah, Madsen, Sullivan, Swidler, and Tipton, 1985). No leader (or therapist), however benevolent, should make these decisions, because individuals know their unique situation best. Hence, values in therapy should be determined by the clients themselves, *relative* to their individual situation, with the therapist remaining neutral as to which values are best. This neutrality supposedly permits clients in therapy to choose their own values, without interference or coercion. Many therapists use the term "tolerance," rather than "neutrality," in this regard but the therapeutic injunction against values interference and coercion is the same.

MODERN PSYCHOTHERAPY

Is this modern reaction to the premodern world—this supposedly enlightened response to the presumed darkness of the Dark Ages—reflected in our psychotherapy values? Psychotherapy reflects modernism not only in affirming the importance of objectivism and relativism, but also in reacting negatively to those who would insert subjective and absolute values into the therapy session. Objectivism, for instance, is a clear theme of past and present formulations of the modern psychotherapy enterprise. Traditional personality theories are viewed as mere speculations until tested empirically. For example, many have viewed psychoanalysis skeptically, until it has justified its therapy techniques in objective ways (Henry, Strupp, Schacht, and Gaston, 1994; Weber, Bachrach, and Solomon, 1985).

However, the clearest approaches to neutrality in this objectivist sense are the recent movements of eclecticism and empirically supported treatment (EST). The most popular form of eclecticism, technical eclecticism, is the notion that science can objectively indicate which techniques of therapy are the most effective for which disorders (Slife and Reber, 2001). No values seem to be necessary in this process; the hard facts of therapy outcome are the adjudicator. EST is another variation of this objectivism (cf. Messer, 2001). Whatever is empirically supported—again, shorn of any value-laden judgments—is presumably what guides the therapist. With eclecticism and EST, then, the modernist strategy of neutrality is clear, because a supposedly value-free method is used for deciding which values and techniques therapists should use.

Relativism, too, has exerted its own brand of neutrality in psychotherapy. As far back as Freud (1912/1963), therapists have been exquisitely sensitive to the use of values in the therapy enterprise, especially personal and private values. The therapist is viewed as having tremendous power over the client. Similar to the kings and cardinals of the premodern era, therapists are viewed as having a power that should not be wielded subjectively or absolutely. This sensitivity explains the clear professional injunctions against "imposing" personal values on a client (American Psychological Association, 1992). Consequently, therapists either work with objectively derived professional values or with values that are relative to the client or the client's culture.

At this point, it seems obvious that current notions of values management are historically situated. Dominant modes of this management are dominant reactions to historical developments, some occurring centuries ago. As we mentioned at the outset, however, profound questions have been raised about these management strategies. These questions are, for the most part, uniquely *theoretical* in nature (which are themselves historically situated). Although empirical research has contributed mightily to this profound questioning, as we will show, the fact that these empirical studies were conducted at all points to the theoretical concerns that spawned them.

THEORY: PROBLEMS WITH STRATEGIES OF NEUTRALITY

Problems with strategies of neutrality began to emerge when theorists examined them more closely (Bergin, 1980; Strupp, 1980). For instance, how is it that such strategies are not themselves values, even personal values? The ethical codes and training modes of therapy make it clear that therapists *should* be or *ought* to be objective and relativistic, the "should" or "ought" of this sentence betraying the moral undertone of objectivity and relativity. One way to put it is that there is nothing neutral about this ethics of neutrality. Asking therapists to *value* being value-free is contradictory, so why not recognize the impossibility of this value-free status?

OBJECTIVISM

Recent scholarship in the philosophy of science has also challenged the value-free status of the scientific method. Although modernist methods have successfully provided "objective" justification for a host of therapeutic techniques, they provide no objective justification for themselves (Curd and Cover, 1998; Slife, in press). That is, there is no empirical justification for empiricism, no scientific validation for science. Empiricism and the philosophy underlying science are just that—philosophies. One could claim that science has been a most successful method, but then such a claim would merely be one's opinion, stemming from one's personal values. No scientific evidence could be gathered for this claim without already assuming the validity of science in the first place. Moreover, there would be all sorts of pre-investigatory values involved in what is considered successful.

Science is actually filled with such values (Slife, in press). What matters (and is valued) in traditional science, for example, is what is observable and replicable. The problem is that there is no empirical evidence for the assertion that this is what should matter in science. Indeed, the history of science itself does not bear these values out, as several historians have noted (e.g., Kuhn, 1970; Feyerabend, 1975), and there are alternative formulations of science, such as qualitative research, that do not assert the same pre-investigatory values (Denzin and Lincoln, 2000). In addition, the doctrines of observability and replicability are not themselves observable and replicable. They are philosophical or moral assertions about what should be valued, and they cannot be supported by scientific evidence, because, again, such values have to be assumed to garner such evidence.

Therapy researchers often present their research as if their methods are the value-free and transparent revealers of the effectiveness of various techniques (Beutler and Clarkin, 1990; Lazarus, 1995). Technical eclectics, for instance, put great stock in an objective method that reveals which techniques work for which disorders, regardless of the theory that spawned the technique. The difficulty is that some therapy theories, such as existentialism (Yalom, 1980), specifically deny that their theory or their practice is about observable techniques, making it impossible to take part in a method that requires observability and replicability. One could claim, of course, that existential therapy *is* observable (e.g., operationalizable), but then one is in danger of studying only the *manifestations* of existential therapy—to fit the method mold—rather than what existentialists consider truly important. Moreover, to believe that the assumptions of method, such as observability, are the most correct or effective in the first place is to make a very unscientific assertion, because this belief must be asserted before investigation even begins.

RELATIVISM

Relativism has similar problems. Relativistic therapists are supposed to work with the values relative to the client (e.g., working with the client's cultural and ethnic values). However, before therapists can identify which cultural values are appropriate and relative to clients, they must approach their clients neutrally. That is, therapists ought to be nonjudgmental and nonpartisan about the values their clients should have. The problem again lies in the demand or moral injunction for therapists to be neutral—the "ought" of the previous sentence. The notion that one "ought to" approach clients in this relativistic manner is itself a value (Fowers and Richardson, 1996). That is, to be tolerant or open to someone's values is to support the values of tolerance and openness.

The paradox of relativism becomes clear when we consider a client who is intolerant or close-minded. What values do relativistic therapists use in this instance? Should relativists adopt the values of the client, as relativism would demand, and abandon their own relativistic tolerance and openness, even to the client? Or should they uphold the values of relativism and thus use and model them during the therapy session, potentially persuading a nonrelativist?

Either way, the paradox of neutrality disallows relativists from fully affirming their relativism.

The existence of these two alternatives raises an interesting empirical question: which alternative do relativistic therapists typically select (however unconsciously)? The research on this question is fairly unequivocal: relativists do not embrace their clients' close-mindedness and intolerance; they attempt to influence their clients to become more open-minded and tolerant (e.g., Jensen and Bergin, 1988; Smith, 1999; Strupp, 1980). In other words, relativistic therapists not only hold specific values, contrary to their relativism, but they also attempt to promote these values with their clients, often without realizing it. Indeed, they rarely view these values as stemming from their own unique philosophical position (relativism)—that is, as their own private values.

Consider the popular multiculturalism movement in psychology, which explicitly extols the value of "cultural relativism" (Sue, Carter, Casas, Fouad, Ivey, Jensen, LaFramboise, Manese, Ponterotto, and Vazquez-Nutall, 1998, p. 4). In the multicultural view, culturally competent therapists are those who respect the culturally different worldviews of their clients "without negative judgments," because all worldviews—all values—are relative and therefore legitimate (Sue et al., 1998, p. 39). This relativistic stance is viewed as preventing value imposition and oppression. However, the multicultural commitment to relativism extends beyond the therapist. The client, too, should be persuaded to value relativistic tolerance and acceptance of multiple worldviews. In other words, relativism is not just something that all therapists should endorse, but something that all clients should endorse as well—as a kind of absolute (or universal) set of values.

The intriguing thing is that this quasi-absolutism violates the relativist ethic about *not* imposing values on clients, regardless of how widely these values are endorsed. Just because these values are widely agreed upon does not make them any less values, or any less imposing when the therapist insists upon them. And there is considerable evidence that these therapists *do* insist upon them (see Kelly, 1990 and Beutler and Bergan, 1991 for review). Indeed, this is the reason some observers view multiculturalism in therapy as a type of cultural imperialism (cf. Fowers and Richardson, 1996). Far from therapy being a neutral technique, and far from therapists working within the client's own value framework, these techniques and these therapists are pushing a very specific culture and a very specific set of values—relativism.

Actually, this attempt to inculcate relativistic values is completely understandable, both from a historical perspective (as reviewed) and from a human nature perspective. In the latter case, it may be natural for people to want to share what they think is good or correct. Relativists would not hold their relativism unless they believed it to be the best and most healthy approach to living. Why not impart this to their clients? Of course, relativistic therapists are not the only therapists to attempt to influence their clients with their own values. The empirical literature on values makes it clear that no therapist is immune from this attempt to influence. As Kelly (1990) puts it in his review of this research, "therapists [are] not value free even when they intend to do so" (p. 171). The reason we point to relativists particularly is that they are *specifically* dedicated to avoiding the imposition of their values on their clients. Yet all empirical indications are that they are like the rest of us—completely value laden.

RESEARCH ON VALUES

The research on therapist values in therapy dates back at least as far as Rosenthal's classical studies over 45 years ago (Rosenthal, 1955) and involves literally scores of studies (e.g., Arizmendi, Beutler, Shanfield, Crago, and Hagaman, 1985; Beutler, 1979; Beutler et al., 1983; Kelly and Strupp, 1992; Martini, 1978). Actually, Rosenthal's findings hold up remarkably well, though the methods have since been improved and refined. Rosenthal essentially found that client scores on a test of moral values changed during therapy, with those clients who were rated as improved becoming more like their therapists, while those rated as unimproved tending to become less like their therapists. In sum, value similarity was highly associated with therapeutic improvement.

Although the meaning of this association was not fully understood until subsequent studies, this essential finding has been confirmed and replicated across many types of experimental designs, therapists, settings, and clients. Larry Beutler has been a leader in this confirmation and replication (Beutler and Bergan, 1991; Beutler, Johnson, Neville, Elkins, and Jobe, 1975; Beutler et al., 1983). Beutler and his colleagues have also shown that *value convergence*, as it has come to be known, is even more important to therapy improvement than a host of other factors, such as therapist credibility and competence (Beutler et al.. 1975). And all sorts of values seem to be important to perceived client improvement—professional values, moral values, and in many studies religious values were pivotal (e.g., Beutler, 1979; Kelly and Strupp, 1992). This last finding is especially intriguing, because it means that for therapy to be successful, clients and therapists have to converge on their *religious* values.

But what is this convergence? It sounds like a mutual and reciprocal relationship between client and therapist. However, as Alan Tjeltveit's (1986) insightful review of this research reveals, this convergence is not some idyllic fusion of horizons. Overwhelmingly, this research indicates that therapists do not change their values during therapy; only clients change their values (Tjeltveit, 1986). One might say that therapists only perceive success in therapy when their clients have come to have values like their own, including their own religious values. As Tjeltveit (1986) puts it, this phenomenon should not be known as "convergence" but rather "conversion" (p. 516). Therapists are essentially converting their clients to their own way of thinking, including their private religious values, and not considering them finished with therapy until they do convert. As Kelly (1990) notes in his review of this research, values convergence (or conversion) does not apply to clients' ratings of their own improvement; it only applies to therapists' ratings of improvement and normality.

The corollary of this finding is that notions of improvement and lack of improvement are bound up with therapists' values. Therapists do not perceive improvement until clients evidence a certain set of values. Another way to say this is that those who are in need of psychotherapy—those who are disordered or abnormal—are those who do not match our values as therapists. If this corollary is startling, it probably should be. It clearly suggests that private therapists' values, even religious values, are vitally involved in professional judgments, including collective judgments, such as the diagnostic system.

The fact is, values are endemic to all worldviews, cultures, theories, and frameworks (O'Donohue, 1989). Unless therapy is done randomly or capriciously—without a system of any kind—then it is value-laden rather than value-free. Interestingly, the eclectics have already tried a form of unsystematic therapy. However, they soon abandoned this "bag of tricks" approach as unthinking and unethical (Slife and Reber, 2001). The upshot is that therapy cannot be conducted without values, both personal and professional. Therapists cannot work with clients without using, and urging them to use, the therapist's values in the process.

Some tough questions follow from this conclusion. For instance, does this mean therapists are doomed to be dogmatic? How are they different from religious missionaries, attempting to convert their clients to their own value system, including their religious values? Does this mean that they cannot truly be open to the value system or culture of their clients? How can client autonomy be preserved? Several insightful scholars have recognized the significance of these questions over the years. As mentioned, Paul Meehl (1959) surmised this problem at an early stage of this research: "Suppose that the empirical research should show that . . . all therapists are crypto-missionaries. Such a finding would present us with a *major* professional and ethical problem" (p. 257).

FAILED SOLUTIONS

Two ways of solving these problems have been proposed: minimizing and matching. Unlike objectivism and relativism, these solutions acknowledge at some level the inescapability of values. However, similar to objectivism and relativism, they underestimate the power of values. A recent book by Tjeltveit (1999) represents the first solution. The essence of this solution is that therapists should minimize their values to the greatest extent possible. They may not be able to eliminate their values for all of the reasons reviewed, but they should strive to come as close as possible to this ideal to protect client autonomy.

The problem with this first "solution" is apparent in the "shoulds" of the last two sentences. Minimization of values is itself a value; protecting client autonomy is itself a value. And neither value is a "minimized" value. Both are full-blown values, in every sense of the term. One cannot minimize a minimization value without getting into the paradox of relativism. That is, one cannot minimize minimization without trying to minimize as little as possible, but then trying to minimize as *little* as possible is to engage in minimization as *much* as possible, and so on, with the same paradoxical result.

Perhaps most tellingly, research shows the same value imposition as the relativist. When therapists embrace minimization and autonomy as their primary values about values, they also urge their clients to embrace these values as well (Smith, 1999). In other words, if therapeutic relationships are thought to work best by minimizing values and protecting autonomy, then why would therapists not presume that other relationships also work best in this manner? After all, such a finding reflects the 45-year history of this research, across all sorts of values. Whatever values are valued, they are the values that are promoted in therapy. The point is that no strategy of neutrality has resolved this values dilemma—not objectivism and not relativism—and no minimization strategy that attempts to approximate this neutrality, as if it were the ideal, will resolve it either.

Another blind alley is the proposal to match clients and therapists (e.g., Kelly and Strupp, 1992). This approach would first assess the values of all clients and their therapists and then match them so that only those with similar values would be working together. The problems with this approach, however, are manifold. First there is the practical problem of getting a valid assessment of a person's values. Any quick review of this research reveals the many challenges in accomplishing this task (Braithwaite and Scott, 1991). Even if this problem could be solved, another line of research indicates that values change from context to context and problem to problem (Walsh, 1995). This changeability would mean that a perfect match in therapy might become decidedly imperfect as the therapy relationship evolves or as either individual in the relationship changes, for any number of reasons.

But how "perfect" can a match in values really be? When those who advocate this approach discuss "value similarity," what does this similarity mean? How similar do therapists and clients have to be to truly *be* matched? Would such a match have to extend to *all* professional, moral, and religious values? Are any two people on this earth really identical in all these ways? The logistics of this matching approach, as well as the empirical and theoretical obstacles, seem insurmountable.

At this point, we have two clear elements of the values dilemma in psychotherapy. First, therapists have an important sensitivity to values imposition that arose in response to, or at least was nurtured by, *historic* value abuses. Second, we have a cogent line of *theoretical* (and empirical) argument that seems to indicate that attempts at value persuasion, in some forms at least, are inescapable. Where does this leave therapists? From the modernist perspective, it must look like an irresolvable dilemma. Therapists cannot eliminate, suspend, or even minimize their values. Indeed, it appears as if they cannot even eliminate value *differences*. In fact, this is the correct conclusion—therapists must have and act on their values, and they must have and act on their value differences. But then what can they do if this conclusion is true? Are they destined, as Meehl (1959) predicted, to being crypto-missionaries, attempting to convert everyone to their own value system? Is there an alternative?

PHILOSOPHY: THREE MISCONCEPTIONS

Fortunately, there is a relatively overlooked alternative philosophic tradition that is a vital source of aid—the hermeneutic tradition. Philosophers such as Hans Georg Gadamer (1960/1995), Jurgen Habermas (1973), and Charles Taylor (1985) advocate a new postmodern attitude toward values. The modernist attitude has therapists fearing and attempting to avoid values, because they assume that values distort our understanding through biases and obstruct our relationships through conflicts. Hermeneuticists, however, contend that therapists should *embrace* rather than fear and avoid our values. They assert that values have been misunderstood because of the modernist overreaction to premodern abuses.

This misunderstanding has resulted in three major misconceptions that we describe in turn: values are bad, values are subjective, and values are independent of one another (Slife, in press). The first misconception is one we have already alluded to—*values are bad*, at least for knowledge advancement (in therapy and research). This modernist value about values is what some hermeneutic philosophers call our "prejudice against prejudice," our bias against biases (Gadamer, 1960/1995). However, these philosophers point out that very little is possible without values, including knowledge advancement, because human experiences and identities require a sense of what matters (Taylor, 1985). Values organize and prioritize our experiential world, making the things that matter stand out and the things that do not matter recede into the background. Values also help define us as individuals. Who we are involves what we stand for. Who we are entails what we consider to be right and good, and wrong and bad (Richardson, Fowers, and Guignon, 1999).

This is ultimately the reason therapists (and researchers) cannot avoid values—values constitute them. Therapists are lost without the direction that values bring. Modern relativists and objectivists are cases in point. Neither could function without their values—openness and tolerance for the relativist, neutrality and impartiality for the objectivist. Interestingly, openness and neutrality are rarely viewed as values, and certainly not as biases. In fact, many people associate these values with the antithesis of values and biases. Make no mistake, however, that they clearly meet the definition of values, because they provide a code of conduct and indicate what is important. Yet the modernist prejudice against prejudice has led therapists to view them as devoid of values.

The second misconception of modernism is that *values are merely subjective.* This is the notion that values stem from the subjectivity of the mind and are added to our experience of the objective world. If a therapist values honesty, for instance, this value is not thought to be *part of* the world, but rather a subjective meaning that the mind *adds to* it. This is one of the reasons therapists have traditionally attempted to avoid values—they wanted to operate solely on the basis of objective experience, without the subjectivity and presumed arbitrariness of biases and values.

Hermeneutic philosophers, however, have long realized that our subjectivity and objectivity cannot be so easily separated (Heidegger, 1926/1962; Taylor, 1985). What we have considered the objective world—the world of our lived experience—is filled with more values than our Cartesian tradition has allowed us to realize. One cannot experience the world without also experiencing values—that some things matter over other things (Taylor, 1985). The rape of a five-year-old girl is publicly reprehensible and objectively consequential. Although context and culture must be taken into account when understanding this event and our response to it, our horror at this small girl's plight is not just an arbitrary feeling that our culture happens to have invented. There is a kind of reality to these feelings and a kind of objectivity to the value of her life. Some values, in this hermeneutic sense, are not solely private and subjective; some values have a public and an intersubjective quality that is vital to recognize.

The last misconception of modernism is that *values are independent of one another.* Many people, for example, assume that the value of open-mindedness is independent of other values, certainly independent of close-mindedness and religious values. However, the hermeneuticist contends that all values are part of a system of values, a web of values, from which they cannot be extricated without losing their meaning. For the therapist to value open-mindedness, for example, is to simultaneously reject the dialectical value of close-mindedness. The very identity of open-mindedness depends on us understanding where this value begins and ends—where it is and where it is not. Although it is true that we cannot act simultaneously on opposite values, dialectical values still define and give meaning to each other (Rychlak, 1994).

The web of values also contains those values that we must *assume* for the particular value to be possible. In the case of open-mindedness, for example, one might assume that open-mindedness is good, moral, and, for a theistic person, godly. In other words, many values are underlain with other moral and religious values. Even if one is not religious, one still has a value position regarding religion—God, for instance—that can underlie other values (Eliade, 1987). After all, to assume that God does not exist, or even that the issue of God's existence is irrelevant, is to have a qualitatively different position from someone who assumes that God *does* exist and that God's existence *is* relevant. The point is that all values are inextricably connected (and underlain) to other values.

Consider our open-minded therapist, again, this time working with a fundamentalist client—a client, let us say, who is close-minded because she believes that God has commanded it. The webbed relation between the therapist's professional values and the client's religious values is particularly evident in this situation. The therapist has several options, ranging from attempting to change the client's close-mindedness to endorsing it. However, to attempt a change in this value is literally to attempt a conversion, because it means a change in her religious beliefs—her beliefs that God says she should be close-minded. On the other hand, to accept and not dispute her close-mindedness is to implicitly endorse her religious beliefs. Either way, the therapist's values have religious implications. The therapist's values are part of the web of such values, whether or not the therapist intends this.

But what do these three "corrected" misconceptions tell us about what it means to embrace values from the hermeneutic perspective? First, values are real, in a sense, and consequential; they are not merely figments of our imaginations or inventions of our minds. They have an aliveness and an energy all their own. Second, this energy is not always an obstacle to the pursuit of knowledge. Indeed, values can be viewed as constituting (and not being separable from) our understanding and identities. And last, values are intimately related to one another. Part of the energy of values is that they require each other for completeness, including oppositional values. Values exist and make sense only in relation to one another. This means that if values constitute our very being, then *we* require each other for completeness; we exist and make sense only in relation to other valuing beings.

This radical sociality is the reason many hermeneutic philosophers have championed dialogue (Gadamer, 1960/1995; Habermas, 1973). Dialogue is the means of interrelating and completing these values. Indeed, this could be the purpose of therapy—to offer an intimate setting in which values and the people who hold them can interrelate and work toward completion. This purpose is a much more positive picture of therapy than the one Meehl (1959) painted when he lamented the problem of values and feared the crypto-missionary role. Indeed, he saw the problem of values as the potential destruction of the therapy enterprise. The hermeneutic perspective on values, in contrast, leads to a justification for and perhaps even a reorientation of therapy. Although the details of this reorientation remain to be worked out (see Smith and Slife, in press, for more details), it seems clear that a hermeneutic perspective provides an understanding of the role of therapeutic values that meets the historical, theoretical, and philosophical challenges of the issues.

CONCLUSION

It is for this reason, too, that we believed the issue of therapeutic values would offer an instructive exemplar of the crossroads of history, theory, and philosophy. Psychotherapists have long known something was wrong with their management of values. Consider Meehl's (1959) warnings over 40 years ago about the potential for crypto-missionaries. However, empirical research alone, as important as it is, has not been able to deal with the problem. The other parts of the knowledge advancement enterprise—history, theory, and philosophy—are required to illuminate the problem, provide a framework for understanding it, and suggest an alternative framework for resolving it.

History has the unique property of providing perspective and illumination. In this case, many therapists had assumed that the need for neutrality was a given, at least until historical analysis illuminated this "given" as *one* view—the modern view—on a long historic road of views. Still, it is theory, in this case, that supplied a framework for this view that led to the values dilemma, only dimly sensed by Meehl and others. Theory examined the underlying assumptions of the current framework in ways that no empirical program could, revealing the reasons for the practical paradoxes and therapeutic tensions. This theoretical analysis also hinted at seeming solutions (see the "Failed Solutions" section earlier in this chapter) that ultimately only revealed the bankruptcy of the old framework. In the case of therapeutic values, then, another framework altogether is warranted. A philosophical understanding of the current framework is thus required, along with an understanding of possible alternative philosophies, such as hermeneutics, for the field to continue to move in a positive direction.

REFERENCES

American Psychological Association. (1992). Ethical principles of psychologists and code of conduct. *American Psychologist, 47,* 1597–1611.

Arizmendi, T. G., Beutler, L. E., Shanfield, S., Crago, M., & Hagaman, R. (1985). Client-therapist value similarity and psychotherapy outcome: A microscopic approach. *Psychotherapy: Theory, Research, and Practice, 22,* 16–21.

Bartlett, R. (1993). *The making of Europe: Conquest, colonization, and cultural change.* Princeton, NJ: Princeton University Press.

Bellah, R., Madsen, R., Sullivan, A., Swidler, A., & Tipton, S. (1985). *Habits of the heart: Individualism and commitment in American life.* Berkeley, CA: University of California Press.

Bergin, A. E. (1980). Psychotherapy and religious values. *Journal of Consulting and Clinical Psychology, 48,* 95–105.

Bernstein, R. J. (1983). *Beyond objectivism and relativism: Science, hermeneutics, and praxis.* Philadelphia, PA: University of Pennsylvania Press.

Beutler, L. E. (1979). Values, beliefs, religion and the persuasive influence of psychotherapy. *Psychotherapy: Theory, Research, and Practice, 16,* 432–440.

Beutler, L. E., Arizmendi, T. G., Crago, M., Shanfield, S., & Hagaman, R. (1983). The effects of value similarity and clients' persuadability on value convergence and psychotherapy improvement. *Journal of Social and Clinical Psychology, 1,* 231–246.

Beutler, L. E., Johnson, D. T., Neville, C. W., Elkins, D, & Jobe, A. M. (1975). Attitude similarity and therapist credibility as predictors of attitude change and improvement in psychotherapy. *Journal of Consulting and Clinical Psychology, 43,* 90–91.

Beutler, L. E., & Bergan, J. (1991). Value change in counseling and psychotherapy: A search for scientific credibility. *Journal of Counseling Psychology, 38,* 16–24.

Beutler, L. E., & Clarkin, J. F. (1990). *Systematic treatment selection: Toward targeted therapeutic interventions.* New York, NY: Brunner/Mazel.

Braithwaite, V. A., & Scott, W. A. (1991). Values. In J. R. Robinson, P. R. Shaver, & L. S. Wrightsman (Eds.), *Measures of personality and social psychological attitudes* (pp. 661–753). San Diego, CA: Academic Press.

Curd, M., & Cover, J. A. (1998). *Philosophy of science: The central issues.* New York, NY: Norton.

Denzin, N. K., & Lincoln, Y. S. (Eds). (2000). *Handbook of qualitative research* (2nd Ed.). Thousand Oaks, CA: Sage.

Eliade, M. (1987). *The sacred and the profane: The nature of religion.* (W. R. Trask, Trans.). San Diego, CA: Harcourt Brace & Co.

Feyerabend, P. (1975). *Against method.* London, UK: Verso.

Fowers, B. J., & Richardson, F. C. (1996). Why is multiculturalism good? *American Psychologist, 51,* 609–621.

Franklin, G. (1990). The multiple meanings of neutrality. *Journal of the American Psychoanalytic Association, 36,* 195–219.

Freud, S. (1963). Recommendations for physicians on the psychoanalytic method of treatment. In P. Rieff (Ed.), *Collected papers* (Vol. 3, pp. 117–126). New York, NY: Collier. (Original work published 1912)

Gadamer, H. G. (1995). *Truth and method.* (J. Weinsheimer & D. G. Marshall, Trans.) (Rev. ed.). New York, NY: Continuum. (Original work published 1960)

Habermas, J. (1973). *Theory and practice* (J. Viertel, Trans.). Boston, MA: Beacon.

Heidegger, M. (1962). *Being and time.* (J. Macquarrie & E. Robinson, Trans.). San Francisco, CA: Harper. (Original work published 1926)

Henry, W. P., Strupp, H. H., Schacht, T. E., & Gaston, L. (1994). Psychodynamic approaches. In A. E. Bergin & S. L. Garfield (Eds.), *Handbook of psychotherapy and behavior change* (pp. 467–508). New York, NY: John Wiley & Sons.

Jensen, J. P., & Bergin, A. E. (1988). Mental health values of professional therapists: A national interdisciplinary survey. *Professional Psychology: Research and Practice, 19,* 290–297.

Jones, W. T. (1969a). *The medieval mind: A history of Western philosophy* (2nd Ed). New York, NY: Harcourt Brace Jovanovich.

Jones, W. T. (1969b). *Hobbes to Hume: A history of Western philosophy* (2nd ed.). San Diego, CA: Harcourt Brace Jovanovich.

Kelly, T. (1990). The role of values in psychotherapy: A critical review of process and outcome effects. *Clinical Psychology Review, 10*, 171–186.

Kelly, T. A., & Strupp, H. H. (1992). Patient and therapist values in psychotherapy: Perceived changes, assimilation, similarity, and outcome. *Journal of Consulting and Clinical Psychology, 60*, 34–40.

Kuhn, T. S. (1970). *The structure of scientific revolutions* (3rd Ed.). Chicago, IL: University of Chicago Press.

Lazarus, A. A. (1995). Different types of eclecticism and integration: Let's be aware of the dangers. *Journal of Psychotherapy Integration, 5*, 27–39.

Leahey, T. H. (2000). *A history of psychology: Main currents in psychological thought* (5th ed.). Upper Saddle River, NJ: Prentice Hall.

Martini, J. L. (1978). Patient—therapist value congruence and ratings of client improvement. *Counseling and Values, 23*, 25–32.

Meehl, P. (1959). Some technical and axiological problems in the therapeutic handling of religious and valuational material. *Journal of Counseling Psychology, 6*, 255–259.

Messer, S. B. (2001). Empirically supported treatments: What's a nonbehaviorist to do? In B. Slife, R. Williams, & S. Barlow (Eds.), *Critical issues in psychotherapy: Translating new ideas into practice* (pp. 3–20). Thousand Oaks, CA: Sage.

O'Donohue, W. (1989). The even bolder model: The clinical psychologist as metaphysician-scientist-practitioner. *American Psychologist, 44*, 1460–1468.

Richardson, F. C., Fowers, B. J., & Guignon, C. B. (1999). *Re-envisioning psychology: Moral dimensions of theory and practice.* San Francisco, CA: Jossey-Bass.

Rogers, C. (1951). *Client-centered therapy: Its current practice, implications, and theory.* Boston, MA: Houghton Mifflin.

Rosenthal, D. (1955). Changes in some moral values following psychotherapy. *Journal of Consulting Psychology, 19*, 431–436.

Rychlak, J. F. (1994). *Logical learning theory: A human teleology and its empirical support.* Lincoln, NB: University of Nebraska Press.

Slife, B. D. (in press). Theoretical challenges to therapy practice and research: The constraint of naturalism. In M. Lambert (Ed.), *Handbook of psychotherapy and behavior change.* New York, NY: Wiley.

Slife, B. D., & Reber, J. (2001). Eclecticism in psychotherapy: Is it really the best substitute for traditional theories? In B. Slife, R. Williams, & S. Barlow, (Eds.), *Critical issues in psychotherapy: Translating new ideas into practice* (pp. 213–234). Thousand Oaks, CA: Sage.

Slife, B. D., & Williams, R. N. (1995). *What's behind the research? Discovering hidden assumptions in the behavioral sciences.* Thousand Oaks, CA: Sage.

Smith, A. F. (1999). From value neutrality to value inescapability: A qualitative inquiry into values management in psychotherapy (Doctoral dissertation, Brigham Young University, 1999). *Dissertation Abstracts International, 60*, 2337.

Smith, A. F., & Slife, B. D. (in press). *Managing inescapable values in psychotherapy.* Thousand Oaks, CA: Sage.

Strupp, H. H. (1980). Humanism and psychotherapy: A personal statement of the therapist's essential values. *Psychotherapy: Theory, Research, and Practice, 17*, 396–400.

Sue, D. W., Carter, R. T., Casas, J. M., Fouad, N. A., Ivey, A. E., Jensen, M., LaFromboise, T., Manese, J. E., Ponterotto, J. G., Vazquez-Nutall, E. (1998). *Multicultural counseling competencies: Individual and organizational development.* Thousand Oaks, CA: Sage.

Taylor, C. (1985). *Human agency and language: Philosophical papers.* New York, NY: Cambridge University Press.

Tjeltveit, A. C. (1986). The ethics of value conversion in psychotherapy: Appropriate and inappropriate therapist influence on client values. *Clinical Psychology Review, 6,* 515–537.

Tjeltveit, A. C. (1999). *Ethics and values in psychotherapy.* London, UK: Routledge.

Walsh, R. A. (1995). The study of values in psychotherapy: A critique and call for an alternative method. *Psychotherapy Research, 5,* 313–326.

Weber, J. J., Bachrach, H. M., & Solomon, M. (1985). Factors associated with the outcome of psychoanalysis: Report of the Columbia Psychoanalytic Research Center Research Project (II). *International Review of Psychoanalysis, 12,* 127–141.

Wilson, G. T. (1995). Empirically supported treatments as a basis for clinical practice: Problems and prospects. In S. C. Hayes, V. M. Folette, R. M. Dawes & K. E. Grady (Eds.), *Scientific standards of psychological practice: Issues and recommendations* (pp. 163–196). Reno, NV: Context Press.

Wilson, G. T. (2000). Behavior therapy. In R. J. Corsini & D. Wedding (Eds.), *Current psychotherapies* (6th ed., pp. 205–240). Itasca, IL: Peacock.

Yalom, I. D. (1980). *Existential psychotherapy.* New York, NY: Basic Books.

CHAPTER FIVE

A THEORY OF PERSONHOOD FOR PSYCHOLOGY

Jack Martin and Jeff Sugarman

PERSONHOOD, AND RELATED TERMS such as being and agency, have not commonly been employed in mainstream disciplinary psychology, although there has been a small but significant surge of interest in these topics in the 1990s, especially among theoretical, social, and personality psychologists. On the other hand, terms such as self and identity seem to saturate much past and contemporary literature in psychology. Of these latter terms, "self" is especially salient. Just how increasingly salient is documented by the results of a recent search of the *PsychInfo* database by Martin (in press). According to this search, the total number of articles in psychology, published during the 100 years from 1901 to 2001, which contained the word "self" in their titles was 45,594. Of these, 18,774 appeared between 1990 and 2001, and more than 10,000 appeared during the 1970s and 1980s. The total number of these articles appearing before 1950 was a comparatively meager 1,434. The 1960s, as might be expected, ushered in the accelerating growth in "self" publications (with 2,904 such articles) that has continued ever since.

With all of this publishing, it might be supposed that psychologists have come to an agreed-upon understanding of what the self is, or at the very least have shown considerable concern with conceptual issues of this kind. Unfortunately, for the most part, nothing could be further from the truth. For much of the 20th century, the most influential theoretical work on the self within psychology had been the single chapter, The "Consciousness of Self," published by William James (1890) in his *Principles of Psychology*. Only more recently have psychologists such as Baumeister (1986), Cushman (1995), Danziger (1997), Freeman (1993), Gergen (1991), Harter (1999), Markus and Nurius (1986), McAdams (1993), Neisser and Fivush (1994), Neisser and Jopling (1998), Paranjpe (1998), Schiebe (1998), and Singer and Salovey (1993), among others, returned to the task of seriously theorizing the self. For this was a task that had been mostly abandoned during the reign of behaviorism in the early to middle part of the 20th century in American psychology, despite several notable attempts by some analytically (Kohut, 1977) and humanistically inclined psychologists (Rogers, 1967), and a few others (e.g., Goffman, 1959; Lecky, 1945; Mead, 1934), to attend carefully to such matters.

However, despite the recent upsurge in theoretical work concerning the self, the vast majority of psychological inquiry purporting to be concerned with the self remains startlingly atheoretical. In lieu of rigorous conceptual work aimed at clarifying what the self might be, one finds empirical study after empirical study employing frequently used operational indicators of self-concept, self-esteem, self-regulation, and self-efficacy, with little apparent concern for the ontological status of the first term in these hyphenated expressions. Outside of the informative work of those relatively few contemporary theorists of the psychological self, referenced in the preceding paragraph, the student of psychology who wishes to know what a self, let alone a person, might be can find little assistance in the majority of that enormous psychological literature described earlier.

Our general purpose in this chapter is to sketch an ontology of personhood that we believe can help inform psychological theorizing about what we are as persons with a sense of, and concern for, ourselves and others. Our specific purposes are threefold. First, we describe and discuss what we regard as the single most important question concerning personhood, a question that has divided scholars since the first days of the Enlightenment. Next, we propose a conceptualization of personhood that includes conceptions of what we regard as the central aspects of personhood, that is, embodied being, identity, agency, and self. Finally, we describe recent theoretical work of our own that has been concerned with the development of personhood as we understand it.

FROM THE ONTOLOGICALLY PRIOR TO THE SOCIOCULTURALLY CONTINGENT PERSON

Prior to the Enlightenment, ancient and medieval conceptions of personhood tended to be theological in the sense of considering the self as a soul-like substance that connects to the divine within a divinely ordained cosmos. Interestingly, the earliest English-language uses of the term "self" (around 1300 CE) were as a personal pronoun ("same I"), that often was set against the will of God. For example, the *Oxford English Dictionary* provides such exemplary historical uses as "Oure own self we sal deny, And floow oure Lord God al-mighty" (Simpson and Weiner, 1989, p. 906), and "Self is the great Anti-Christ and Anti-God in the world" (Simpson and Weiner, 1989, p. 907).

During the Enlightenment, most historians of psychology (e.g., Danziger, 1997; Harré, 1998; Toulmin, 1977) have associated the initiation of more contemporary Western conceptions of self with the rise of empiricism and its accompanying brand of mental philosophy. In this regard, John Locke's (1694/1959) *Essay Concerning Human Understanding* (the second edition, published in 1694) is taken as a point of departure, because in this work Locke examined personal identity entirely in secular terms. Some (e.g., Danziger, 1997) have gone so far as to imply that until the famous chapter of William James's (1890), "The Consciousness of Self," Locke's essay dominated and determined the direction of English-language discussions of personhood for almost two centuries. Frequently overlooked in this standard version is the work of Locke's immediate predecessor, Thomas Hobbes. Like Locke, Hobbes emphasized what has come to be regarded as the ontological priority of personhood—the idea that human nature is essentially fixed prior to society in the history of humankind, and, by implication, prior to socialization in the development of any individual human being.

We take Hobbes as the progenitor of many of the ideas that subsequently have proven so influential in the psychological study of personhood. For not only did Hobbes (1962) promote the idea of an ontologically prior person, but he also married this idea to doctrines of a physiologically reductive determinism and a dissolutionist approach to the question of human agency. Hobbes's metaphysics held that human nature is entirely reducible to materialistic circumstances consisting of matter in motion, which possessed the capacity for self-direction, with the continuation of its own motion being the ultimate end of the human machine. As an appetitive machine, all behaviors of the person are automated responses to appetite and aversion (i.e., motions toward and away from objects classified as good or evil, respectively). The dominant appetite governing human behavior is power, with all other appetites being instrumentally and strategically devoted to this end.

At its most fundamental (i.e., physiological) level, Hobbes held that human life is a struggle of individual contestants to subordinate others to their wills. Hobbes's original state of human beings (a kind of imagined, historically primitive condition of human beings, of which Locke, Rousseau, and others had their different versions) was a war of all against all. For Hobbes, this primitive state was resolved by a Leviathan who governs a polis contracted by self-interested individuals for purposes of peace and personal security. Moreover, this contractarian arrangement was aided and abetted by a human agency (individual capability for deliberation and action) understood as a calculation of probabilities that particular actions will satisfy desires, a view that was to influence later generations of liberal utilitarians that included Jeremy Bentham and John Stuart Mill. However, Hobbes's version of agency dissolved the debate between strict determinism and free will by reducing deliberative choice and action to the internal motions of the physiologically constituted person.

In Hobbes's (1962) famous seventeenth-century debate with Bishop Bramwell, he argued that our ordinary sense of freedom, as an absence of coercion, compulsion, or constraint, is not at all incompatible with determinism. This is because we are free when we are self-determining, and we are self-determining when nothing prevents us from doing what we will. Consequently, we can be free in the sense of intending and doing what we will, even if our intentions and actions are necessitated by antecedent circumstances. Moreover, Hobbes declared that determinism actually is required in order to make coherent sense of the idea of freedom as self-determination. For in the absence of determination, resultant conditions of chaos hardly could be viewed as an adequate context for purposeful self-determination. He therefore concluded that any kind of mysterious freedom that might be incompatible with determinism was simply unintelligible, a point of view iterated ever since by various compatibilists in response to a succession of allegedly mysterious libertarian conceptions such as noumenal selves, nonoccurrent causes, transempirical egos, and the like.

In Thomas Hobbes, we thus find all of the essentialism, naturalism, reductive determinism, and certitude forming the classic portrait of ontologically prior personhood conceived in the interests of a Baconian science of the individual. For Hobbes, basic human needs, capabilities, desires, and motivations were all formed within each individual independently of social interactions and historical traditions.

> . . . [The] causes of the social compound reside in men as if but even now sprung out of the earth and suddenly, like mushrooms, come to full maturity without all kinds of engagement to each other. (Hobbes, 1962, Vol. 1, p. 109)

Anyone familiar with the reductive functionalism currently favored in contemporary cognitive and neuroscience will recognize the persistence of the Hobbesian legacy in today's mainstream psychology.

Nonetheless, Hobbes and his successors have not been unopposed. Since neoliberals such as Thomas Hill Green and Leonard Trelawny Hobhouse first renounced atomistic conceptions of the person during the latter part of the 19th century, a wide variety of scholars (including many Marxists, sociologists, cultural anthropologists, hermeneuts, feminists, narrativists, poststructuralists, and postmodernists) have eschewed the ontologically prior self. In its place, they have offered various versions of a socioculturally contingent self wherein both the conception and actuality of personhood are understood to be constituted by human sociocultural (especially relational and linguistic) practices. A prototypic statement of socioculturally contingent personhood is Tiryakian's (1962) summary of Durkheim's view that

> . . . instead of collective life arising from the individual, the individual personality is a product of society. If there is nothing in social life which is not found in the minds of individuals, it is because almost everything found in the latter has its source in social life. Collective beliefs are manifestations of an underlying reality which transcends and yet is immanent in the individual. It transcends him because society does not depend on any particular individual for reality, and because its temporal span is greater than that of any individual. At the same time, society is immanent because it is the individual who is the ultimate vehicle of social life. (p. 22–23)

Many scholars who have forsaken the ontologically prior person also have jettisoned commitments to fixed, natural, and essential components of human nature. The new socioculturally spawned person is held to be highly mutable, artifactual, and without a recognizable center that holds across diverse societies and cultural traditions. Interestingly, while adamantly refusing reductions of socioculturally contingent personhood to biology, neurophysiology, or other natural kinds, several of these more recent perspectives (e.g., some versions of Marxism and postmodern social constructionism) have come surprisingly close to eliminating individual personhood by reducing it to its supposed societal and cultural determinants and constituents.

Within psychology, the still dominant ontologically prior conceptions of personhood are increasingly challenged by narrative (e.g., Polkinghorne, 1988), rigorous humanistic (e.g., Rychlak, 1988), cultural (e.g., Marsella, DeVos, and Hsu, 1985), feminist (e.g., Hare-Mustin and Marecek, 1990), critical (Tolman, 1994), pragmatic (e.g., Barone, Maddux, and Snyder, 1997), and discursive (e.g., Harré and Gillet, 1994) approaches that champion different versions of the socioculturally contingent person. Some such psychological perspectives also appear to have little room for psychological agency reflective of an individual's own authentic deliberations, choices, and intentional acts. For example, as Kenneth Gergen (1991) says, "Under postmodernism, processes of individual reason, intention, moral decision making, and the like—all central to the ideology of individualism—lose their status as realities" (p. 241). The same point is echoed by Lovlie (1992): "[T]aken at face value, it [postmodernism] seems to eliminate a basic presupposition of psychology and education: the idea of an autonomous and intentional agent" (p. 120).

Not surprisingly, the strong polarization between traditional atomistic individualism (which assumes ontologically prior personhood) and holistic socioculturalism (which assumes socioculturally contingent personhood) has encouraged a considerable amount of "middle-ground" theorizing. Some such work (e.g., Fairfield, 2000; Martin and Sugarman, 1999a) has attempted to marry a sociocultural perspective on personhood with a kind of emergent agency constituted by sociocultural practices, conventions, and means, but not reducible to such sociocultural constituents. It is our own version of such "middle ground" theorizing to which we now turn. However, before offering our approach as a hopefully viable theory of personhood for psychology, we first need to become more precise about the way in which we will use the term personhood, and related terms such as embodied being, identity, agency, and self.

A BRIEF CONCEPTUALIZATION OF PERSONHOOD

Our conception of a person (or psychological person) is an identifiable, embodied individual human with being, self, and agentic capability. The adjective identifiable references the physical characteristics and social identity of a person. Social identity refers to those socially constructed and socially meaningful categories that are appropriated and internalized by individuals as descriptive of themselves and/or various groups to which they belong (e.g., female, African American, soccer player, attorney, mother, community leader, and so forth). The adjective embodied captures the sense of a physical, biological body in constant contact with the physical and sociocultural life-world. Being refers to the existence in such a life-world of a single human being (an individual). Importantly, the manner of such being is historically and socioculturally effected within traditions of living. Self, for us, is *not* a substantive entity but a particular kind of understanding that discloses and extends a person's being and activity in the world. It is that compelling comprehension of one's unique existence that imbues individual experience and action in the world with significance and provides a phenomenal sense of being present.

Finally, agency, in our conception of personhood, has two aspects, the latter of which conforms to standard philosophical conceptions of the reflective, deliberative agent capable of intentional action in accordance with his or her own authentic desires and choices (e.g., Frankfurt, 1971). More generally, however, we consider agency to refer to the activity of a person in the world, and claim that the philosopher's (and our own) reflective, deliberative agency emerges from prereflective activity as part of the developmental unfolding of an individual life within a collective life-world. It is to this developmental emergence of reflective, deliberative agency and self that we now turn.

A DEVELOPMENTAL THEORY OF SITUATED, AGENTIC PERSONHOOD

Our developmental theory of situated, agentic personhood rests upon three neo-ontological perspectives. We use the term "neo-ontological," because none of these views assumes the kind of fixed, prior essences typical of traditional attempts to posit the existence of entities such as "reality" or "person." Thus our theory is contingent, not prior. However, it does ascribe a real, irreducible agency to the psychological person that is not commonly found in other contemporary, contingent theories of personhood. The three neo-ontological perspectives in question concern: (1) our assumptions concerning "levels of reality"; (2) our "underdetermination" argument for agency; and (3) our construal of self as a particular kind of understanding that discloses and extends a person's being and activity in the world. In what follows, we discuss each of these perspectives before turning to a brief sketch of our developmental theory of situated, agentic personhood.

LEVELS OF REALITY

A common philosophical understanding of reality is rendered in terms of existence independent of human perception and conception. In such terms, the physical and biological world may be taken as unquestionably real, the reality of psychological phenomena is highly debatable, and sociocultural practices fall somewhere in between. Another commonplace in much scholarly work in the more empirical of the social sciences is that physical and psychological (mental) phenomena are arrayed along a continuum of some sort that makes it possible to reduce mental phenomena back to the physical kinds from which they spring (phylogenetically and ontogenetically).

In Martin and Sugarman (1999b), we offered an alternative conceptualization of relations between what we termed physical, biological, sociocultural, and psychological levels of reality. In this alternative understanding, psychological phenomena such as reasons and intentions are held to be real, not by virtue of being mind-independent, but by virtue of the influence they exert on actions in the world that may affect self and others. Secondly, physical, biological, sociocultural, and psychological phenomena are not understood as arrayed along a single continuum privileged by the physical, but are assumed to be levels of reality that are nested within each other in accordance with a general historical unfolding. In particular, psychological phenomena are understood to be nested within sociocultural practices from which the former are constituted, while both psychological and sociocultural phenomena are nested within biological and physical levels of reality.

While biological and physical levels of reality, including human bodies, are necessary requirements for psychological phenomena and constrain what is psychologically possible, psychological phenomena cannot be reduced to these levels of reality. This is because psychological phenomena also require sociocultural practices for their more specific constitution within particular historical traditions and forms of life.

THE UNDERDETERMINATION OF HUMAN AGENCY

More recently, we have relied on our understanding of the foregoing levels of reality to formulate an argument for the existence of *human agency*, which is for us (in addition to *self understanding*) one of the two defining aspects of personhood. We take human agency to be the deliberative, reflective activity of a human being in framing, choosing, and executing his or her actions in a way that is not fully determined by factors and conditions other than his or her own authentic understanding and reasoning. As such, agency is a kind of self-determination.

In Martin and Sugarman (2001a), we argue that the only factors or conditions, other than agency (self-determination), that might determine human choice and action, aside from explicit coercion that does not always exist, are: (1) physical/biological (e.g., neurophysiological) states and processes; (2) sociocultural rules and practices; (3) unconscious processes over which an agent has no control; or (4) random (chance) events. Assuming that these options exhaust plausible possibilities for explaining human choice and action (other than the positing of human agency understood as self-determination in the manner we have specified in our definition of agency), the elimination of each and all of these options as fully determinate of human choice and action will establish the underdetermination of human agency by factors and conditions other than agency (in our sense of self-determination) itself.

Our argument against full physical/biological determinism starts with the observation that human actions are meaningful. Meaning refers to the conventional, common, or standard sense of an expression, a construction, or a sentence in a given language, or of a nonlinguistic signal or symbol. Therefore, the meaningfulness of human actions requires sociocultural rules and practices, the most important of which are linguistic or language-related. Consequently, the only way in which human choice and action could be determined entirely by biological/neurophysiological states and processes is if the sociocultural rules, practices, and conventions are determined by or reducible to such states and processes. Such a full reduction of society and cultures to physical biology seems highly implausible, rather like attempting to explain the activity of baseball players without reference to the rules and regulations of the game of baseball.

To see why full sociocultural determinism of agency also fails, it is important to note that socioculturally governed meanings change over historical time. Such change could not occur if current sociocultural rules, conventions, and practices were fully determinate of meaning and, therefore, of meaningful human action. Thus, current sociocultural rules, conventions, and practices cannot be fully determinate of meaningful human action, but must be at least partially open-ended. Further, it seems highly likely that the potentially open-ended nature of whatever conventional sociocultural meanings are operative at any given time allows for the development of personal understanding and possibilities for action that may contribute significantly to sociocultural change. However, allowance of this kind is not determination.

Moreover, despite ongoing sociocultural change, a good deal of order is discernible in sociocultural conventions, rules, and practices. Because randomness cannot account for order, the sociocultural meaning that is required for human action cannot be random. Finally, humans are at least partially aware of many of their choices and actions in ways that converge and coordinate with the observations, accounts, and activities of others. Unconscious processes alone cannot account for such awareness and coordination of human choice and action.

Having eliminated full biological and cultural determination of human action, and argued against random chance and unconscious processes alone, we are left with the possibility that human choice and action, at least in part and sometimes, result from the authentic (irreducible) understanding and reasoning of human agents. The *underdetermination* of human agency by these other conditions and factors does not mean that human agency is undetermined, only that it figures in its own determination. Such self-determination means that human agency is not reducible to physical, biological, sociocultural, and/or random/unconscious processes, even though all of these may be required and/or help to constitute it.

Of course, it might be argued that some combination of physical/ biological, sociocultural, chance, and/or unconscious factors and conditions might provide a fully deterministic account that does not require self-determination. Indeed, this may be a logical possibility if one assumes some kind of generative (not strictly additive) interactivity among these various conditions and factors. However, without an exacting empirical demonstration of precisely such a generative effect (preferably one displayed at the level of everyday events, not one based speculatively on microparticulate chaos, as recently proposed by Kane, 1998), such possibilities amount to little more than gestures of faith that assume a determinism that is complete without self-determination. Consequently, they seem to us only to beg the question.

Thus concludes our argument for the underdetermination of human agency. The reason that this argument by elimination is important for our current purposes is because we believe that any viable theory of psychological personhood must offer an explanation of human agency in nonreductive terms. This is, of course, precisely what our developmental theory of emergent, agentic personhood attempts to do. However, before turning directly to such theorizing, a few words will help clarify further our conception of self as a kind of understanding.

Self As Understanding

The second of our two defining aspects of personhood is self-understanding or, more specifically, our conception of self as the understanding of particular being (Martin and Sugarman, 2001b). In our view, understanding is a process through which the physical, sociocultural, and eventually the psychological world is revealed, both tacitly and explicitly. That part of a person's understanding that uncovers aspects of her or his particular being in the world is self-understanding (self). Self is an ever-changing, dynamic process of understanding particular being. This said, self, as a core, necessary aspect of personhood, is related to particular identity, embodied being, and deliberative, reflective agency in ways that give it an existential and experiential grounding. This grounding ensures some necessary degree of stability within an overall pattern of processural change. As related to these other aspects of personhood, self is recognizable to itself, even as it shifts and evolves. As such, self as an understanding of particular being is capable of taking aspects of itself (e.g., beliefs, desires, reasons, values) as intentional objects. When such second-order, self-reflective capability emerges within the contextualized, developmental trajectory of an individual life, full-fledged psychological personhood is attained (cf. both Merleau-Ponty, 1962 and Taylor, 1985). Such persons are potentially capable of influencing, to some extent, those sociocultural contexts that are indispensable to their own development as persons.

We realize that the foregoing introductions to our conceptions of levels of reality, the underdetermination of agency, and self as understanding may be difficult to grasp at an initial reading. However, in the following brief description of our developmental theory of emergent personhood (Martin and Sugarman, 1999a), we believe that these three neo-ontological perspectives, and their interrelations, will be clarified.

Our Developmental Theory

At the beginning of individual human life, the infant is equipped with nothing more than primitive, biologically-given capabilities of limited motion and sensation (e.g., nonreflective movements and sensations associated with feeding and physical discomfort) and the prereflective ability to remember, in a very limited physical manner, something of what is encountered and sensed. However, the human biological infant both matures and develops within her or his inescapable historical and sociocultural context. This sociocultural world of linguistic and other relational practices comes increasingly to constitute the emergent understanding of the developing infant. Within this life-world, nested within the ever-present biological and physical world, caregivers and others interact with the infant in ways that furnish the developing infant with the various practices, forms, and means of personhood and identity extant within the particular society and culture within which the infant exists. Psychological development now proceeds as the internalization and appropriation of sociocultural practices as psychological tools, that is, vehicles for language and thought, much in the manner envisioned by Vygotsky (1978, 1934/1986) (also see Harré, 1998 for a neo-Vygotskian account). In this way, developing psychological persons come to talk and relate to themselves in much the same way as others have talked and related to them. In so doing, they become engaged in both the ongoing, always present sociocultural practices in which they are embedded and those appropriated, internalized linguistic and relational practices that they now employ as a means for thinking and understanding.

With such appropriation and internalization and the thinking and understanding that it enables, the individual's mode of being is transformed from one of prereflective activity to one in which reflective, intentional agency is possible. (Vehicles for such appropriation and transformation include a wide variety of contingent processes that psychologists have labeled reinforcement, observational learning, and so forth. However, our theoretical treatment of such "vehicles" differs sharply from that found in the more reductive accounts of behavioral and social-cognitive psychologists [also see Degrandpre, 2000].) The psychological person is a biological individual who becomes capable of understanding some of what the life-world (in its history, culture, and social relations and practices) and her or his being in it consists. Open to the life-world, the psychological person gradually becomes capable of increasingly sophisticated feats of recollection and imagination. Concomitant with these capabilities of projecting backward and forward in time is the gradual understanding of one's embodied being in the world as a center of experiencing, understanding, intending, and acting. In this way, "self" understanding emerges and continues to develop within the historical, sociocultural contexts into which humans are born as biological individuals but come to exist as psychological persons.

Such psychological persons are capable of reflective, intentional thought and action directed outward and inward. The self now has emerged as a kind of interpreted, reflexive understanding that discloses and extends particular, individual existence. When this occurs, thought and action are no longer entirely determined by the sociocultural practices from which they initially were constituted and within which they continue to unfold. Given the inevitably unique history of individual experience within a life-world, and the capacity for self as reflexive, interpretive understanding of experience in that world, psychological persons are underdetermined by their constitutive, sociocultural, and biological origins. This does not mean that psychological persons are undetermined, only that together with biological, cultural, and situational determinants, the "self" understanding and deliberations of such persons may, and frequently do, enter into their determination. Even as psychological persons continue to be formed by the relational and discursive practices in which they are embedded, they also come to contribute to those practices in innovative ways that reflect a self-interpreting agency. As Rychlak (1997) might say, as agents, we are capable of framing "transpredications" (alternative possibilities) that draw upon but purposefully transform what we have experienced and learned as participants in sociocultural and linguistic practices and forms of understanding.

For us, self as understanding and agency as self-determination are the hallmarks of psychological personhood. Together they give rise to what we regard as a uniquely human capability—deliberative, reflective activity in framing, choosing, and executing actions. While never outside of the determining influence of relevant physical, biological, and sociocultural (especially relational and linguistic) factors and conditions, the psychological person is underdetermined by such other factors and conditions and capable of entering into the framing, choosing, and execution of actions, both experienced and innovative.

CONCLUDING REMARKS

The approach to personhood that we have described in this chapter is socioculturally contingent, yet reserves a genuine agency and self-understanding that cannot be reduced to their sociocultural origins or to any pregiven physical/biological properties, processes, or structures of the human body or brain. It is a personhood nested within physical, biological, and sociocultural reality, both historically and ontogenetically. As such, it refuses extreme forms of both atomism and holism and charts a middle course between physical/ biological reductionism and sociocultural determinism. In this sense, it fits within a view of psychological phenomena as irreducibly situated within traditions of living that have unfolded socially and culturally within the physical and biological world. It thus preserves a unique disciplinary ground for psychological studies, assuming the kind of reconfiguration of such studies envisioned by theoretical psychologists such as Richardson, Fowers, and Guignon (1999).

Due primarily to space limitations, perhaps we have not focused sufficiently on features of identity, those socially constructed and meaningful categories that are appropriated and internalized by individuals as descriptive of themselves and/or various groups to which they belong. We also have not pursued possible political and moral ramifications of the conception and theory of personhood that we have advanced. However, some brief mention of these matters might help readers consider possible social, political, and ethical ramifications of our kind of personhood.

Our account of personhood, with its closely related conceptions of agency and self-understanding, does not view human action as purely procedural and rule-governed instrumental activity that somehow is given antecedently to sociocultural and historical contexts. In light of the developmental framework that we have described, our reasons for judging and acting come largely from our having been initiated into a life-world comprised not only of means and practices for reflection but also of goods and ends that contribute substance and direction to our deliberations. This sociocultural and historical life-world, replete with meanings, identifications, and significances, is an ever-present tacit background to all of our attempts to deliberate and understand.

In contrast to a view of deliberation that hinges on instrumental rationality, we pose our conceptions of understanding and self-understanding. Individuals deliberate and exercise choice not simply for the instrumental gratification of desires, but to create possibilities for an existence that is both meaningfully connected to the life-world and something of their own agentic making. The development of a capacity for reflective, explicit understanding makes it possible for us to achieve some measure of critical distance from tradition and from our own niches and ascribed identifications, and, in so doing, critique and revise our practices, ends, and, inevitably, ourselves. From this perspective, the political individual is not a transcendent, rational chooser but rather, an enculturated yet emergent, agent capable of individually and collectively pursuing possibilities that might go somewhat beyond those already enacted in public and civic life.

In pointing briefly and generally to the possible sociopolitical and moral consequences of our theory of personhood, we explicitly want to draw attention to the obvious but frequently neglected fact that disciplinary psychology, in its practice and research, has an enormous social impact (Prilleltensky, 1994). Increasingly, contemporary Westerners understand themselves through the discursive lenses of psychology (Woolfolk, 1998). Moreover, Western systems of liberal and social democracy are animated by particular conceptions of the individual person and his or her rights and responsibilities (e.g., Fairfield, 2000; Rose, 1996). Consequently, the way in which disciplinary psychology conceives of and understands personhood has important implications beyond the confines of psychology per se. By proposing a situated, agentic conception of the person as both socioculturally contingent, yet capable of taking up relevant social practices as psychological resources and wielding these in a reflective, deliberative manner, we hope to offer a viable and attractive alternative to more extreme ontologically prior and socially deterministic perspectives. Hopefully at least some of what we have said here will encourage other psychologists to consider carefully their own conceptions of personhood and the possible implications of these conceptions both within and beyond the disciplinary borders of psychology.

REFERENCES

Barone, D. F., & Maddux, J. E., & Snyder, C. R. (1997). *Social cognitive psychology: History and current domains.* New York, NY: Plenum.

Baumeister, R. F. (1986). *Identity: Cultural change and the struggle for self.* New York, NY: Oxford University Press.

Cushman, P. (1995). *Constructing the self, constructing America: A cultural history of psychotherapy.* Reading, MA: Addison-Wesley.

Danziger, K. (1997). *Naming the mind: How psychology found its language.* London, UK: Sage.

Degrandpre, R. J. (2000). A science of meaning: Can behaviorism bring meaning to psychological science? *American Psychologist, 55,* 721–739.

Fairfield, P. (2000). *Moral selfhood in the liberal tradition.* Toronto, ON: University of Toronto Press.

Frankfurt, H. (1971). Freedom of the will and the concept of a person. *Journal of Philosophy, 67,* 5–20.

Freeman, J. (1993). *Rewriting the self: History, memory, narrative.* London, UK: Routledge.

Gergen, K. J. (1991). *The saturated self.* New York, NY: Basic Books.

Goffman, E. (1959). *The presentation of self in everyday life.* Garden City, NY: Doubleday.

Hare-Mustin, R. T., & Marecek, J. (1990). *Making a difference: Psychology and the construction of gender.* New Haven, CT: Yale University Press.

Harré, R. (1998). *The singular self: An introduction to the psychology of personhood.* London, UK: Sage.

Harré, R., & Gillet, G. (1994). *The discursive mind.* Thousand Oaks, CA: Sage.

Harter, S. (1999). *The construction of the self: A developmental perspective.* New York, NY: Guilford.

Hobbes, T. (1962). *The English works of Thomas Hobbes* (W. Molesworth, Ed.). London, UK: Scientia Aalen.

James, W. (1890). *Principles of psychology.* New York, NY: Henry Holt.

Kane, R. (1998). *The significance of free will.* Oxford, UK: Oxford University Press.

Kohut, H. (1977). *The analysis of the self.* New York, NY: International Universities Press.

Lecky, P. (1945). *Self-consistency: A theory of personality.* New York, NY: Island Press.

Locke, J. (1959). *An essay concerning human undersanding.* New York, NY: Dover. (Second edition originally published 1694)

Lovlie, L. (1992). Postmodernism and subjectivity. In S. Kvale (Ed.), *Psychology and postmodernism* (pp. 119–134). Thousand Oaks, CA: Sage.

Markus, H. R., & Nurius, P. (1986). Possible selves. *American Psychologist, 41,* 954–969.

Marsella, A., DeVos, G., & Hsu, F. L. K., (Eds.). (1985). *Culture and self: Asian and Western perspectives.* New York, NY: Tavistock.

Martin, J. (In Press). *Educating selves.* Manuscript in preparation.

Martin, J., & Sugarman, J. (1999a). *The psychology of human possibility and constraint.* Albany, NY: State University of New York Press.

Martin, J., &Sugarman, J. (1999b). Psychology's reality debate: A "levels of reality" approach. *Journal of Theoretical and Philosophical Psychology, 19,* 177–194.

Martin, J., & Sugarman, J. (2001a, June). *Agency, compatibilism, and psychology.* Paper presented at an invited conference on Determinism, Munich, Germany.

Martin, J., & Sugarman, J. (2001b). Is the self a kind of understanding? *Journal for the Theory of Social Behavior, 31,* 103–114.

McAdams, D. (1983). *The stories we live by: Personal myths and the making of the self.* New York, NY: William Morrow.

Mead, G. H. (1934). *Mind, self, and society: From the standpoint of a social behaviorist.* Chicago, IL: University of Chicago Press.

Merleau-Ponty, M. (1962). *Phenomenology of perception* (C. Smith, Trans.). London, UK: Routledge & Kegan Paul. (Original work published 1945)

Neisser, U., & Fivush, R. (Eds.). (1994). *The remembering self: Construction and accuracy in the self-narrative.* Cambridge, UK: Cambridge University Press.

Neisser, U., & Jopling, D. (Eds.). (1998). *The conceptual self in context.* Cambridge, UK: Cambridge University Press.

Paranjpe, A. (1998). *Self and identity in modern psychology and Indian thought.* New York, NY: Plenum.

Polkinghorne, D. E. (1988). *Narrative psychology.* Albany, NY: State University of New York Press.

Prilleltensky, I. (Ed.). (1994). *The morals and politics of psychology: Psychological discourse and the status quo.* Albany, NY: State University of New York Press.

Richardson, F. C., Fowers, B. J., & Guignon, C. (1999). *Renewing psychology: Beyond scientism and constructionism.* San Francisco, CA: Jossey-Bass.

Rogers, C. (1967). *On becoming a person.* London, UK: Constable.

Rose, N. (1996). *Inventing our selves: Psychology, power, and personhood.* Cambridge, UK: Cambridge University Press.

Rychlak, J. F. (1988). *The psychology of rigorous humanism* (2nd ed.). Malabar, FL: Kriegar.

Rychlak, J. F. (1997). *In defense of human consciousness.* Washington, DC: American Psychological Association.

Schiebe, K. E. (1998). *Self studies: The psychology of self and identity.* New York, NY: Praegar.

Simpson, J. A., & Weiner, E. S. C. (1989). *Oxford English dictionary* (2nd ed.). New York, NY: Oxford University Press.

Singer, J. A., & Salovey, P. (1993). *The remembered self: Emotion and memory in personality.* New York, NY: The Free Press.

Taylor, C. (1985). *Human agency and language: Philosophical papers* (Vol.1). Cambridge, UK: Cambridge University Press.

Tiryakian, E. A. (1962). *Sociologism and existentialism: Two perspectives on the individual and society.* Englewood Cliffs, NJ: Prentice-Hall.

Tolman, C. (1994). *Psychology, society, and subjectivity.* London, UK: Routledge.

Toulmin, S. (1977). Self-knowledge and knowledge of the "self." In T. Mischel (Ed.), *The self: Psychological and philosophical issues* (pp. 185–214). Oxford, UK: Blackwell.

Vygotsky, L. S. (1978). *Mind in society: The development of higher psychological processes* (M. Cole, V. John-Steiner, S. Scribner, & E. Souberman, Eds.). Cambridge, MA: Harvard University Press.

Vygotsky, L. S. (1986). *Thought and language* (A. Kozulin, Trans.). Cambridge, MA: The Massachusetts Institute of Technology Press. (Original work published 1934)

Woolfolk, R. L. (1998). *The cure of souls: Science, values, and psychotherapy.* San Francisco, CA: Jossey-Bass.

Chapter Six

Self-Esteem and the Demoralized Self
A Geneaology of Self Research and Measurement

Scott Greer

Ful wys is he that kan hym selven knowe.
—Chaucer, *The Canterbury Tales*

INTRODUCTION AND TECHNÉ

ONE OF THE MOST ESSENTIAL and, ironically, problematic concepts for psychology is the concept of the "self." While the self is a well known and traversed concept within the personality area, it is also an integral (if theoretically implicit) part of many psychological theories; aspects of social, health, abnormal, and clinical psychology, as well as others, are based on a Western conception of an individualized self. After a "disappearing act," as

Gordon Allport called it, during the heyday of behaviorism, the concept of "self" began to again permeate psychological discourse with the decline of behaviorism and the rise of more client-based practices that both appealed and applied to people's experience. Since the late 1950s and early 1960s, self research has exploded in terms of the number of theories about the self, as well as the number of measures and tests of the self and self-related constructs. Kitano (1989) reported that over 30,000 articles included the term "self" in the title, about 6,500 of which specifically used "self-esteem," clearly the most intensively studied area in self research. However, with all of this research activity, and with its central place among several areas in psychology, there is no consensus as to what terms such as self, self-concept, self-esteem mean or refer to, or how they should be defined within psychological research (Byrne, 1996; Hattie, 1992; Wylie, 1974, 1989). To make matters worse, even the use of the terms is inconsistent: some use "self" and "self-concept" interchangeably; others simply use either self or self-concept and do not differentiate between the two; and others still may use "self-concept" to mean "self-esteem." This may be (or should be) somewhat surprising, considering how fundamental this concept is to psychology. Wylie (1968, 1974, 1989) and Byrne (1996) have noted this rather obvious omission and have repeatedly upbraided psychologists for failing to define these terms. What results, unfortunately, is a theoretical and terminological quagmire, and only recently have some psychologists begun to pay attention to their conceptual language (e.g., Byrne, 1996). Not only does the lack of a clear definition pose problems in interpreting the results of research, but coordinating results with other studies also becomes impossible. Furthermore, in the past 10 to 15 years, a growing number of writers have, on a theoretical level, questioned the validity of this frequented notion, calling our attention to its cultural and historical embeddedness and leaving the nagging feeling that there is no actual "self" behind our discourse about it (e.g., Cushman, 1990; Gergen 1991).

Thus it would seem that despite the fact that the notion of a self (as well as the related "self-concept" and "self-esteem") has become a central part of Western identity, the abundance of empirical self research has failed to ascertain what the self is, or even if we actually have one. The self has been described as both "empty" and "saturated," but as a viable concept for empirical research, it might be best described as "dead." Although there is still a considerable amount of *theoretical* discussion regarding the self, the empirical literature all but ignores this concept, with most researchers considering it a "philosophical question" (Ross, 1992).

With this discrepancy in mind, this chapter presents a genealogical study of the self to discover the reasons for its failure as an empirical target, taking the point of departure to be current self research. In discussing the evolution of Michel Foucault's historiography, Dreyfus and Rabinow (1983) differentiate between an "archaeology," which is a more or less direct historical analysis of discourse and praxis, and a "genealogy," which emphasizes the conditions that limit, enable, or otherwise alter the context under which a particular discourse is made possible. This notion and use of "genealogy" are based on the work of Nietzsche (e.g., *Genealogy of Morals*, 1887/1968), which has more recently been taken up by Foucault (e.g., *Discipline and Punish*, 1977). In a similar Foucauldian vein, Nikolas Rose (1988, 1996) and Philip Cushman (1995) have also presented genealogical analyses of the importance and influence of social and economic context upon the production of psychological knowledge, and these too have been instructive for this chapter.

In keeping with this genealogical approach, the status of the self as an object *of investigation* is not so much what is addressed here; rather, our inquiry focuses on the self as an object *for investigation*. Starting with current practices of measurement, this chapter presents a history of the "measured self" or the "self-as-practiced." By casting the self as an object that is co-constructed through disciplinary activity, this approach not only raises questions about the meanings of self terms but presents a "questioning" (to borrow Heidegger's 1954/1977 phrase) that places the very notion of a self in question and, moreover, in a position to be deconstructed. While the concept of self obviously has a long history before psychology, this chapter will attempt to show that the "disciplining of the self" by psychology, through its investigative practices, has substantively changed its meaning, both within the field and as a psychological concept for public consumption. So not only do we have to acknowledge the role of the larger social and historical context in which this (presumed) entity exists, but, at a more specific level, in order to discuss the meaning of the self in psychological research, we must first consider its genealogy through the methodological and investigative practices that have represented and measured this construct. In this way, the roles of history and historiography in psychology and psychological research are argued to be of prime importance, and perhaps even a necessary, reflexive part of research.

In addition, this questioning extends into the nature of what psychology has actually produced as an empirical, socially practiced object of knowledge, to what uses and ends this knowledge is applied, and how both past and present contexts shaped the construction of this knowledge. In this analysis, various theories and concepts of self are placed in a social and historical context, and the history of "theorizing the self" becomes deconstructed as a form of disciplinary activity. The complete results of this are broad indeed and too vast to discuss here. This chapter concludes with one of the main themes that emerged from this genealogy of the "measured self": "self-esteem as moral judgment," or the uncovering of the moral dimension of human conduct in the empirical (and amoral) discourse of esteem.

METHOD

In conducting a genealogy, we begin by considering the present context, which is contemporary self research and the current practices that define and represent the "self." First, this involves understanding the self in the context of "mainstream" empirical self research. To do this, I conducted an intensive investigation into the current practices of self measurement and assessment. This included extensive research into a number of reviews of the self literature (e.g., Byrne, 1996; Crowne and Stevens, 1961; Demo, 1985; Hattie, 1992; Ross, 1992; Wylie, 1968, 1974, 1989) and a computer search through the *PsycINFO* index, covering material from January 1967 to August 1999. The results of these searches provided a basis for identifying the most popular self measures, how and where they are used, and by whom. Based on this, further research was conducted into specific self measures and the way in which they are used in various forms of research practices (e.g., educational testing, rehabilitation, and vocational assessment). The results obtained through the *PsycINFO* searches were confirmed by Byrne (1996) and Wylie (1989): the *Tennessee Self-Concept Scale* registered the most "hits" by far at 580. The *Piers-Harris Self-Concept Scale* was second, with 480 hits, and the *Rosenberg Self-esteem Scale* came in third, with 385 hits. Other well-known self measures were well behind this degree of popularity: these included Harter's (1982) *Self-Esteem Scale* (168 hits), Coopersmith's (1959) *Self-Esteem Inventory* (162), Marsh's and Shavelson's (1985) *Self-Description Questionnaire* (96), *Pictorial Scale of Perceived Competence* (39), and *Body Esteem Scale* (34), and Bracken's (1992) *Multidimensional Self-Concept Scale* (34).

CURRENT USES, MEANINGS, AND PRACTICES OF SELF RESEARCH

From an analysis of these measures and their use in psychological practice, a number of points emerged regarding the current meanings of the self. As noted above, aside from theoretical discussions about the self, the "empirical" literature has very little to say about this concept. What becomes immediately apparent is that so-called "self research" is actually about *self-esteem,* which is often referred to as "self-concept." In fact, measures of "self-concept," while the most popular self term, are more accurately understood as the person's evaluation of his or her self. There seem to be few, if any, measures of self that assess anything except the concept of esteem or self-evaluation (also noted by McGuire, 1984). Simply put, self measures are measurements of "esteem."[1]

Conceptually, the distinctions among self, self-concept, and self-esteem are fairly straightforward. Theoretically, the "self" signifies the person as agent, or as William James (1890/1950) described it, the "I." Following James's analogy, the self-concept would then be the "me," my perception of myself, or a system of self perceptions (e.g., Markus and Nurius, 1986, and "possible selves"). James (1890/1950) also described self-esteem and even presented a "formula" for its calculation as one's "successes divided by one's pretensions." While some self researchers have acknowledged James's formulation of esteem, very few (if any) follow it explicitly. However, what *has* become virtually universally accepted is that self-esteem refers to one's evaluation of one's self, usually defined as a set of beliefs and attitudes about one's self-concept (Byrne, 1996).[2]

How, then, did the focus on—some might say preoccupation with—self-esteem in psychology arise? And, furthermore, what happened to the "self" as a psychological construct? And why the confusion—and profusion—of self terms? Before attempting to answer these questions, it should be noted that, clearly, our contemporary "esteem culture" has been determined by a vast assortment of factors. These range from the social and political to the philosophical and methodological, and a full analysis and discussion of our "esteem culture" well exceeds the boundaries of this chapter. For our purposes, the focus is on psychology as a disciplinary body and its connection to the larger social arena: how has esteem been conceived of to fit into this boundary, and what functions has it served?

THE EMERGENCE OF SELF IN MODERN PSYCHOLOGY

We will begin by considering the historical roots of the self as it was first understood and used in North American psychology, where the first major self theorist was William James (Hergenhahn, 2001). The concept of "self" as found in James's writings, can be traced to, and to a certain extent contrasted with that of Immanuel Kant. As noted in his famous *Principles of Psychology* (1890), James had studied Kant fairly extensively, and he noted that Kant (1781/1965) had made a distinction between an "ego" and a "self" (das Ich and das Selbst).

Unlike those before him, Kant did not equate "self" with "ego." For Kant, the self was used in an active, epistemological sense—usually equated more with a "knower." The self was also a term that was more associated with the "appearances," things of which we can have some knowledge, but never certainty or truth. The ego, on the other hand—such as the "transcendental ego"—belonged to the "things-in-themselves," a realm we know could logically exist, but to which we have no direct access (Kant, 1781/1965). In this sense, the ego was more of an abstraction representing a unity of consciousness. Kant's position was in direct contrast to Hume's. The latter had argued that there is no self, that our experience only gives us a sense of continuity, but that we cannot logically conclude that this is evidence of a core, singular self.[3] Kant countered that the diversity of our experience (or different senses of self) presupposes a unity of mind (i.e., the "transcendental ego") that provides a foundation for our conscious awareness.

One of James's main interests was consciousness itself, but he wanted to avoid both the epistemological split inherent in the Kantian view of the world, as well as giving the impression that "American psychology" was recapitulating "German philosophy."[4] British and American philosophy of mind and psychology during the 19th century actually paid a great deal of attention to "consciousness," which was understood as the individual's experience. James Mill, J. S. Mill, Alexander Bain, and William Hamilton all discussed consciousness and speculated on its nature, but there was little direct attention paid to the "self" per se (Murray, 1988). However, the topic of consciousness was to serve as the backdrop for William James's lengthy consideration of the self in his *Principles of Psychology* (James, 1890/1950). His treatment of the self stands as one of the first in-depth explorations of the self in North American psychology.

According to James, the existence of consciousness itself serves to distinguish between the "knower," or the conscious subject, and the "known," which is the object(s) of consciousness. For James, there was no "mind-body dualism" or "subject-object" split; there was only experience, which is the fundamental quality of all existence. The act of "knowing" simply expresses a relationship between two aspects of experience. Furthermore, what is a "knower" in one situation can, in another, become the "known"—again, eschewing the subject-object dichotomy (James, 1890/1950).

As Hume had much earlier argued, James saw the self as an aggregate of perceptions. Unlike Hume, however, the "I," which is the knower of these perceptions, is not a compilation of experience but a thought which can itself be known (or perhaps "sensed") through reflection, if only vaguely. Perhaps this thought is a "pure ego" or "unity of consciousness" (based on Kant), which could mean that James did implicitly distinguish between a self and an ego. More importantly, James makes a fundamental distinction—and is one of the earliest to do so in "psychology"—between the self-as-knower and the self-as-known; this would eventually become the distinction between the self and self-concept, respectively. However, this distinction is not between two different "things" but refers to two perspectives on, or types of, experience.

It is also important to note that, after Kant, the ego and self "went their separate conceptual ways" for the most part: the "self" became increasingly used in English-speaking countries, whereas the "ego" was retained in the German tradition. Part of the reason for this undoubtedly lies in the conflict between the rationalist (German) and empiricist (British) traditions and what each considered objective knowledge, with the ego being a more rationalist/ transcendent concept and the self more tied to the empirical act of observation. In any event, the German distinction between "das Selbst" and "das Ich" was not a tradition shared by most 18th- and 19th-century British philosophers. In English, the term "ego" only became widely used in the early 20th century as a result of the popularization of psychoanalysis and the translation of "das Ich" into English. While the terms now have different technical meanings within certain areas of psychology (e.g., psychoanalysis), these do not correspond to their original distinction introduced by Kant.

The positivism that came to predominate through much of North American psychology's early history (i.e., the early 20th century) resulted in a decline in theories and research on the self. The self is obviously not an observable phenomenon, and such ideas were regarded by positivists as too speculative and not the proper subject matter for a "science." By the 1950s, the grip of positivism had loosened somewhat, and there was once again some discussion of the self. Allport (1943), McClelland (1951), Rogers (1951), and Maslow (1965) each posited a "self" construct and successfully argued for its relevance in psychology. As Wylie (1968) notes, in most cases writings on the self were reintroduced to psychology through the clinical area, where behaviorism had had relatively limited success. While some of the behavior modification principles were indeed highly successful, the range of problems encountered in therapy could often not be adequately addressed from a behavioristic standpoint, and, moreover, the role of the client's experience began to take on greater importance in treatment. Carl Rogers (1951), for example, noted that initially he had *not* set the notion of a "self" as an explicit focus for his therapy. However, it was his *clients* who continually brought up and referred to this concept in their therapeutic sessions. Accordingly, as the ban on unobservables was gradually lifted from psychological discourse, writing and research on the self skyrocketed.

DISCIPLINARY ACTIVITY: REFRAMING THE SELF

Although the self was successfully resurrected by the late 1950s, it was *not* the same understanding of personhood that was found at the beginning of the 20th century. First, the interest in "consciousness" and its experiential qualities had almost completely vanished, and would be substantially reframed through the cognitive and information-processing revolution (Bruner, 1990). Second, the construction and understanding of the "social" underwent a substantial revision as well. Earlier in the century, psychologists such as James and Baldwin and sociologists such as Mead and Cooley had much more in common in terms of the ontogeny and development of the self; the "social" arena was more an expression of the social nature of human beings rather than a set of factors or variables that were overlaid on top of a core individual entity. In this earlier view, consciousness itself was seen as evolving socially. The information-processing paradigm, however, stressed the development and role of individual mental processes. The relationship between the social and the self thus changed, as psychology became more focused on the practical prediction, intervention, and control of the individual, thus bringing about a more individualistic focus to theorizing about the self (Morawski, 2000). To paraphrase Bruner (1990), the "social" went from a co-constitutive process that constructs "meaning" to a set of essentially psychological mechanisms located "in the head" processing "information."

These changes also involved a variety of other changes in method and professional practice, most of which were designed to reflect a new methodologically self-conscious concern with objective assessment and measurement. Danziger (1990) notes that while the "history of science" is usually conceived as an interplay between theory and practice, studies on scientific research (e.g., Latour, 1987) suggest that concepts and the methods and practices that are used to investigate them have (at the very least) distinguishable, and in some cases, separate traditions. This appears to be the case throughout the history of self research.

For example, while the utility of the notion of a self was becoming apparent to a growing number of clinicians, the recognized and accepted types of methods for psychological research were still heavily influenced by positivism and neo-positivism. Clearly a blatantly experiential and nonobservable concept such as the self did not fit within psychology's scientific discourse. As noted above, Rogers (1951) pointed out that it was only after the concept of self proved to be integral for client-centered therapy that researchers began wanting an empirical definition of the term. Rogers was somewhat loathe to provide such a definition, because he believed such boundaries painted the self as a "structure" rather than a "process," which he believed was more accurate of people's experience. Yet there had to be a compromise, whereby the self would be accepted as valid and legitimate methodologically but still retain its utility in psychological practice. As a result, new methods for measuring the self evolved, such as Raimy's (1943, 1948) "checklist" for describing the self-concept.

Victor Raimy's research represents some of the earliest attempts to understand the self empirically in a clinical context (Rogers, 1951; Combs, 1999). His notion of self was based on the writings of Kurt Lewin and Gestalt psychology, as can be clearly seen from his definition of the self-concept, as "a learned perceptual system which functions as an object in the perceptual field" (Raimy, 1948, p. 154). To tap the "self-concept" (or what is more properly called self-esteem), Raimy developed a checklist where the person rated self-referential statements. These were then classified by judges into one of three categories: approval of self, disapproval of self, or ambivalence toward self. A six month follow-up reclassification was conducted to check for reliability.

On the one hand, Raimy's study was groundbreaking in that it represents one of the first measures to draw upon phenomenological theory as a conceptual basis for the self (Crowne and Stephens, 1961). On the other hand, it is also significant in that it operationalized the self into self-referential statements (behavior). This transformation of a holistic, experiential notion of self into an empirical methodological context helped bring about, and could be seen as a signal of, the rise of self-concept research. Further efforts to understand the self along these lines soon followed with the development of the Q-sort by William Stephenson (1953), which was quickly picked up and elaborated by Rogers and Dymond (1954). Almost immediately after-ward, as though quenching a long drought, there was a "flash flood" of self-rating methods in the early and mid-1950s, most using an adjective checklist or self-rating scale, for example, *Index of Adjustment and Values* (Bills, Vance, and McLean, 1951), *Adjective Check-list* (Gough, 1955),[5] *Interpersonal Check List* (LaForge and Suczek, 1955), *Self-Rating Inventory* (Brownfain, 1952), *Attitudes Towards Self and Others Questionnaire* (Phillips, 1951), and *Berger Self-Acceptance Scale* (Berger, 1952).

Again, this research activity reflected the general clinical finding that in order to understand personality and behavior change, one had to address the experience of the person. However, the "experiential" and "phenomeno-logical" were now constructed, for the purposes of research practices, in an "objective," linear, ordinal, and serial fashion—or as a data set that was suitable to aggregate statistics. The call for empirical research that provided this type of data became a clear trend in personality research (and psycho-logical research in general). For instance, in 1945 the journal *Character and Personality* issued a policy statement stipulating that it would be giving greater weight to "empirical papers" rather than to theoretical or historical ones, and it changed its name to the *Journal of Personality*, perhaps reflecting a concern for more "objective" and "scientific" research (Zener, 1945; also see McAdams, 1997).

Disciplinary changes such as these led to transformations of many psychological/mentalistic concepts into observable "operational definitions," which are framed in more behavioral and thus quantifiable terms. As can be seen in the research and measures of Raimy (1948), Bills (et al., 1951), Brownfain (1952), Phillips (1951), and Berger (1952), as well as others, this interest in the self resulted in a substantive transformation of the concept. The *concept* of self was now a scientific "*construct*," and was a basis for tests of "self-acceptance," "self-worth," or self-esteem. A substantial part of this transformation undoubtedly lies in the changing context in which the per-son was theorized: in clinical practice, as we see clearly described by Rogers (1951) and later Wylie (1974), the self-as-knower represented features that were integral to therapy, whereas the same could not be said of an experi-mental situation. In the context of empirical personality research (and the "individual differences" paradigm), the agentic self-as-knower proved inac-cessible, yet the products of self (i.e., its perceptions, evaluations, etc.) *could* be tapped through self-report questionnaires (McAdams, 1997).

It is curious and even ironic that the first step toward a "measured self" often was made not by the experimentalists but by the clinicians themselves, who maintained a holistic and an experiential understanding of self (e.g., Raimy and Rogers). As this trend grew, however, the "measured self" was no longer just interpreted in a clinical context by therapists who viewed the person as an organized whole. Instead, these measures soon became tools for more widespread consumption and application, where they would be increasingly used by researchers without the same general horizon of understanding regarding the self as the clinicians at the time (see Pervin, 1990; McAdams, 1997; Wylie, 1989). This process proved truly transformative: research on the self (i.e., now framed as the self-concept or self-esteem) began to be carried out from the perspective of North American personality psychology rather than within the context of humanistic, phenomenological, or psychodynamic clinical theory. The transformative process was thus twofold: the redefinition of self into the more behavior-focused "self-concept" and "self-esteem," and the change in interpretative contexts from clinical and ideographic to experimental and nomothetic.

The self, then, was no longer an agent or a knower but was reframed and reworded as a testable and measurable compilation of perceptions about how one viewed oneself. The constructs of self-concept and self-esteem are therefore the direct descendants of the self in that they represent its first operationalization in contemporary personality research and a disciplinary turn away from the realm of the self as an experiencing social and moral entity. In essence, the problem of agency and moral judgment became "invisible" or rather transformed into the language of North American personality psychology.

Self-concept and self-esteem, on the other hand, offered a much better fit for the type of "paper and pencil rating game" prescribed by ordained disciplinary practices. In this scheme, the person simply rated her or his sense of esteem in a particular area on a linear scale (usually a five- or seven-point Likert scale).[6] The concept of self—with all of its moral, agentic, social, and historically situated qualities—was now simply reduced to "How I feel about myself" (the subtitle of the *Piers-Harris Children's Self-Concept Scale*; see Piers and Harris, 1964, 1984). The Piers-Harris scale is an example of the transformation of the self as found in most later self measures, in that it posits and claims to address a "phenomenological self-concept" (i.e., is still theoretically connected to a notion of self), yet the measure only consists of *80 true/false questions!*[7] This makes clear just how severely truncated the notions of "phenomenological" and experiential had (and have) become in self-concept research (also see Jennings, 1986).

DISCIPLINARY JUSTIFICATION: CONSTRUCT VALIDITY

As discussed by Cushman (1995), Danziger (1990), and Rose (1996), as well as by others, we can interpret psychology's disciplinary activity following World War II as clearly geared toward meeting an increased demand from the private sector for certain types of psychological knowledge. "Self-report behavior," as found through paper and pencil tests, became an objective and an acceptable—not to mention a primary—source of psychological knowledge. As psychological research became increasingly applied, it frequently dealt with large numbers of people, and the utility of questionnaire-type data (i.e., aggregate data) precipitated the rise and acceptance of question-naires as a psychological method. The entire notion that psychological tests could render mental attitudes, beliefs, or desires in objective terms became, as it is now, an accepted practice.

However, it is important to note that this is *a reversal* of the positivists' sanctioned criteria for "scientific objectivity" before the arrival of "construct validity" (cf. Cronbach and Meehl, 1955) in the mid-1950s. It was, of course, no coincidence that construct validity and other new criteria for defining the "objective" were created around this time for aggregate questionnaire-based data, giving official disciplinary credence to these practices (Rogers, 1995). By the 1960s, the reframing of the self as "self-concept" and "self-esteem" was a part of this larger process, reflecting an emphasis on operationalization and quantification, thus making our "psychological inte-rior" more accessible for scientific and social application and consumption.

However, even the "self-concept" did not make an ideal object for research. For one, open-ended questionnaires tapping how people think of themselves are difficult to standardize and cause difficulties when looking for individual differences. It is also difficult to build an empirical model of the self-concept in this way. What was of real interest to psychologists was "esteem," or the idea that our self/self-concept contained an evaluative component that could be manipulated to affect behavior. How much we esteem our "selves" carries the promise of great practical utility—child development, socialization, personality, work and family stress, and a myriad of clinical applications all point to "esteem" as a crucial variable (c.f., Wylie, 1968, 1974, 1989). Moreover, and as noted earlier, esteem was the concept that caught psychologists' attention in the first place (*viz.,* earlier measures of "self-acceptance" or "self-worth"), not only in its presumed utility to change behavior, but it fit the empirical methodological bill much better than any other aspects of the self. In rating self-esteem, the researcher usually provides the categories; it is forced choice. Moreover, esteem can be con-ceptualized in an ordinal, serial, and linear fashion, making it amenable to psychology's "individual differences" paradigm and aggregate methods and statistics. Thus esteem has come to be understood as a quantity, or set of quantities, that is not only associated with the self-concept, but is often referred to *as* "self-concept."

On a related front, the results of empirical esteem research *appears* to examine it at the level of the individual. However, the almost exclusive reliance on aggregate data and the use of inferential statistics places the emphasis unmistakably on the *overall characteristics of the group.* The individual's experience and the qualities of the individual person's esteem are not rep-resented as psychological knowledge but as "data" in the calculation and construction of esteem. "Esteem" is therefore not so much psychological knowledge about the individual as it is *statistical knowledge* about a sample of the population. Danziger (1979, 1990) has noted how the use of aggregate data in North American psychological practices often conflates psychological knowledge (e.g., knowledge about an individual's mental processes) with statistical knowledge (e.g., knowledge about how a group responded to a set of questions). Accordingly, "esteem" as a psychological variable is, in a meaningful way, co-constructed by the methods used to collect and analyze the data. Perhaps "esteem" is better understood as representing a form of disciplinary knowledge about aggregate self-evaluative responses or, at the very least, a set of disciplinary practices concerning the way that these responses are obtained, understood, and used.

DISCIPLINARY PRODUCT: ESTEEM AS A "TRAIT"

An important part of this "death and transfiguration of the self" is that questions regarding the self became interpreted within the hegemony of North American personality research; thus self research became included as part of the individual differences paradigm (Hattie, 1992; McAdams, 1997; Ross, 1992). Significantly, this has led to the investigation and representation of self-esteem as a "personality trait." In this view, people have esteem in a similar way that they have other traits, such as agreeableness, conscientiousness, extraversion, and so on.

Obviously the trait approach fits well with the individual differences paradigm and the aggregate nomothetic model of personality research espoused by mainstream psychology (as described above). This type of data also provides a basis for the "discovery" of the factors (*viz.,* factor analysis) constituting self-esteem (or self-concept). While there is not room to discuss the genealogy of psychological knowledge as "statistics-driven trait psychology," it is important to note that such practices have been applied to the person's physical and mental characteristics since the time of Francis Galton and James Cattell (Hergenhahn, 2001). Such practices were later ingrained in American psychology by personality researchers such as Raymond Cattell (McAdams, 1997). Cattell (1946, 1950) developed a quantitative system of prediction based on traits, roles, and states, called a "specification equation," where each element was weighted according to its present influence on the situation. The point is, psychologists researching the self in postwar America found themselves (pardon the pun) with a large accessible population and an increasing demand by private and public sectors for aggregate psychological knowledge (Danziger, 1990; McAdams, 1997; Pervin, 1990). Armed with construct validity and new statistical techniques such as factor analysis, the mandate was set for establishing knowledge about the self—albeit particular kinds of knowledge about particular aspects of identity. As the construct of esteem was evolving from the agentic self in psychotherapeutic practice to a personality variable in empirical research, it became at the same time caught up in the individual differences "industry" in personality psychology and would soon be represented as (just) another personality trait.

Even a cursory glance at the contemporary literature overwhelmingly shows this to be the case, to an almost exclusive degree (e.g., Brinthaupt and Erwin, 1992; Burns, 1979; Byrne, 1996; Demo, 1985; Wylie, 1989).

DISCUSSION AND CONCLUSION

Based on this genealogy of self research, I submit that the concept of self raises issues that one cannot simply ignore, as behaviorism had ignored mental states, nor is an answer to be found in transforming or reframing the self into behavioral operational definitions of self-concept or self-esteem. The notion of a self in its philosophical and early psychological history (i.e., the modern self) has traditionally involved qualities such as agency, intentionality, and consciousness (e.g., Descartes, Leibniz, Kant, Freud, etc.). Despite their differences, what each of these theories has in common is a theory of self (or ego) that establishes the foundation of agency and moral judgment (Greer, 1999). In other words, the self or ego is not only the seat of consciousness in these views, but awareness of our actions clearly has moral implications, just as our awareness of moral codes does in governing our future conduct. As a result, consciousness and agency are tied to moral judgment (as discussed in Taylor, 1989). (These modern theories of morality and self obviously inherited a Christian emphasis on the soul as the source of our moral being.)

However, the transformation of self into self-concept and self-esteem in American personality research has left these qualities of the self either unaddressed (because they are not empirical questions) or in an uncertain or indeterminate state. In short, the questions of agency, intentionality, reflexivity, and moral judgment are gaps left behind in the wake of the disciplinary transformation of the self. Some may argue that these are in fact addressed by contemporary self theory through the current decision-making models of cognitive psychology and information-processing. However, I believe that this argument falls short, particularly with respect to the notion of esteem as a trait of the "de-moralized self." I will first consider the problems with esteem as a trait and then turn to a more general critique of moral reasoning as information-processing.

"Esteem as a personality trait" is untenable because traits are not products of thought, nor a set of generated perceptions. Rather, self-concept and self-esteem are (if anything at all) the *result* of reflexivity and consciousness, and their existence must be understood as emanating from behavior and cognition rather than a *cause* of or upon it (although when discussing reflexivity, the causation is often reciprocal). As such, the assumption that "self-esteem" is a real, fixed, naturally occurring, normally distributed "variable" seems perverse. This is, of course, connected to the further belief that this "esteem variable" accounts for a percentage of the variance in behavior—which, at this point, no longer makes sense.

The presence and influence of the trait paradigm and the cognitive revolution of the 1950s and 1960s can also be seen as part of the shift away from self and the involvement of self in awareness and consciousness. Consider, for example, the subtle but important rewording of "self-acceptance" as "self-concept." The notion of "self-acceptance," such as found in early self and personality measures (e.g., Brownfain, 1952; Berger, 1952; Gough, 1955), was at least implicitly understood as an attitude posited by a self. With the advent of cognitive psychology and information-processing models, however, the concept of a hierarchical information-processing system replaced the intentional and meaning-generating qualities of the self. On the other hand, what was meaningful and relevant about the self to the consumers of psychological knowledge was recast into the more accessible and testable traits of self-concept and self-esteem. The self, in other words, became "reduced" to self-concept and self-esteem. What is even more striking is that the qualities of self that involved intention, moral judgment, and reflexivity that were once *required* for acts such as self-acceptance or evaluation were reconstituted under an information-processing approach and represented as *products* (e.g., the self-concept and self-esteem) of cognitive processes.

While the role of agency, as well as intentionality and moral judgment, has traditionally involved a theory of self, recent theories of cognitive and information-processing have bypassed a homuncular self-as-knower. Instead, issues of "moral reasoning" that are inherent in self-evaluations are understood along the lines of social comparisons and "present self" versus "ideal self" discrepancies (e.g., the Marsh-Shavelson model; see Shavelson, Hubner, and Stanton, 1976; Shavelson and Bolus, 1982; Shavelson and Marsh, 1986). These comparison-based perceptions are schema-driven inferences about the quality of our actions, resulting in an experience conceptualized as self-concept or self-esteem (e.g., Piers and Harris, 1964, 1984). Along these lines, others see self-esteem as represented in terms of various "possible selves" (Markus and Nurius, 1986), thus depicting self-esteem as a schematized set of "reflected appraisals" (to coin Mead's phrase).[8] Thus current self research suggests that our self-esteem is primarily based on appraisals from others, which are understood within a set of codified social rules adopted from our environment. These rules and past appraisals are represented as internalized self-schemata in either a present or future context (how do I feel about myself now, and how would I like to see myself in the future?). For example, I helped an elderly lady across the street, therefore I am a good person (or at least I did something that "good" people do). Recent research also argues that esteem is therefore not a global attitude toward the self, but is best understood as "multidimensional"; that is, as a collection of behavior-specific attitudes: I have high social esteem, but low academic (math) esteem, and so forth (e.g., Bracken, 1992; Byrne, 1996; Marsh, 1986a, 1986b, 1990).

However, if one rejects the idea that self-esteem and self-concept can be properly understood as traits, then the roles of agency, intentionality, and moral judgment are regarded as *enabling* the construction of (rather than simply contained in) a self-concept. Furthermore, the questions then return to some of the original (and I believe perennial) concerns of being human. More specifically, we first have to recognize that the act of esteem is essentially *a moral act*: as defined, it is an evaluation or appraisal of our (or others') conduct, judging it good or bad, competent or impotent, free or bound. However, in cognitive and information-processing theories, which eschew a self, the question of moral judgment has been rendered invisible by the language of data, schemata, and esteem, rather than a language that addresses "meaning," "conduct," and "moral judgment" on its own terms. The act of "esteeming" both self and others is not described or understood as an essentially moral act or judgment in this view, but simply as an evaluation of information (or data), which is not unlike any other type of information-processing. In other words, human conduct is not grounded in a moral domain, but becomes "moralized" through a particular type of cognitive mediation of data (which I see as a form of "psychologism"). Our current empirical models of self-concept thus apparently agree with Shakespeare: "Nothing is good or bad, except that thinking makes it so." This is a surprisingly normative and relativistic moral theory for a field that posits objective realism. Ironically, morality and meaning are understood as radically subjective, and become a matter of perception, representation, and perspective. Actions themselves do not have any "real" moral qualities and are in fact not "moral" at all unless they have been perceived and represented by consciousness. Therefore, it is the psychological representation of action that essentially defines and denotes the moral act.

Alternatively, I argue that the notion that human conduct and discourse have an inherent moral quality is one that is difficult to deny, suppress, or (in this case) restate as something else (such as esteem). The idea of a moral dimension, which involves discourse about personal identity, is part of what it means to be, to exist. The concept of identity, regardless of what conception of self one uses (or does not use), implies an "inescapable moral framework" (as described by Heidegger, 1926/1962; and more recently, Taylor, 1989). Thus questions and issues involving identity and the means by which we define that identity are inherently moral, social, and historical in nature. For example, it is not just that I now frame a certain portion of my moral questions in terms of individual esteem rather than the quality of my soul in the eyes of God (*viz.*, personal salvation), but that the *sources of esteem* in this social context represent the acquiring and having of "esteem" in a particular way. As a result, psychological research that defines the construction and representation of esteem as a product of ahistorical, acontextual, and amoral processes must clearly be called into question.

More specifically, the view I propose here argues that instead of cloaking the moral dimension within psychological variables such as esteem, contemporary accounts of moral action and judgment should focus on:

(1) as Taylor (1989) suggests, the language of moral understanding as the "sources" of moral judgment; (2) the social and historical context and the networks of relations that draw upon this language (e.g., the "esteem" culture); (3) a decognitivizing of moral judgments as schematic representations and inferences based on self and social perceptions; and, most significantly, (4) a relocation of moral discourse in terms of not only language (as a source of social/moral meaning), but as inherent to the various social and cultural systems that use this language in various forms of discourse and social praxis. Further, social and disciplinary practices in the social sciences must be addressed—specifically the means (i.e., technology) by which self-knowledge is represented and communicated.

I maintain that future research would greatly benefit by considering esteem a product of both individual and social activities. The horizons of meaning for esteem become more full and perhaps "authentic" when set within a discourse that recognizes the importance of the social, moral, and historical dimensions of conduct. The absence of any of these aspects in current self research indicates that we have yet to really ask questions about *the act of esteeming itself*: "What does it mean to 'esteem' or 'be esteemed'?" I would suggest that when we understand esteem as a form of moral conduct, we are recognizing our conduct as a type of social and moral discourse grounded in our responsibility and relationship to each other (e.g., what makes me feel good is inextricably bound to the fact that I exist in this world with "you"). I believe how we characterize or theorize these acts is indeterminate, and that perhaps they do not have any essential qualities themselves (i.e., social, individual, transcendental). What we do know "a priori" is that they will be part of an ongoing discourse regarding the various dimensions of human existence—the social, moral, and historical, for example. Eventually I see this as a part of the question of being: what it means to be, to exist, and to experience this existence as being-in-the-world. To articulate this question, however, we must (to paraphrase Heidegger) better understand the "house" (i.e., our language) "in which being dwells."

NOTES

1. There is, to be sure, a tremendous literature—including a number of measures—on an assortment of self-related terms, for example: self-efficacy, self-monitoring, self-presentation, self-discrepancy, self-regulation, self-deception, self-handicapping, self-determination, and so on. However, this vast and sprawling literature follows from a later and somewhat different origin. As discussed later, the measures of self-concept and self-esteem are more directly connected to the concept of a self and are in a significant sense the conceptual heirs to—or even replacements for—the self.

2. Of course, this only holds true for those who recognize the difference between self and self-concept.

3. Hume's argument, in fact, has some contemporary proponents, such as Markus and Nurius (1986), who argue for the existence of a plurality of "possible selves" instead

of a singular self. Various information-processing theories of self also favor a network versus a homuncular model.

4. Consciousness was also central to Wundt and German psychology at around the same time. Wundt considered part of his research to be on immediate conscious experience; that is, the use of, among other methods, "introspection" (i.e., as internal perception) was focused on consciousness (Danziger, 1980).

5. This was to be part of the basis for the *California Psychological Inventory* (Gough, 1957).

6. In early measures of esteem, the terms "self-acceptance" or the rather culturally embedded notion of "self worth" are often used (Crowne and Stephens, 1961; Wylie, 1968).

7. All of the major self-concept/self-esteem scales use the Likert or true/false format; for examples, see *Piers-Harris Children's Self-Concept Scale* (Piers and Harris, 1964); *Self-Description Questionnaire I-III* (Marsh, 1992a, 1992b, 1992c); *Tennessee Self Concept Scale* (Fitts, 1965); *Rosenberg Self-Esteem Scale* (Rosenberg, 1965).

8. Some of the more popular self-concept/self-esteem measures (e.g., Rosenberg, 1965) are theoretically linked to Mead (Greer, 1999).

REFERENCES

Allport, G. W. (1943). The ego in contemporary psychology. *Psychological Review, 50*, 451–476.

Berger, E. M. (1952). The relation between expressed acceptance of self and expressed acceptance of others. *Journal of Abnormal Social Psychology, 47*, 778–782.

Bills, R. E., Vance, E. L., & McLean, O. S. (1951). An index of adjustment and values. *Journal of Consulting Psychology, 51*, 257–261.

Bracken, B. A. (1992). *Multidimensional Self-Concept Scale*. Austin, TX: Pro-Ed.

Brinthaupt, T. M., & Erwin, L. J. (1992). Reporting about the self: Issues and implications. In T. M. Brinthaupt & R. P. Linka (Eds.), *The self: Definitional and methodological issues* (pp. 137–171). Albany, NY: State University of New York Press.

Brownfain, J. J. (1952). Stability of the self-concept as a dimension of personality. *Journal of Abnormal Social Psychology, 47*, 597–606.

Bruner, J. (1990). *Acts of meaning*. Cambridge, UK: Cambridge University Press.

Burns, R. B. (1979). *The self-concept: Theory measurement, development, and behavior*. New York, NY: Longman.

Byrne, B. (1996). *Measuring the self-concept across the life span: Issues and instrumentation*. Washington, DC: American Psychological Association.

Cattell, R. B. (1946). *Description and measurement in personality*. New York, NY: World Book.

Cattell, R. B. (1950). *Personality: A systematic, theoretical, and factual study*. New York, NY: McGraw-Hill.

Chaucer, G. (1987). *The Canterbury tales* (N. Coghill, Trans.). New York, NY: Penguin Books.

Combs, A. (1999). *Being and becoming: A field approach to psychology*. New York, NY: Springer-Verlag.

Coopersmith, S. (1959). A method for determining types of self-esteem. *Journal of Abnormal Social Psychology, 59*, 87–94.

Cronbach, L. J., & Meehl, P. (1955). Construct validity in psychological tests. *Psychological Bulletin, 52*, 281–302.

Crowne, D. P., & Stephens, M. W. (1961). Self-acceptance and self-evaluative behavior: A critique of methodology. *Psychological Bulletin, 58*, 104–121.

Cushman, P. (1990). Why the self is empty: Toward a historically situated psychology. *American Psychologist, 45*, 599–611.

Cushman, P. (1995). *Constructing the self, constructing America: A cultural history of psychotherapy.* Reading, MA: Addison-Wesley.

Danziger, K. (1979). The social origins of modern psychology. In A. R. Buss (Ed.), *Psychology in social context* (pp. 27–45). New York, NY: Irvington.

Danziger, K. (1980). The history of introspection reconsidered. *Journal of the History of the Behavioral Sciences, 16*, 241–262.

Danziger, K. (1990). *Constructing the subject: Historical origins of psychological research.* Cambridge, UK: Cambridge University Press.

Demo, D. (1985). The measurement of self-esteem: Refining our methods. *Journal of Personality and Social Psychology, 48*, 1490–1502.

Dreyfus, H., & Rabinow, P. (1983). *Michel Foucault: Beyond structuralism and hermeneutics* (2nd Ed.). Chicago, IL: University of Chicago Press.

Fitts, W. H. (1965). *Tennessee Self-Concept Scale: Manual.* Los Angeles, CA: Western Psychological Services.

Foucault, M. (1977). *Discipline and punish: The birth of the prison* (2nd Ed., A. Sheridan, Trans.). New York, NY: Vintage.

Gergen, K. J. (1991). *The saturated self.* New York, NY: Basic.

Gough, H. G. (1955). *Reference handbook for the Gough adjective check-list.* Berkeley, CA: University of California Institute of Personality Assessment and Research.

Gough, H. G. (1957). *California psychological inventory: Manual.* Palo Alto, CA: Consulting Psychologists Press.

Greer, S. (1999). *Making $ense out of the self: A social constructionist perspective on the history and measurement of the self.* Unpublished doctoral dissertation. Toronto: York University.

Harter, S. (1982). The Perceived Competence Scale for Children. *Child Development, 53*, 87–97.

Hattie, J. (1992). *Self-concept.* Hillsdale, NJ: Erlbaum.

Heidegger, M. (1962). *Being and time.* (J. Macquarrie & E. Robinson, Trans.). New York: Harper and Row. (Original work published 1926)

Heidegger, M. (1977). The question concerning technology. In D. F. Krell (Ed.), *Martin Heidegger: Basic writings* (pp. 283–317). New York, NY: Harper and Row. (Original work published in 1954)

Hergenhahn, B. R. (2001). *An introduction to the history of psychology* (4th Ed.). Belmont, CA: Wadsworth.

James, W. (1950). *Principles of psychology* (2 vols). New York, NY: Dover. (Original work published 1890)

Jennings, J. L. (1986). Husserl revisited: The forgotten distinction between psychology and phenomenology. *American Psychologist, 41*, 1231–1240.

Kant, I. (1965). *Critique of pure reason* (N. K. Smith, Trans.). New York, NY: St. Martin's Press. (Original work published 1781)

Kitano, H. (1989). Alcohol and drug use and self-esteem: A sociocultural perspective. In A. Mecca, N. Smelser, and J. Vasconcellos (Eds.), *The social importance of self-esteem* (pp. 294–326). Berkeley, CA: University of California Press.

LaForge, R., & Suczek, R. F. (1955). The interpersonal dimension of personality: III. An interpersonal check list. *Journal of Personality, 24*, 94–112.

Latour, B. (1987). *Science in action.* Cambridge, MA: Harvard University Press.

Markus, H., & Nurius, P. (1986). Possible selves. *American Psychologist, 41*, 954–969.

Marsh, H. W. (1986a). Verbal and math self-concepts: An internal/external frame of reference model. *American Educational Research Journal, 23*, 129–149.

Marsh, H. W. (1986b). Global self-esteem: Its relation to specific facets of self-concept and their importance. *Journal of Personality and Social Psychology, 51*, 1224–1236.

Marsh, H. W. (1990). The structure of academic self-concept: The Marsh/Shavelson model. *Journal of Educational Psychology, 82*, 623–636.

Marsh, H. W. (1992a). *Self-Description Questionnaire (SDQ) I: A theoretical and empirical basis for the measurement of multiple dimensions of preadolescent self-concept. A test manual and research monograph.* Macarthur, New South Wales, Australia: University of Western Sydney, Faculty of Education.

Marsh, H. W. (1992b). *Self-Description Questionnaire (SDQ) II: A theoretical and empirical basis for the measurement of multiple dimensions of adolescent self-concept. A test manual and research monograph.* Macarthur, New South Wales, Australia: University of Western Sydney, Faculty of Education

Marsh, H. W. (1992c). *Self-Description Questionnaire (SDQ) III: A theoretical and empirical basis for the measurement of multiple dimensions of late adolescent self-concept. A test manual and research monograph.* Macarthur, New South Wales, Australia: University of Western Sydney, Faculty of Education.

Marsh, H. W., & Shavelson, R. J. (1985). Self-concept: Its multifaceted, hierarchical structure. *Educational Psychologist, 20*, 107–125.

Maslow, A. H. (1965). Some basic propositions of a growth and self-actualization psychology. In C. L. Stacey, & M. F. DeMartino (Eds.), *Understanding human motivation* (Rev. Ed., pp. 26–47). Cleveland, OH: World Publishing Co.

McAdams, D. (1997). A conceptual history of personality psychology. In R. Hogan, J. Johnson, & S. Briggs, S. (Eds.), *Handbook of personality psychology* (pp. 3–39). San Diego, CA: Academic Press.

McClelland, D. C. (1951). *Personality.* New York, NY: Holt, Rinehart, & Winston.

McGuire, W. J. (1984). Search for the self: Going beyond self-esteem and the reactive self. In R. A. Zucker, J. Aronoff, & A. I. Rabin (Eds.), *Personality and the prediction of behavior* (pp. 73–120). New York, NY: Academic Press.

Morawski, J. (2000). Social psychology a century ago. *American Psychologist, 55*, 427–430.

Murray, D. (1988). *A history of western psychology.* (2nd Ed.). Englewood Cliffs, NJ: Prentice Hall Inc.

Nietzsche, F. (1968). On the genealogy of morals. In W. Kaufmann (Ed. & Trans.), *Basic writings of Nietzsche* (pp. 449–599). New York, NY: Random House. (Original work published 1887)

Pervin, L. (1990). A brief history of modern personality theory. In L. Pervin (Ed.), *Handbook of personality: Theory and research* (pp. 3–18). New York, NY: Guilford Press.

Phillips, E. L. (1951). Attitudes towards self and others: A brief questionnaire-report. *Journal of Consulting Psychology, 15*, 79–81.

Piers, E. V., & Harris, D. B. (1964). Age and other correlates of self-concept in children. *Journal of Educational Psychology, 55*, 91–95.

Piers, E. V., & Harris, D. B. (1984). *Piers-Harris children's self-concept scale: Revised manual.* Los Angeles, CA: Western Psychological Services.

Raimy, V. C. (1943). *The self-concept as a factor in counseling and personality organization.* Doctoral dissertation, Ohio State University.

Raimy, V. C. (1948). Self reference in counseling interviews. *Journal of Consulting Psychology, 12,* 153–163.

Rogers, C. R. (1951). *Client-centered therapy.* New York, NY: Houghton Mifflin.

Rogers, C. R., & Dymond, R. F. (1954). *Psychotherapy and personality change: Coordinated studies in the client-centered approach.* Chicago, IL: University of Chicago Press.

Rogers, T. B. (1995). *The psychological testing enterprise: An introduction.* Pacific Grove, CA.: Brooks/Cole.

Rose, N. (1988). Calculable minds and manageable individuals. *History of the Human Sciences, 1,* 179–200.

Rose, N. (1996). *Inventing our selves: Psychology, power, and personhood.* Cambridge, UK: Cambridge University Press.

Rosenberg. M. (1965). *Society and the adolescent self-image.* Middletown, CT: Wesleyan University Press.

Ross, A. (1992). *The sense of self: Research and theory.* New York: Springer.

Shavelson, R. J., & Bolus, R. (1982). Self-concept: The interplay of theory and method. *Journal of Educational Psychology, 74,* 3–17.

Shavelson, R. J., & Marsh, H. W. (1986). On the structure of the self-concept. In R. Schwarzer (Ed.), *Self-related cognitions in anxiety and motivation* (pp. 305–330). Hillsdale, NJ: Erlbaum.

Shavelson, R. J., Hubner, J. J., & Stanton, G. C. (1976). Self-concept: Validation of construct interpretations. *Review of Educational Research, 46,* 407–441.

Stephenson, W. (1953). *The study of behavior: Q-technique and its methodology.* Chicago, IL: University of Chicago Press.

Taylor, C. (1989). *Sources of the self: The making of the modern identity.* Cambridge, MA: Harvard University Press.

Wylie, R. (1968). The present status of self theory. In E. F. Borgatta & W. W. Lambert (Eds.), *Handbook of personality theory and research* (pp. 728–787). Chicago, IL: Rand McNally & Company.

Wylie, R. (1974). *The self-concept* (Rev. ed.). Lincoln, NB: University of Nebraska Press.

Wylie, R. (1989). *Measures of self-concept.* Lincoln, NB: University of Nebraska Press.

Zener, K. (1945). A note concerning editorial reorientation. *Journal of Personality, 14,* 1–2.

CHAPTER SEVEN

CULTURAL TURNS IN PSYCHOLOGY

Karen M. Seeley

FOR MORE THAN A CENTURY, the discipline of psychology has sought truths that transcend culture, race, ethnicity, and history. Convinced that psychic unity exists, and that its general laws and specific features could be determined through scientific inquiry, psychologists set out to discover them. Many contemporary psychologists in the United States remain committed to a discipline that is unified and univocal (Gergen, 1997), exhibiting a "fascination with universals and the reductionistic desire to explain human beings by a limited number of principles" (Greenfield, 2000, p. 572). Yet others now consider such commitments inadequate for the task of under-standing human behavior in a world where cultural complexity, multivocality, and disunity thrive. Indeed, it is no longer necessary to venture far afield to encounter cultural diversity, nor must one be an anthropologist to work in unfamiliar cultural worlds. Today's psychologists commonly find themselves teaching, experimenting, and practicing in settings that are culturally, ethni-cally, and racially diverse. As they confront the practical demands that multiculturalism and globalization have made upon their discipline, they must concede that psychology's universalizing principles cannot account for the extensive variations in cognition, emotion, perception, psychopathology, and human development that have been found among populations within the United States and abroad. And as psychology spreads across the globe, they must acknowledge that psychologists in other nations find their assumptions, concepts, and methods irrelevant and inappropriate, and take their doctrine of psychic unity, a doctrine originally invoked to counter racializing theories of mind (Jahoda, 1992), as an assertion of Euro-American hegemony.

For much of their discipline's history, the majority of psychologists in the United States avoided such considerations, choosing to exclude culture from their studies of mind. Although cultural psychologies were proposed at the discipline's inception and reemerged at various points throughout its history, they remained outside its mainstream. For example, Wilhelm Wundt (1921), who founded scientific psychology, also proposed a *Volkerpsychologie*, or people's psychology, for the study of higher-level mental functions. Wundt viewed these functions as social phenomena, and as culturally and histori-cally contingent, and he advised that they be investigated ethnographically rather than experimentally. But while Wundt considered both his experi-mental and *Volker* psychologies equally important, so that one was incom-plete without the other, the psychologists who brought his work to the United States left his culturally oriented *Volkerpsychologie* behind (Cole, 1996; Jahoda, 1992). Preferring to establish the legitimacy of their newly created discipline, these psychologists emulated the harder sciences, recreating their laboratories, adapting their instruments, and appropriating their methods. By constructing the means of psychological knowledge production as removed from the social, economic, and political contexts in which it occurred, they positioned their discipline to share the hard sciences' claims to objectivity, universality, and cultural neutrality.

Just as psychologists situated their discipline beyond the boundaries of culture and time, they studied their subjects in laboratories, extracted from the historical, social, political, and economic circumstances that shaped their daily lives. Stripped of their everyday identities and configured as culturally . neutral collections of physiological processes, psychology's subjects were made to portray an essential and universal human nature (Schwartz, 1992). Having constructed their subjects as culture-free, and having constructed culture as largely irrelevant to mental functioning, psychologists had little motivation to examine the relationships between culture and mind, to study human behavior in various cultural surrounds, or to consider the cultural specificity of disciplinary theories and practices.

Recently, however, with the emergence of the field of critical psychol-ogy (Fox and Prilleltensky, 1997), and with increasing postmodern chal-lenges to the objectivity and impartiality of all sciences (Proctor, 1991), including the hard ones, some psychologists have begun to examine their discipline's embeddedness in specific historic and social surrounds. These psychologists now contend that psychological theories, rather than emanat-ing from spaces beyond culture and history, are formulated in particular times and places and embody local and era-specific moralities, priorities, and concerns, namely, those of the modern West. They maintain that psychological concepts, rather than addressing universal concerns, refer only to the specific American social problems requiring the sorting, measuring, ranking, and labeling of persons that they were designed to solve (Danziger, 1997). They claim that psychology's methods and instruments, rather than being scientific and culture-free, are so culture-bound that they may be inappropriate for use outside the industrialized West (Greenfield, 1997). And they view the discipline's fundamental unit of analysis, the self-contained individual, as a culturally specific construction of the person that may be rarely encountered, or at least differently configured, in non-Western worlds (Sampson, 1989).

If psychologists are beginning to acknowledge that their discipline is grounded in the assumptions and circumstances of the West, they also are starting to recognize that the United States exerts an inordinate influence on psychology around the world. For much of psychology's history, the United States has dominated the field, providing the most prestigious academic institutions to train psychologists, the most sophisticated equipment to support their research, the greatest number of publication outlets to disseminate their findings, and the most plentiful resources to sustain their professional projects and organizations. The United States remains the world's primary producer of psychologists; more than half the world's psychologists are American, and half of the world's psychological researchers reside in the United States (Rosenzweig, 1992). Moreover, the United States exports its psychological knowledge to the rest of the world in the form of development projects, academic conferences, textbooks and journals, college curricula, psychotropic medications, and international students, who attend universities in the United States before returning home to teach or otherwise apply what they have learned (Moghaddam, 1987). This transfer of psychological knowledge is emphatically unidirectional; although American psychologists distribute their knowledge internationally, they remain largely uninfluenced by the psychological theories and findings produced in other parts of the world (Moghaddam, 1990).

Psychology's monoculturalism is all the more remarkable because multiculturalism is far from a new phenomenon. Although perhaps to an extent different from contemporary globalization, numerous societies have long been culturally, ethnically, and racially diverse. Even Freud's Vienna, which was often portrayed as culturally homogeneous, recently has been described as "a veritable cultural crossroads where polylingualism and polyglottism were more or less the order of the day" (Amati-Mehler, Argentieri, and Canestri, 1993, p. 19). Freud's psychoanalytic consulting room itself was a cultural crossroads; as his reputation grew, people from all over Europe, and from as far away as the United States, journeyed to Vienna to be healed by him. Yet despite Freud's extensive psychoanalytic work with patients whose homelands and native languages differed from his, he neglected to examine questions of culture in his theories of mind. Gilman (1993) speculates that Freud's insistence on the universality of psychoanalysis was designed not only to establish the scientific status of his discipline but to counter the opinion, predominant in late 19th-century European medicine, that the Jewish mind was inherently diseased. Freud was trained in a medical community where respected physicians and experts in psychiatry openly discussed the fact of Jewish mental instability in public lectures and central texts. Prevailing views of Jews as genetically predisposed to a variety of incapacitating mental disorders implied that Freud, as a Jew, was potentially insane, compromising his scientific objectivity and authority.

Whether 20th century American psychologists, many of whom were recent immigrants or members of religious, racial, or ethnic minorities, had similar motivations for creating universalizing models of mind cannot be fully examined here. It is plausible that, like Freud, they chose to proclaim psychic unity and to refrain from investigating the relationships between culture and psychology to spare themselves the possibility of being identified as deviant or defective. But it is also the case that these generations of psychologists considered the principles of psychic unity progressive in their anti-evolutionism and viewed Western intellectual projects, and especially positivistic science, as sources of universal and natural truths. Inhabiting academic environments in which the Western premises of their discipline remained largely unquestioned, these American psychologists not only neglected to examine the relationships between culture, behavior, and mind, but also failed to study populations outside their national borders, or to invite members of minority communities into their experimental spaces. Unlike anthropologists, fellow social scientists who deepened their understandings of human beings by living and studying in other societies, psychologists preferred to investigate subjects who lived closer to home, if not in their own backyards. Indeed, the majority of subjects in psychological research have been from the United States, and the field's subjects of choice have been students at American colleges and universities, most of whom have been White and male (Sears, 1986).

In theory, psychologists could regard the cultural, racial, and ethnic identities of their research subjects as unimportant, inasmuch as given subjects were merely "the media through which abstract laws of behavior expressed themselves" (Danziger, 1990, p. 94). Throughout the history of psychology, however, its practitioners discouraged the use of non-White subjects (Graham, 1992), devalued research on ethnic and racial minorities within the United States (S. Sue, 1999), and dismissed considerations of what culture-inclusive research might entail (Greenfield, 1997). As Fish (2000) has remarked, psychologists who have sought to expand their understandings of human behavior have been more inclined to study guinea pigs, pigeons, and rats than non-Whites and non-Westerners.

Basing their findings on such culturally, ethnically, and racially re-stricted samples might have made psychologists wary of attributing universal validity to them. Instead, they chose to make attributions of universality selectively. Constructing White Americans as qualified to represent persons all over the world, regardless of their culture, race, or ethnicity, psychologists in the United States accorded research on Whites universal value and significance and allowed it to dominate psychological discourse. Contras-tively, they constructed non-Westerners and non-Whites as being incapable of representing Whites or others outside of their particular ethnic and racial groups. Psychologists thus marginalized research on these subjects, viewing it as significant only to the specific communities studied—as inherently ungeneralizable (S. Sue, 1999).

After a century of psychological theorizing, experimentation, and practice, such ethnocentric logics have begun to take their toll. Psychologists increasingly realize that their discipline's restrictive theories and practices guarantee a poverty of psychological knowledge about everyone other than White middle-class Americans—in other words, about most of the world's inhabitants. They also realize that their disciplinary universals are likely to produce evidence of deficits and abnormalities among those not studied. As criticism of the discipline has intensified, there has been disagreement as to whether psychology is more accurately described as exclusionary, racist, oppressive, colonialist, or simply obsolete (Gergen, Gulerce, Lock, and Misra, 1996; Hall, 1997; Marsella, 1998; Moghaddam, 1987). There is growing agreement, however, that psychology's ethnocentric logics compromise its ability to speak with authority and impartiality about human behavior.

The following sections examine recent moves to correct such disci-plinary flaws and limitations by developing culturally inclusive approaches to psychological theory and practice. After briefly critiquing previous efforts by psychologists to take culture into account, this chapter considers three still-emerging cultural turns in psychology: cultural psychology, multicultural psychology, and indigenous psychologies.

CULTURE AND PSYCHOLOGY

Though most psychological research conducted in the United States during the last century failed to attend to culture, a small percentage of studies tried to take culture into account. Like most research in psychology, however, the majority of these studies have been based on the erroneous premise that culture fails to deeply penetrate the core of what it means to be human. These studies have been further flawed by conceptualizations of culture that lack substance and depth. Some psychologists have reduced culture to a label, asking subjects to respond only to a question or two regarding their race, ethnicity, or nationality, or to fill out checklists composed of preselected cultural categories. Similarly, psychotherapists' intake forms have required patients to fill in their nationality or ethnicity, but have neglected to request key information concerning their histories of migration, cultural adaptation, and linguistic formation. Because cultural labels have been viewed as suggesting "a vast assortment of stereotyped cultural characteristics" (Jacobsen, 1988, p. 137), they have permitted practitioners to presume cultural knowledge of subjects and patients and, in effect, to avoid deeper investigation. Moreover, although such labels have specified subjects' ethnicities, they often have had no real impact on practice. In laboratory settings, they rarely have influenced experimental design, data collection, or data analysis. In clinical settings, they frequently have had little bearing on diagnosis and treatment (Seeley 2000). Throughout the discipline's history, when psychologists have reduced culture to something as thin as a label, it frequently has disappeared.

Other psychologists—specifically cross-cultural psychologists, who since their subdiscipline's inception in the mid-20th century have examined culture's effects on behavior—constructed culture as a variable in the scientific sense of the term. Cross-cultural psychologists generally have embraced conventional disciplinary perspectives and methods but have been distinguished by their research in non-Western settings, where they have sought empirical evidence supporting psychological universals. Cross-cultural psychologists constructed culture as a variable by defining selected features of the environments in which they worked as antecedents that produced measurable effects in dependent variables such as perception, memory, and motivation. One classic study in Africa, for example, conceptualized culture as the scarcity of right-angled, "carpentered," constructions in the local surround, shaping subjects' perceptions of optical illusions (Segall, Campbell, and Herskovitz, 1966). Confining culture to the external environment and encapsulating it within the specific variables examined allowed cross-cultural psychologists to control it. Although culture produced effects and responses for them to measure, it did not otherwise seep into their research. In this subdiscipline's perspective, culture was unrelated to the concepts tested, the instruments that tested them, the psychologists who administered the instruments, and the experimental situation itself—despite the fact that all were of Euro-American origin (Greenfield, 1997; Morawski, 1997). Cross-cultural psychologists commonly concluded that the psychological phenomena they investigated would indeed be universal were it not for the interference of culture. Just as conceptualizing culture as a label restricted the kinds of cultural knowledge psychologists produced, defining culture as a variable failed to advance psychological understandings of the complex and profound interactions between culture and mind.

PSYCHOLOGY'S CULTURAL TURNS

While psychologists continued to conduct scientific studies that employed impoverished conceptions of culture or, more frequently, that neglected culture, race, and ethnicity entirely, the world around them changed. In recent years, constructionist and interpretive theories and methods have profoundly affected a variety of academic disciplines, challenging conventional positivistic approaches. In addition, globalization and multiculturalism have been deeply felt both outside the academy and within it, intensifying demands for psychologists to transform their assumptions and practices. Recognizing the significance of these changes, some psychologists have begun to assert that their discipline requires nothing short of a "multicultural revolution" (Sue, Bingham, Porche-Burke, and Vasquez, 1999, p. 1061) if it is to retain its relevance and authority.

The discipline is responding with unprecedented conviction and momentum. The American Psychological Association has strengthened its commitments to producing research on diversity and to training culturally competent practitioners. Many contemporary psychologists seek to undo their discipline's monoculturalism and ethnocentrism. As psychologists turn their attention to diverse populations and to a range of issues beyond their usual purview, they have begun to seek new theoretical and methodological approaches that incorporate cultural investigation. Psychology thus appears to be making a cultural turn—or, more accurately, several cultural turns.

The rest of this chapter critically examines three of contemporary psychology's cultural turns. Each turn has distinct and particular agendas. Further, each differently defines culture, differently interprets what it means to bring culture into psychology, and differently imagines how this might be accomplished. While it is beyond the scope of this chapter to examine psychology's cultural turns in detail, or to critically analyze research within them, the following sections address the problems they have identified, the objectives they have expressed, and the directions they have charted.

CULTURAL PSYCHOLOGY

Cultural psychology, the first cultural turn examined here, claims an affinity with anthropology, urging psychologists to adopt this discipline's complex conceptualizations of culture and its ethnographic methods of inquiry. Contemporary cultural psychology has two main strands. The cultural psychology proposed by Bruner (1990), a psychologist who once conducted laboratory studies on cognition, contends that because human minds are realized through culture, "it is impossible to construct a human psychology on the basis of the individual alone" (p. 12). This strand of cultural psychology conceives of individual minds as fundamentally social entities that cannot be understood apart from the cultural systems of symbols and meanings in which they are situated, and of which they are composed. Derived in part from Vygotskian notions as to the mediation of all mental activities by cultural symbols and tools (Vygotsky, 1978), this cultural psychology lends itself to research on cognition. It has been primarily applied in the spheres of education and human development, where it has incorporated narrative approaches (Bruner, 1997). A similar insistence on the interconstitution of culture and mind underlies the second strand of cultural psychology, as set forth by Shweder (1990, 1997, 1999), an anthropologist, who describes cultural psychology not as a subfield of psychology but as an interdisciplinary field between psychology and anthropology. Shweder's cultural psychology, which resembles latter-day psychological anthropology (e.g., Behar, 1993; Lutz, 1988; Shore, 1996), has been implemented in studies of the self, emotion, morality, sexuality, language, and psychopathology, as well as in cognition and human development (Shweder, 1991; Shweder, 1992; Shweder, Goodnow, Hatano, LeVine, Markus, and Miller, 1997; Shweder, 1998; Stigler, Shweder, and Herdt, 1990).

While cultural psychology is not a unified field, its basic principles are largely shared by those who practice it. Cultural psychology rejects the mental mechanism prevalent in late 20th century American psychology, asserting the impossibility of analytically separating culture and mind and decontextualizing subjects for psychological investigation. Demanding fundamental transformations in psychology's construction of the person, it conceptualizes culture not as secondary to biology in forming human minds but as constitutive of selfhood. Deeply indebted to Geertz's (1973) meaning-centered approaches to culture—and perhaps to his example of radically transforming anthropology—cultural psychology urges mainstream psychologists to reclaim their place among the humanities by replacing scientific methods with interpretive theory and qualitative research strategies.

While cultural psychology denies neither the existence of psychological universals nor the primacy of academic psychology, it intends to decenter them by examining significant psychological differences, as well as wholly different psychologies, across cultures. Thus Shweder (1999) advocates discovery of the "distinctive psychologies associated with alternative ways of life" (p. 64), while Bruner (1990) describes Western scientific psychology as one of many ethnopsychologies, or "folk" accounts, of "what makes human beings tick" (p. 13). Decentering disciplinary tendencies toward universalization and univocality also entails transforming the means by which psychologists produce knowledge. Instead of transporting standard psychological categories abroad and testing them in contrived experimental situations, cultural psychology recommends that practitioners conduct ethnographic research in non-Western sites to identify indigenous categories of self, behavior, and mind. By encouraging investigations of community members' representations of themselves and their experiences in their own languages and categories, cultural psychology promotes psychological explorations from the "native's point of view" (Geertz, 1973).

Through its importation of anthropological theory and method, cultural psychology identifies new areas of psychological inquiry and facilitates research on topics that cannot be studied experimentally. Cultural psychology also counters disciplinary parochialism and insularity by reviving established traditions of collaboration between psychologists and anthropologists (Bock, 1999), and by stimulating interdisciplinary exchange between psychologists and linguists, philosophers, political scientists, literary critics, historians, and biologists. Although cultural psychology offers expanded understandings of culture, race, and ethnicity, it is unclear whether mainstream psychologists will readily take advantage of them. Psychologists may suspect that cultural psychology's multivocality masks a cultural relativism in which "everything is as significant, and thus as insignificant, as everything else" (Geertz, 1984/2000, p. 46), which would challenge their discipline's universal theories and findings. They may find ethnographic accounts impressionistic and subjective, introducing noise that should be silenced through the techniques of science. And they may not wish to work in cultures that are foreign and distant, even though they may believe that conducting psychological studies in non-Western settings would immeasurably deepen disciplinary knowledge of culturally diverse populations.

Only time will tell whether psychologists will willingly step "into the metaphysical frameworks of the people [they] study" (Shweder, 1999, p. 70), let alone into their nations and neighborhoods. There are indications, however, that cultural psychology may appeal primarily to anthropologists interested in psychology rather than to psychologists concerned with culture, race, and ethnicity. Indeed, despite cultural psychology's commitments to meaning-centered conceptions of culture, ethnographic depth and detail, and local categories and concepts, one of the most influential articles produced within the field violates them all. Markus and Kitayama's (1991) "Culture and the Self: Implications for Cognition, Emotion, and Motivation" divides all the world's cultures into two broad, schematic, and mutually exclusive categories, the interdependent and the independent—new glosses for the non-Western and the Western—and assigns highly stereotyped patterns of self, thought, and feeling to each. Though entirely unlike the cultural psychology many have envisioned, this article has captured the psychological imagination. Its frequent citation by psychologists suggests that it represents culture in a form they can tolerate, allowing them to "explain human beings by a minimum number of principles" (Greenfield, 2000, p. 572), and sparing them the need to rethink their conventional perspectives and to become deeply acquainted with the psychologies of others.

MULTICULTURAL PSYCHOLOGY

While cultural psychology's impact on the psychological mainstream appears limited, multicultural psychology, the second cultural turn, seems to enjoy a growing influence. Some suggest that its emerging strength reflects not only heightened interest in multiculturalism in the United States, but the discipline's recent internal diversification, including the election of the American

Psychological Association's (APA) first Asian-American president, and of psychologists of color to head five other APA divisions (Fish, 2000; D. W. Sue, 1999). This intraorganizational diversification may also explain why multicultural psychology, though less theoretically elaborated than the two other psychologies discussed in this chapter, conveys a stronger "sense of mission" (Fowler, 2001, p. 9). Indeed, multicultural psychology is more than an intellectual project, as it encompasses work in social advocacy and expresses profound moral commitments to the ideals of tolerance, human rights, and social justice (Fowers and Richardson, 1996).

Both cultural psychology and multicultural psychology strive to develop culturally inclusive perspectives and approaches, yet they construct inclusion differently. Unlike cultural psychology, which promotes international research, multicultural psychology's interests are domestic, focusing on American ethnic and racial diversity and on studies of minority populations within the United States. Moreover, when compared to cultural psychology, multicultural psychology's conceptions of culture are at once expanded and reduced. Multicultural psychology defines culture more broadly to include minority groups based on sexual orientation, age, gender, social class, and disability, as well as on ethnicity and race (Pedersen, 1991). At the same time, rather than exploring the particular features of distinct ethnic and racial groups, multicultural psychology tends to reduce the rich cultural variety of the United States society to a few rudimentary categories, such as Asian, African-American, and Hispanic. Accordingly, the "Asian" category equally describes Hmong refugees from rural Laos and Indian expatriates from urban Bombay, and research findings based on Korean or Japanese subjects are extended to all "Asians." Such conceptions of culture also emphasize generic and fixed behaviors and beliefs that members of each category supposedly share, rather than cultural fluidity, specificity, and heterogeneity, allowing practitioners to become "culturally competent" by mastering preestablished bodies of information portraying group worldviews and practices. Notions of cultural competence have been applied to clinical practice as well, so that psychotherapists are expected to acquire cultural knowledge of their ethnic and minority patients to more effectively treat them (Seeley, in press).

In addition to their divergent conceptions of culture, cultural psychology and multicultural psychology have markedly different objectives. In contrast to cultural psychology, which considers itself apolitical, multicultural psychology's politics are at the heart of its agenda. For many multicultural psychologists, generating theoretical knowledge is less important than advocating for economic equality and social justice (D. W. Sue, 1999). Multicultural psychology's push to establish plural psychological standards serves the similar real world ends of displacing universal psychological standards and norms that have legitimized the subjugation of minorities (Fowers and Richardson, 1996). Further, this cultural turn fosters disciplinary diversification by extending the ideals of multiculturalism to all aspects of organizational infrastructure, research, practice, and training, mandating the ethnocultural education of psychologists, the hiring of minorities, and the recruitment of faculty and students of color who are underrepresented in the field.

Multicultural psychology clearly has made itself an ambitious agenda. To accomplish its objectives, however, may require more sophisticated conceptions of culture than those currently in use—conceptions so elastic that they trivialize the concept of culture, so superficial that they perpetuate cultural stereotypes, and so simplistic that they cannot account for bicultural and biracial individuals. Realizing its agenda may also require new research methodologies or "alternative ways of knowing" (Sue et al., 1999, p. 1065). Indeed, although multicultural psychology encourages investigations of culture-specific psychologies and has diversified research samples to include subjects of color, the articles published in recent volumes of *Cultural Diversity and Ethnic Minority Psychology*, the field's principal journal, demonstrate this subdiscipline's continued uncritical use of traditional psychological concepts, procedures, and methods. Many multicultural psychologists have failed to consider that standard psychological instruments travel poorly across cultures (Greenfield, 1997; Shweder, 1990) and cannot accurately capture local concerns and ways of being. Further, they have failed to develop novel strategies for studying bilingual subjects, so that issues of language and translation, which are central to research in multicultural psychology, remain undertheorized.

Although quantitative studies using standard psychological categories, measures, and instruments are predominant in multicultural psychology, recent years have seen the creation of richly detailed, culture-specific psychologies, as current work by African-American psychologists demonstrates. Some African-American psychologists have theorized indigenous models of psychological functioning, elaborating ideals of selfhood drawn from a shared African heritage (Azibo, 1996; Myers, 1993; Parham, White, and Ajamu, 1999). Others have investigated difficulties particular to African-American development, proposing models of identity formation that consider the psychological consequences of racism and discrimination and suggest therapeutic strategies for their remediation (Carter, 1995; Cross, 1991; Helms, 1993). While some Afrocentric psychologies predate the emergence of multicultural psychology and thus developed outside its frameworks, this subdiscipline may now provide psychologists of color with a newly supportive and energized base from which to expand their investigations.

INDIGENOUS PSYCHOLOGIES

Though the domination of psychology by the United States persists around the globe, there are signs that its grip may be loosening. Psychology has begun to internationalize, albeit unevenly, as evidenced by the growing numbers of psychologists abroad—including many who were educated in the United States (Lunt and Poortinga, 1996). As psychology spreads, it assumes a variety of forms. In some countries, psychologists import Western theories and practices and apply them uncritically (Adair and Kagitcibasi, 1995), while in others, they combine them with traditional philosophies of human behavior (Mays, Rubin, Sabourin, and Walker, 1996). Elsewhere, psychologists—even those trained in the West—have rejected Western academic psychology entirely, for reasons that are both cultural and political. Some psychologists from developing and decolonizing nations have determined that Western psychology is so "enmeshed with Euro-American values that champion rational, liberal, individualistic and abstract ideals" (Kim, 1995, p. 666) that it can neither perceive culturally-specific psychic phenomena, explain local subjectivities, nor address important social issues. Others assert that all Western psychologies, including cultural and multicultural psychology, perpetuate the hegemony of the United States, exporting scientific knowledge to serve its national interests and subordinating indigenous cultural, religious, and intellectual heritages (Gergen et al., 1996; Leung and Zhang, 1995). Consequently, these psychologists have begun to create indigenous psychologies, representing a third cultural turn.

Because many indigenous psychologies are still in their early stages, and because they are practiced in a variety of countries and languages, it is difficult to accurately characterize their diverse projects and aims or to predict how they will be elaborated theoretically. However, it is possible to identify the distinctive features that the separate psychologies constituting this third cultural turn share. Indigenous psychologies, which generally conceptualize cultures in national terms, involve "the scientific study of human behavior (or the mind) that is native, that is not transported from other regions, and that is designed for its people" (Kim and Berry, 1993, p. 2). In contrast to the dominant model in cultural psychology, where Western academics travel abroad to study the psychologies of others, indigenous psychologies generally have been developed and practiced by psychologists who belong to the societies they study. Grounded in local conceptions of selfhood and behavior, these psychologies also commonly address pressing regional concerns such as poverty and illiteracy. Indigenous psychologists implement research strategies that aspire to scientific validity and reliability, but that incorporate "individual, social, cultural and temporal variations . . . into the research design" (Kim and Berry, 1993, p. 4). Some reject Western psychology's "methodological individualism" (Kim, 1995, p. 666) in favor of culturally congruent research approaches that facilitate investigations of social groups and that promote socioeconomic change rather than personal growth (Moghaddam 1990). While these psychologists "affirm the need for each culture to develop its own indigenous understandings" (Kim and Berry, 1993, p. 3), many also claim that their objective is not to promote cultural relativism but to discover universal psychological laws. To this end, they have developed the "cross-indigenous approach," a two-stage process whereby the culturally-specific psychic phenomena discovered in the first phase of study are then compared to results from other cultures to identify psychological universals (Kim and Berry, 1993).

Indigenous psychologies are exemplified by recent work in Korea, where psychologists have begun to develop a scientific psychology based on the cultural primacy of social groups rather than individuals. Central to this project is an analysis of the Korean term *woori*, which is roughly translatable as the English "we" but which references group identifications and feelings of oneness with others. Research has begun to explore the place of *woori* in Korean emotions, notions of self, and social relations (Choi, Kim, and Choi, 1993). Alternatively, recent work on the indigenous psychology of the Philippines promotes "the decolonization of the Filipino psyche" and the flowering of "national consciousness" (Enriquez, 1993, p. 155). In this psychology, the basic unit of analysis is not the isolated individual but interrelated individuals, reflecting what are taken to be fundamental Filipino conceptions of shared identity, of selves that include others, and of human interdependence. Some work in this region has implemented indigenous methods of data collection, reproducing cultural norms of social interaction to provide investigators with greater access to local subjects (Enriquez, 1993).

The growing excitement concerning indigenous psychologies is not unaccompanied by controversy. Indigenous psychologists are divided as to whether their aim is to establish distinct cultural psychologies or to identify psychological universals (Adair and Kagitcibasi, 1995), with some contending that turning local principles into universal laws necessarily incurs significant losses in cultural meaning. Mainstream psychologists have found fault with the local emphasis of indigenous psychologies, denouncing them as "nativist" (Fowers and Richardson, 1996, p. 614) bodies of knowledge that support essentializing notions of cultural authenticity, promote isolationism, and narrowly focus on regional problems. In nonindustrialized countries, indigenous psychologies face practical obstacles to their development. Because indigenous psychologists tend to be from the most Westernized sectors of their societies and to have been trained abroad, they may not be attuned to the norms and needs of traditional social groups. Inadequate research funding, lack of laboratory equipment, and a shortage of psychology students and teachers also impede disciplinary growth (Leung and Zhang, 1995). While efforts are underway to remedy these problems, solutions are neither clear nor immediate.

CONCLUSION

If the three cultural turns in psychology examined in this chapter differ in their specific theoretical orientations, approaches, and aims, they are united in the view that mainstream psychology must fundamentally transform itself to respond to the needs of multicultural and globalizing societies. Cultural, multicultural, and indigenous psychologists concur that culture, race, and ethnicity must be given significant places in psychology, and that disciplinary aspirations to uniformity and univocality should be laid to rest. The psychologies they envision are practiced in numerous cultural sites by regionally as well as Western-trained psychologists who study diverse populations, investigate indigenous concepts, employ interpretive theories, create locally appropriate methods, and produce distinct bodies of knowledge, which they publish in a variety of languages.

How might American psychologists respond to this altered disciplinary scene? Perhaps the contention that cultural psychology is too "radical" (Geertz, 1984/2000, p. 196) for the psychological mainstream applies to multicultural and indigenous psychologies as well. Indeed, because they undermine disciplinary certainties, these cultural turns may be destabilizing in several ways; they disrupt positivistic modes of theorizing, displace universalizing models and claims, and raise unsettling questions as to the discipline's purpose and as to whose interests it serves. Moreover, the implementation of hermeneutic approaches, diversification of practitioners, institutions, and training, and indigenization of theory and method are unlikely to create a harmonious psychological pluralism. Rather, they may produce a "clash of cultures . . . a clash of values, of logics, and of conceived worlds and personhood" rooted in "incommensurate" historical traditions (Gergen et al., 1996, p. 499). Psychology's cultural turns thus may intensify intercultural competition for disciplinary power and influence, ultimately diminishing the United States' domination of the field. Whether American psychologists will abandon their usual advantage and insularity to participate in intercultural dialogues and to import psychological knowledge produced abroad is uncertain. To date, indigenous psychologists who have collaborated with American psychologists have found them reluctant to consider non-Western perspectives and to work with psychologists from other countries "as equals" (Kim, 1995, p. 674).

However difficult and destabilizing, the transformations that psychology's three cultural turns propose are necessary for psychology's continuing relevance and growth. Their emphases on culturally, ethnically, and racially diverse subjects, local psychological realities, multiple psychologies, and interdisciplinary collaboration offer the discipline fresh perspectives. By encouraging psychologists to adopt interpretive theoretical perspectives, complex conceptions of culture, and new methods of cultural inquiry, they ensure that the range of psychological phenomena investigated will be expanded, and that the discipline's understandings of culture, race, and ethnicity will be enriched. Although these cultural turns fail to define psychology's purpose and function in simple terms, in their insistence that culture is inseparable from mind, and that "all psychology is cultural" (Bock, 1999, p. 255), they suggest new possibilities for creating and applying psychological knowledge. Psychology's cultural turns therefore promise to revitalize the field: "to confront, discompose, energize, and deprovincialize . . . , and thus drive the enterprise erratically onward" (Geertz, 1984/2000, p. 199).

REFERENCES

Adair, J., & Kagitcibasi, C. (1995). Development of psychology in developing countries: Factors facilitating and impeding its progress. *International Journal of Psychology, 30,* 633–641.

Amati-Mehler, J., Argentieri, S., & Canestri, J. (1993). *The babel of the unconscious: Mother tongue and foreign languages in the psychoanalytic dimension.* Madison, CT: International Universities Press.

Azibo, D. A. (1996). *African psychology in historical perspective and related commentary.* Trenton, NJ: Africa World Press.

Behar, R. (1993). *Translated woman: Crossing the border with Esperanza's story.* Boston, MA: Beacon.

Bock, P. (1999). *Rethinking psychological anthropology: Continuity and change in the study of human action.* Prospect Heights, IL: Waveland Press.

Bruner, J. (1990). *Acts of meaning.* Cambridge, MA: Harvard University Press.

Bruner, J. (1997). *The culture of education.* Cambridge, MA: Harvard University Press.

Carter, R. T. (1995). *The influence of race and racial identity in psychotherapy.* New York, NY: John Wiley.

Choi, S., Kim, U., & Choi, S. (1993). Indigenous analysis of collective representations. In U. Kim & J. Berry (Eds.), *Indigenous psychologies: Research and experience in cultural context* (pp. 193–210). Newbury Park, CA: Sage.

Cole M. (1996). *Cultural psychology: A once and future discipline.* Cambridge, MA: Harvard University Press.

Cross, W. (1991). *Shades of black: Diversity in African-American identity.* Philadelphia, PA: Temple University Press.

Danziger, K. (1990). *Constructing the subject: Historical origins of psychological research.* New York, NY: Cambridge University Press.

Danziger, K. (1997). *Naming the mind.* Thousand Oaks, CA: Sage.

Enriquez, V. (1993). Developing a Filipino psychology. In U. Kim & J. Berry (Eds.), *Indigenous psychologies: Research and experience in cultural context* (pp.152–169). Newbury Park, CA: Sage.

Fish, J. (2000). What anthropology can do for psychology. *American Anthropologist, 102,* 552–563.

Fowers, B., & Richardson, F. (1996). Why is multiculturalism good? *American Psychologist, 51,* 609–621.

Fowler, R. (2001, April). Multicultural summit. *APA Monitor,* p. 9.

Fox, D. & Prilleltensky, I. (1997). *Critical psychology: An introduction.* London, UK: Sage.

Geertz, C. (1973). *The interpretation of cultures.* New York, NY: Basic Books.

Geertz, C. (2000). *Available light: Anthropological reflections on philosophical topics.* Princeton, NJ: Princeton University Press. (Original work published 1984)

Gergen, K. (1997). The place of the psyche in a constructed world. *Theory & Psychology, 7,* 723–746.

Gergen, K., Gulerce, A., Lock, A., & Misra, G. (1996). Psychological science in cultural context. *American Psychologist, 51,* 496–503.

Gilman, S. (1993). *Freud, race and gender.* Princeton, NJ: Princeton University Press.

Graham, S. (1992). Most of the subjects were White and middle-class: Trends in published research on African-Americans in selected APA journals, 1970–1989. *American Psychologist, 47,* 629–639.

Greenfield, P. (1997). You can't take it with you: Why ability assessments don't cross cultures. *American Psychologist, 52*, 1115–1124.

Greenfield, P. (2000). What psychology can do for anthropology. *American Anthropologist, 102*, 564–576.

Hall, C. (1997). Cultural malpractice: The growing obsolescence of psychology with the changing U.S. population. *American Psychologist, 52*, 642–651.

Helms, J. (1993). *Black and white racial identity*. Westport CT: Praeger.

Jacobsen, F. (1988). Ethnocultural assessment. In L. Comas-Diaz & E. Griffith (Eds.), *Clinical guidelines in cross-cultural mental health* (pp.135–147). New York, NY: John Wiley.

Jahoda, G. (1992). *Crossroads between culture and mind*. Cambridge, MA: Harvard University Press.

Kim, U., (1995). Psychology, science and culture: Cross-cultural analysis of national psychologies. *International Journal of Psychology, 30*, 663–679.

Kim, U., & Berry, J. (1993). *Indigenous psychologies: Research and experience in cultural context*. Newbury Park, CA: Sage.

Leung, K., & Zhang, J. (1995). Systematic considerations: Factors facilitating and impeding the development of psychology in developing countries. *International Journal of Psychology, 30*, 693–706.

Lunt, I., & Poortinga, Y. (1996). Internationalizing psychology: The case of Europe. *American Psychologist, 51*, 504–508.

Lutz, C. (1988). *Unnatural emotions: Everyday sentiments on a Micronesian atoll and their challenge to Western theory*. Chicago, IL: University of Chicago Press.

Markus, H., & Kitayama, S. (1991). Culture and the self: Implications for cognition, emotion and motivation. *Psychological Review, 98*, 224–252.

Marsella, A. J. (1998). Toward a "Global-Community Psychology." *American Psychologist, 53*, 1282–1291.

Mays, V., Rubin, J., Sabourin, M. & Walker, L. (1996). Moving toward a global psychology: Changing theories and practice to meet the needs of a changing world. *American Psychologist, 51*, 485–487.

Moghaddam, F. (1987). Psychology in the three worlds: As reflected by the crisis in social psychology and the move toward indigenous Third-World psychology. *American Psychologist, 42*, 912–920.

Moghaddam, F. (1990). Modulative and generative orientations in psychology: Implications for psychology in the Three Worlds. *Journal of Social Issues, 46*, 21–41.

Morawski, J. G. (1997). White experimenters, white blood and other white conditions: Locating the psychologist's race. In M. Fine, L. C. Powell, L. Weis, & L. M. Wong (Eds.), *Off-white: Readings in race, power and society* (pp. 13–28). New York, NY: Routledge.

Myers, L. J. (1993). *Understanding an Afrocentric worldview*. Dubuque, IA: Kendall/Hunt.

Parham, T., White, J. L., & Ajamu, A. (1999). *The psychology of blacks: An African-centered perspective*. Upper Saddle River, NJ: Prentice Hall.

Pedersen, P. (1991). Multiculturalism as a generic approach to counseling. *Journal of Counseling and Development, 70*, 6–12.

Proctor, R. (1991). *Value-free science? Purity and power in modern knowledge*. Cambridge, MA: Harvard University Press.

Rosenzweig, M. R. (1992). Psychological science around the world. *American Psychologist, 47*, 718–722.

Sampson, E. (1989). The challenge of social change for psychology: Globalization and psychology's theory of the person. *American Psychologist, 44,* 914–921.

Schwartz, T. (1992). Anthropology and psychology: An unrequited relationship. In T. Schwartz, G. White, & C. Lutz (Eds.), *New directions in psychological anthropology* (pp. 324–349). New York, NY: Cambridge University Press.

Sears, D. O. (1986). College sophomores in the laboratory: Influences of a narrow data base on social psychology's view of human nature. *Journal of Personality and Social Psychology, 51,* 515–530.

Seeley, K. M. (2000). *Cultural psychotherapy: Working with culture in the clinical encounter.* Northvale, NJ: Jason Aronson.

Seeley, K. M. (In Press). Cases in short-term intercultural psychotherapy: The uses of ethnographic inquiry. *Social Work.*

Segall, M., Campbell, D., & Herskovitz, M. (1966). *The influence of culture on visual perception.* Indianapolis, IN: Bobbs-Merrill.

Shore, B. (1996). *Culture in mind: Cognition, culture and the problem of meaning.* Oxford, UK: Oxford University Press.

Shweder, R. (1990). Cultural psychology: What is it? In J. Stigler, R. Shweder, & G. Herdt (Eds.), *Cultural psychology: Essays on comparative human development* (pp. 1–43). New York, NY: Cambridge University Press.

Shweder, R. (1991). *Thinking through cultures: Expeditions in cultural psychology.* Cambridge, MA: Harvard University Press.

Shweder, R. (1992. The cultural psychology of the emotions. In M. Lewis & J. Haviland (Eds.), *Handbook of emotions* (pp. 417–431). New York, NY: Guilford Press.

Shweder, R. (1997). The surprise of ethnography. *Ethos, 25,* 152–163.

Shweder, R. (Ed.). (1998). *Welcome to middle age! (And other cultural fictions).* Chicago, IL: University of Chicago Press.

Shweder, R. (1999). Why cultural psychology? *Ethos, 27,* 62–73.

Shweder, R., Goodnow, J., Hatano, G., LeVine, R., Markus, H., & Miller, P. (1997). The cultural psychology of development: One mind, many mentalities. In W. Damon (Ed.), *Handbook of child psychology* (Vol. 1, pp. 865–938). New York, NY: John Wiley.

Stigler, J., Shweder, R., & Herdt, G. (Eds.). (1990). *Cultural psychology: Essays on comparative human development.* New York: Cambridge University Press.

Sue, D. W. (1999). President's corner: The National Multicultural Conference and Summit and upcoming events. *Focus: Notes from the Society for the Psychological Study of Ethnic Minority Issues, 11,* 1–2.

Sue, D. W., Bingham, R. P., Porche-Burke, L., & Vasquez, M. (1999). The diversification of psychology: A multicultural revolution. *American Psychologist, 54,* 1061–1069.

Sue, S. (1999). Science, ethnicity and bias: Where have we gone wrong? *American psychologist, 54,* 1070–1077.

Vygotsky, L. (1978). *Mind in society: The development of higher psychological processes.* Cambridge, MA: Harvard University Press.

Wundt, W. (1921). *Elements of folk psychology.* London, UK: Allen & Unwin.

Chapter Eight

Feminists Rethink Gender

Meredith M. Kimball

The more we look, the less natural sex looks. Everywhere we turn, every aspect of sex seems to be saturated with cultural needs and priorities. Mother Nature has Mankind's fingerprints all over her.

—Wilchins, *Read My Lips,* p. 51

Think of the feminist toolbox as having everything—master's tools, new tools, and old tools that can be deployed for new purposes. Use the toolbox: spend energy on deciding which tools to use, not only on how to equip the box.

—O'Barr, *My Master List for the Millennium,* p. 1207

FEMINIST PSYCHOLOGISTS have thought critically about gender[1] during periods of feminist political action. The discipline of psychology, as it has been traditionally practiced, does not encourage social critiques. However, when supported by broader movements for social change, some psychologists have used the tools of psychology to create social critiques of gender. Two periods of history in North America have seen feminist political action and feminist critiques of gender. The first was from the establishment of psychology departments in the late 1800s through 1920, with the strongest critiques published in the 1910s (Kimball, 1995). After 1920, these critiques largely vanished from the discipline. This was in part due to the increasing emphasis on the universal laws of behavior within the discipline (Danziger, 1990), however, I would argue that the more important social change was that feminist political coalitions broke down after suffrage campaigns were successful. In the late 1960s, with the rise of second-wave feminisms, psychologists once again began to construct critiques of gender. Over the past 30 years, feminisms and feminist critiques of gender have continued to challenge traditional conceptions of gender, both within the discipline and in the wider society.

This chapter is organized around four themes: (1) gender as variable: challenging exclusions; (2) gender as power: challenging individualisms; (3) gender in context: challenging essentialisms; and (4) gender as social construction: challenging dualisms. Each theme focuses on a reconstruction of gender that both challenges a traditional conception of gender within psychology and supports a feminist political agenda. As with all categories, the boundaries between these themes are not mutually exclusive. Individual psychologists work across the themes, and many of the examples of research that I will discuss fit into more than one theme. As with all categories, they obscure differences within and similarities across categories. Thus I offer these themes with the purpose not of definitive classification, but rather as a heuristic that I find useful for understanding some of the diversity of feminist critiques within psychology. Others have proposed conceptualizations of feminist psychology that are both similar and different to mine (Crawford and Marecek, 1989; Marecek, 2001a; Unger, 1998). In each formulation, as in this one, the various categories are "coexisting, interdependent, and mutually informing" (Crawford and Marecek, 1989, p.149).

Furthermore, I would argue that the critique of gender in each theme is partial with both intellectual and political strengths and limitations. Each is more useful in some contexts and more dangerous in others. Therefore, psychologists and feminists need a variety of critiques of gender in order to generate useful knowledge and create social change. What is critical to understand is which critique is most useful in a particular context, and that even the most useful critique for the situation has its weaknesses.

The themes I use here are, I would argue, useful, if partial, constructions for examining the variety of critiques of gender, that have been the focus of feminist psychologists. I do not conceptualize them as stages. These themes do not in any logical or structural sense form a sequence, that is, each does not follow in some logical way from the previous one, as required in stage theory.

Furthermore, there is no necessary empirical sequence in their appearance, either within the discipline or in the work of individual psychologists. Because "gender as variable" was the primary theme of early 20th century critiques of gender and one of the first to resurface in the late 1960s, it is possible to see the other themes as progressing beyond this starting point. However, I do not think this is useful because, as I will show, it is as relevant a critique today as it was in 1910 or 1970. All four themes are important, all are partial with strengths and limitations, and all are necessary.

The relationship I do see among these themes is a political continuum with "gender as variable" the most conservative and "gender as social construction" the most radical challenge to the discipline of psychology as traditionally practiced. Thus "gender as variable" challenges psychology's exclusion of gender in the construction of knowledge and women in the practice of the discipline. However, it does not challenge the basic tenets of the discipline, particularly the beliefs that good science reflects reality, the individual is the central focus of study, and universal laws, or at least generalizations across individuals and situations, are desirable. Each of the other themes challenges at least one of these central tenets. "Gender as power" challenges the centrality of the individual and brings in the importance of larger social structures. Both of these first two themes remain focused on single dimensions (either individual or social) and seek to make generalizations about gender across individuals or situations. The third theme, "gender in context," challenges the essentialism in both of the first two themes by demonstrating that individual and social variables are dependent on the specific situations in which they are observed. "Gender as social construction" is the most radical theme, not only because it rejects traditional objectivity, but also because as a gender critique it fundamentally undermines the assumptions of two and only two genders, which is basic to all the other critiques.

GENDER AS VARIABLE: CHALLENGING EXCLUSIONS

The critiques of the early feminist psychologists were largely focused on challenging the ways in which science was used to exclude women from professional life (Kimball, 1995; Shields, 1975, 1982). Thus they challenged theories of greater male eminence through greater male variability (Hollingworth, 1914), faulty methodology used in the study of sex differences (Hollingworth, 1916a, 1918, 1919; Woolley, 1910, 1914), and the problems for women of combining motherhood and professional work (Hollingworth, 1916b, 1918; Hull, 1917). They shared with their colleagues a faith in science to present an accurate picture of sex differences. However, unlike most of their male colleagues who argued that important sex differences rooted in biology prevented most women from success in male-dominated fields, these feminists critics argued that once proper methodologies were employed, differences either would prove small or rooted in early socialization, and therefore should not block women from entering and being successful in psychology and other professions.

Feminist psychologists in the early 1970s were quick to renew this critique, often without an awareness of the work of earlier psychologists. During the past 30 years, critiques that focus on gender as a variable have led to research that examines discrimination based on perceived gender, the debate around the study of sex/gender differences and similarities, the participation of women within the discipline of psychology, and the interaction of gender with other variables.

Some of the first studies critical of gender were experimental analogue studies of discrimination. A classic in this area is the study by Linda Fidell (1970), in which it was clearly shown that academics were less likely to say that they would hire a woman than a man where the only difference was the name on the curriculum vitae (CV). This and similar studies were important because they showed the effect of discrimination in a controlled situation where one could not argue there were subtle but important differences between the man or woman as often happened, and still happens, in everyday evaluations. A recent study by Rhea Steinpreis and her colleagues showed that sex discrimination still occurs when academic CVs are evaluated (Steinpreis, Anders, and Ritzke, 1999). In a study very similar to Fidell's, 30 years ago, they sent CVs that had been used to apply either for a job or early tenure to male and female academics. The female's application CV was rated less likely to be offered the job, and her research, teaching, and service experiences were rated as less adequate than the male's application CV. There were no interactions with the gender of the rater. Encouragingly there were no main effects, in the ratings of the tenure CV, perhaps due to a ceiling effect, because this was a strong CV that had been used to apply for early tenure. Even though the ratings were not different, there were more cautionary comments written in the margins for the female tenure candidate.

A major emphasis in the study of gender as a variable has been the massive research project of measuring gender/sex differences and similarities. This area has also been the center of a feminist debate concerning the usefulness of gender as an axis of comparison (Kimball 1995, 2001). One of the most useful constructions to come out of this area of research has been meta-analytic techniques (Eagly, 1987; Hyde, 1994). Using a series of effect sizes from different studies, it is possible to summarize the size of gender differences in an area without relying on statistical significance that is dependent on sample size. In addition to an overall or average effect size, meta-analytic studies can and do analyze for heterogeneity among the effect sizes. As far as I am aware, every meta-analysis of gender similarities and differences has found heterogeneity of effect sizes which requires attention to methodological variables such as the measurements used, and to social variables such as race and class which modify gender effects. Another useful contribution to the study of gender similarities and differences has been attention to distributions of scores in quantitative studies. Olga Favreau (1997) has argued that distributions, which often are not normal, are as important in understanding similarities and differences as means or effect sizes. Certainly if all published studies that compared women and men included both information about effect sizes and distributions of scores in cases where these are not normal, we would have much more complex and contextually accurate descriptions of gender similarities and differences.

Feminists psychologists have also critiqued the exclusion of women from the discipline of psychology and discrimination against them as students and professionals. Before 1970, women were a minority of psychologists and underrepresented in positions of power within the discipline (Hogan and Sexton, 1991). With the rise of feminist political activity in the late 1960s and early 1970s, feminist psychologists began to organize both separate organizations, such as the Association for Women in Psychology (Tiefer, 1991), and lobby groups, sections, and divisions within major psychological associations in several Western countries (Mednick and Urbanski, 1991; Pyke, 2001; Unger, 2001). In both Canada and the United States, task forces and status of women committees were formed that lobbied for many reforms such as blind review, women's representation on governing bodies, psychology of women curriculum, and gender-neutral language policies (Hogan and Sexton, 1991; Pyke, 2001). As a result of this political activity within the discipline, women have achieved some advances. They now comprise the majority of graduate students in psychology, although they remain a minority in all academic ranks, noticeably so in the highest ranks. Women are well represented as first authors of articles in professional journals and on editorial boards, but often underrepresented as editors of major journals. Women have made progress, but remain underrepresented as fellows, members of executive committees, and presidents of major psychological organizations (APA, 2000; Gurevich, 2001; Hogan and Sexton, 1991). Journals such as *Sex Roles, Psychology of Women Quarterly,* and *Feminism and Psychology* have become major outlets for studies of gender, however, other journals continue to have only a minority of articles focusing on women and an infinitesimally small proportion of articles claiming a feminist orientation (Boatswain, Brown, Fiksenbaum, Goldstein, Greenglass, Nadler, and Pyke, 2001).

In addition to focusing on the inclusion of gender as an important variable and of women in the discipline, feminist psychologists have increasingly become aware of how gender interacts with other variables. It is never the case that a person acts as only a woman. She also acts as a person with race, age, sexual orientation, certain abilities, and so on. At times these other variables may be more important than her gender and may influence more strongly her opportunities, exclusions, and political identifications, creating similarities with some men and differences from some women. Examples of the importance of these interactions abound. Disabled women are four times more likely to divorce after developing a disability and one-third to one-quarter are as likely to marry as disabled men (Gerschick, 2000). Middle-class girls come up against the middle-class, White framework and expectations for the first time in adolescence, whereas poor and minority girls have struggled against this framework since children (Tolman and Brown, 2001). For both mathematics achievement (Hyde, Fennema, and Lamon 1990) and in the endorsement of feminist beliefs (Henley, Meng, O'Brien, McCarthy, and Sockloskie, 1998), gender differences are larger for White samples than for minority samples. Older White men are more likely to commit suicide than older White women, but older White women are equally or more likely to be the recipients of assisted suicide or euthanasia. In contrast, African-American women are less likely than African-American men to commit suicide and are absent from the known cases of assisted suicide or euthanasia (Canetto, 2001). Minority men and women come to therapy with a different time orientation than White, middle-class women and men, necessitating different therapeutic strategies (Wyche, 2001). The continued predominance of university students as participants in studies in psychology (Wintre, North, and Sugar, 2001) severely limits our understandings of gender in interaction with other variables, critical to challenging the exclusions that limit knowledge about gender and women's participation in psychology. Any single difference, including gender, will become less important as we explore more differences (Unger, 1992).

Given my argument that each of the feminist reconstructions of gender discussed here is partial with both strengths and limitations, I will conclude this section with an analysis of the strengths and limitations of forming a critique around gender as a variable. One of the main strengths of this critique is that it is located solidly within the disciplinary norms of psychology. The study of gender differences is here to stay, therefore, it is important that a feminist analysis remains engaged with gender similarities and differences research. Furthermore, in many areas such as medicine, gender is critical to improving quality of life, and a consideration of gender has been mandated by some funding agencies, especially in the area of health (Rabinowitz and Martin, 2001).

Experiments, as in gender attribution studies, are powerful because they permit causal links. Although they alone may not convince people, they provide a unique piece of the overall picture. For example, the combination of evidence of discrimination from experimental studies of CVs (Steinpreis, et al., 1999), with demographic evidence of wage and hiring discriminations (Gilbert and Rader, 2001) is powerful. When we further understand that women and other minorities are unlikely to see their own situation as reflecting discrimination, and that people are very unlikely to see any single case as indicative of discrimination (Clayton and Crosby, 1992), the power of experimental analogue studies is heightened. Women have made progress in many areas, but exclusion remains an important feminist concern. For example, women have made immense progress since the 1960s in professional fields such as medicine, law, and business. In contrast, their participation in trades has remained minuscule and virtually unchanged (Cole, Zucker, and Duncan, 2001).

On the other hand, there are important limitations to consider when evaluating the gender as variable critique. Experiments are necessarily limited and may not reflect people's everyday decisions. Meta-analyses are limited to quantitative studies and to the operationalizations, samples, and experimental contexts used by other researchers. If the samples are university students, the relationship of age to gender for the area reviewed cannot be known. Furthermore, the statistics behind meta-analysis and the complexity of interpreting the findings reduce the potential of these studies to influence social policy (Kimball, 2001). Finally, an underlying assumption of meta-analysis is that science is cumulative, and that one can add up past findings to arrive at a clear picture of gender similarities and differences (Marecek, in press).

The single greatest limitation of this critique is that the focus of analysis is the individual. When one is studying gender as a single variable, it is all too easy to assume that the picture that emerges is due to essential characteristics that apply to all, or most, women and men. This leads to several dangerous consequences: missing differences among women and among men, reinforcing a dualistic conception of gender, missing the importance of institutional forces, and assuming stable, internal characteristics that remain constant across situations (Hare-Mustin and Marecek, 1994).

GENDER AS POWER: CHALLENGING INDIVIDUALISMS

Feminist psychologists have consistently argued that one problem with the study of gender similarities and differences is that power differences between women and men are ignored. A common suggestion has been that one can interpret sex differences more usefully as power differences (Bohan, 1993; Marecek, 1995; Unger 1998). The basic argument is that men behave differently than women because they hold more power and are supported in their power by institutional sexism. Many behaviors that are thought to be typical of women are also common to others in subordinate positions. Nancy Henley (1977) pioneered this approach in her early work on nonverbal behaviors. Feminist therapists have argued that women's mental disorders are culture-bound and specifically related to their subordinate status (Marecek, 2001b). Many gender differences that have been found in heterosexual couples have been replicated in same-sex couples with the common finding that the person with more power in a same-sex couple is more likely to behave in ways similar to males in heterosexual couples (Lips, 1991). Experimental work also has shown the importance of power over gender, so that behavior patterns such as interpersonal sensitivity are associated with those assigned less powerful roles, whether these people are male or female (Snodgrass, 1992). People in power, whether men or women, attend to stereotypes when evaluating subordinates, whereas people with less power attend to information that challenges stereotypes when evaluating their superiors (Goodwin and Fiske, 2001).

The greater power associated with men is also reflected in the almost automatic assignment of male in situations where female is not specified. Animals, unless otherwise specified, are regularly referred to as "he." Male names are more often used to specify letters verbally, for example, "P as in Peter." Suzanne Kessler and Wendy McKenna (1978) found that human figures with various sex-specific visual cues were identified as male 69 percent of the time if male genitals were covered. This attribution went to 96 percent when a penis was visible. In contrast, female attributions went from 31 percent to 64 percent when a vagina was added. A vagina plus long hair and breasts were necessary to bring the rate of female attribution to 95 percent. The authors argue that the basic social rule is to see a person as male, making male the primary construction, and that "the only cultural genital is the penis" (p. 154). In the medical literature on intersexed infants, an enlarged clitoris is described very negatively but is not as likely to call into question a gender assignment of female as a small penis is to lead to questions about a gender assignment of male (Kessler, 1998, pp. 35–38). Men who violate expected gender roles are evaluated as more poorly adjusted in all areas of life, whereas a gender role deviant woman is not. One explanation for this discrepancy is that women gain and men lose status by taking on cross-gender characteristics (Kite, 2001).

Gender is not the only axis of power. As with the critique of gender as variable, feminist psychologists who analyze gender as power have also attended to the interaction of various dimensions of power and domination. The only institutions in U. S. society that include a majority of people of color are prisons (Yamamoto, 2000). Girls and women of color are more likely to speak out against and challenge discrimination and violence against women than are White, middle-class girls and women (Fine and Carney, 2001). Employed professional women consistently do more housework than their husbands (Gilbert and Rader, 2001) but also often depend on minority women as domestics who support White women's employment at the expense of their own families (Fine and Carney, 2001). Women are more likely than men to be held legally accountable for a failure to protect, however, women with the fewest resources are most likely to be held accountable (Fine and Carney, 2001).

Power is also a critical aspect of research studies and therapeutic encounters. Feminist psychologists have applied power analyses to their own activities of therapy and research. Acknowledging the power imbalance between therapist and client and working with the paradox between empowering the client and the structural power of the therapist have been critical aspects of feminist therapies (Marecek, 2001b, Worell and Johnson, 2001). Researchers also usually have power over their participants, and critical attention has been directed to some of the ethical issues this raises, such as how researchers can both respect and challenge women's taken-for-granted experiences (Kitzinger and Wilkinson, 1997), and how much participants should contribute to the analysis of the data (Jones, 1997). Power also enters the therapy and research contexts through the values of the psychologist, which has led to a rejection of traditional notions of objectivity and the introduction of the concept of reflexivity. Mary Crawford and Ellen Kimmel (1999) define both a personal reflexivity that examines how our identities and work influence each other and a functional reflexivity that involves a sociological perspective of psychology as a discipline and how dominant paradigms and powerful institutions support each other. These reflexivities have led feminist psychologists to challenge some aspects of traditional psychological methodologies. One way has been through the strong endorsement of qualitative research as equally or more important than the quantitative methodologies that have marked traditional psychology. Qualitative work often involves a more intimate relationship between the researcher and participants and thus makes clearer the need for understanding how the researcher enters the processes of analysis and interpretation of data. It also raises questions about traditional concepts of validity and reliability. However, as several feminist psychologists have pointed out, qualitative research is not the opposite of quantitative, and the two forms should not be conceptualized as a hierarchy. Although the assumptions underlying quantitative and qualitative research are different and in some ways incommensurate, they are both attempts to construct knowledge. Neither words nor numbers speak for themselves. Researchers always must convince audiences of the trustworthiness of their analyses, interpretations, ethical procedures, and generalizations (Henwood and Pidgeon, 1995; Marecek, 2001a; Rabinowitz and Martin, 2001).

The strengths of conceptualizing gender as power are in the importance of drawing attention to social inequalities and dominations and showing how they influence individual social interactions. Except for some areas of social psychology, this analysis is often missing from psychology and serves to strengthen our explanatory power. It also challenges psychology's focus on the individual, both as an isolated participant whose behavior is determined only by experimental manipulations and as a researcher who is the model of the disinterested and objective observer.

The limitations of conceptualizing gender as power are twofold. First, as it challenges one of the central tenets of psychology, the focus on the individual, it is harder to integrate into the discipline. In a recent survey, 55 percent of methodology texts did not mention qualitative research, and only 28 percent described quantitative and qualitative research without invoking a hierarchy between the two. Furthermore, all but one of the texts either did not discuss the researcher/participant relationship or described this relationship as one of unproblematic hierarchy (Campbell and Schram, 1995). Second, by rejecting individual gender and choosing instead social and institutional definitions of gender, a dichotomy is set up in which only one level of gender is legitimate. These two levels of gender are not mutually exclusive but interactive (Unger, 1998). Just as it is essentialist to assume that women are different from men, it is also essentialist to assume that women have less power than men. Not only do some women have more power than some men, but individual women and men respond differently to the presence of institutional sexism depending on many factors, including contexts, personalities, values, and past learning, all of which are important for explaining observed diversities of behavior and resistance.

GENDER IN CONTEXT: CHALLENGING ESSENTIALISMS

Both of the first two themes, by focusing on single dimensions—the individual or the social—risk essentialisms. All generalizations involve the search for similarities across different individuals or situations and are therefore essentialist arguments. Most feminist psychologists would not argue against all generalizations, but have become more critical of broad or unquestioned generalizations within psychology as often making dangerously essentialist arguments. Even pro-feminist generalizations, such as violence against women "could happen to anyone," have come to "It could happen to those in power," leading to the invisibility of poor women and women of color as victims of violence (Richie, 2000, p. 1135). To some extent, by including the interaction of gender with other aspects of individuals or dimensions of power, the dangers of essentialisms within each perspective are reduced but not eliminated.

The critique that locates gender in context, however, goes beyond simple interactions of variables or axes of power to examine the effect of more specific contexts on gender. The concept of "intersectionality" that originated in legal studies has been used to theorize the intersection of identities. The search is not just for how gender interacts with major social identities such as race, but how these interactions may be different for women and men and across different times and social contexts. Furthermore, gender identity may interact with some other identities (e.g., parent, gardener). Even more specifically, the interconnectedness of two identities such as woman and parent may be salient in some situations and irrelevant in others (Deaux and Stewart, 2001).

Specific behaviors that have been linked to individual gender differences or to differences in male and female power have, when contextualized, proved to be more situationally specific and complex. Tag questions and conversational interruptions are cases in point. Women and subordinates tend to use more tag questions and interrupt others less. However, both men and women use tag questions less in competitive situations and more in contexts that call for facilitating others. Those in powerful roles use tag questions to solicit responses from subordinates. Those with less power use them to seek reassurance. Men do not interrupt more than women in all contexts, nor do they use all forms of interruptions more. In naturalistic settings, men do use more intrusive interruptions (LaFrance, 2001).

The same behavior can take on different meanings depending on context. Silence has often been interpreted as indicating a lack of self-confidence and therefore a lack of "voice" that women acquire when empowered. However, silence can also signify defiance or resistance (Tolman and Brown, 2001). Women's aggression is often interpreted to mean a lack of emotional control, whereas similar behavior in men is seen as a means of control (White, Donat, and Bondurant, 2001).

Qualitative research creates a context that is particularly useful for bringing out women's interpretations of their experiences that may not match theoretical explanations based on power relations or individual traits. Thus women with eating disorders do not often invoke the "culture of thinness" as the cause of their eating disorder. Rather, they cite periods of severe emotional strain as a trigger and disordered eating as a way to manage emotional stress (Marecek, 2001a, 2001b). Both men and women in heterosexual relationships who endorse equality tend to define it in terms of respect or support, not division of labor, which remains unequal (Dion and Dion, 2001).

Of particular interest to feminist psychologists are conceptualizations of context that open the door to social change. Gender differences in mathematics performance have been described by feminists as nonexistent or small (Hyde et al., 1990), as occurring in standardized tests but not in classroom grades (Kimball, 1989), and as smaller than many school, ethnic, or class or cultural differences (Kimball 1995). All of these arguments exist in the realm of individual gender. Recently, a further contexualization of gender differences in mathematics performance has suggested a much more situationally specific factor that may account for most or all of the observed differences, at least for some groups of students. Claude Steele (1997) introduced the concept of stereotype threat to explain the poorer intellectual performance of disadvantaged groups. Stereotype threat operates when a negative stereotype about a group to which one belongs is made evident. It operates for people who have survived structural obstacles that face their group and who have achieved success and identification with the intellectual domain being tested and where tasks are difficult enough to be at the edge of their ability. It is not an internalized sense of inferiority or a part of the psychology of stigmatized groups, and it can have an effect even if people do not believe that the stereotype applies to them.

Empirical support for the effectiveness of stereotype threat is strong. In several studies students who were taking university math courses were tested on difficult math questions under several conditions. Where stereotype threat was introduced by either saying nothing about gender differences or explicitly referring to gender differences that favored males, women performed worse than men. On the other hand, where gender difference was specifically countered by telling participants that women did as well as men, women performed as well as men (Spencer, Steele, and Quinn, 1999; Walsh, Hickey, and Duffy, 1999). One does not have to draw specific attention to group differences. In several studies a race or gender prime was sufficient to result in performance differences. Thus Asian women primed to think of their Asian identity did better on a math test than Asian women primed to think of their identity as females (Shih, Pittinsky, and Ambady, 1999). Blacks who were told that a difficult verbal test was diagnostic or who were primed to think of their racial identity did less well than Whites, however, when not primed to think of race or told the test was not diagnostic of ability, they performed similarly to Whites (Steele and Aronson, 1995). Stereotype threat can be generated and can affect performance of dominant groups as well. White males who were told of research that shows Asians perform better than Whites, did less well on a difficult math test than White males who were told the test was one of mathematical ability (Aronson, Lustina, Good, and Keough, 1999). Furthermore, in several studies there is a nonsignificant but consistent decrement across studies of dominant group performance under conditions of low stereotype threat (Spencer et al., 1999).

The power of a contextual variable such as stereotype threat is a very useful feminist concept because it does not require assumptions about biology or socialization. Indeed, it is as plausible an explanation for the Benbow and Stanley (1980) results as any that have been offered (Spencer et al., 1999). It is specific to situations and therefore can be changed. Unfortunately, given the pervasiveness of negative stereotypes, the attempts to reduce stereotype threat must be made consistently, since exemptions from the stereotype in one situation will not easily generalize to new settings (Steele, 1997).

The strength of contextualizing gender is that it leads to a much richer and more powerful understanding of gender. It is a powerful tool for deconstructing stereotypes. It also can be useful to people in their everyday lives. For example, to know that in heterosexual couples wives are more likely to demand and husbands to withdraw is much less useful in relationship negotiations than to know that both men and women are more likely to demand when they are trying to change something in the relationship and to withdraw when their partner wants change (LaFrance, 2001).

One limitation of contextualizing gender is that by focusing ever more on specifics, generalizations become more difficult and, in the extreme, impossible. This may be a useful limitation for a broad concept such as gender, but it does go against the grain of the discipline and of popular thinking. It is difficult to communicate complexity within the context of an academic article, and even more so within the context of a media bite. Theories that focus on single issues and seek to reduce complexity have made their mark on psychology, other academic disciplines, and popular culture. Therefore, one must be aware of the importance of guarding against misinterpretation and must work creatively to communicate complexity.

GENDER AS SOCIAL CONSTRUCT: CHALLENGING DUALISMS

Approaching gender as a social construct takes the contextualization of gender one step farther and asks questions about how we arrive at the categories of female and male in the first place. The other three critiques take these categories for granted. Social constructionism asks how people, scientists included, create as natural the categories of sex and gender that come to feel like a part of their innermost selves. Both linguistic and institutional processes are examined in order to explore this question (Hare-Mustin and Marecek, 1994; Kessler and McKenna, 1978). Critical to a social constructionist view is the concept of gender as performance. Gender is not natural or automatic, although it may feel that way to individuals. Rather, through dress, language, verbal exchanges, and nonverbal behaviors, people create themselves as male or female and actively read others' performances in terms of dualistic gender. So powerful is this process that once a person is perceived as male or female, almost any other cue will be read as consistent with the original attribution (Kessler and McKenna, 1978; Wilchins, 1997).

The concept of social construction of gender has led to questioning the duality of gender, the naturalness of heterosexuality, and the distinction between sex and gender.

Once gender is defined as performance, then gender as a fixed and natural category is called into question. Everyone passes, and passing is practiced by both the actor and the perceiver. There is no single characteristic that one can use with 100 percent accuracy to distinguish woman from man, male from female (Kessler and McKenna, 1978; Wilchins, 1997). Transsexuals do not all choose surgery, thus a penis may be a physical attribute of a female as well as a male. Intersexuals who are routinely subjected to surgery during infancy and childhood to create genitals that fit into medical definitions of genital and gender dualities are protesting this process, and many support the idea of nondualistic constructions of gender (Kessler, 1998). Although some transsexuals are invested in creating and living within the natural attitude toward gender, some are also challenging these categories, resisting identities as male, female, or transsexual (Devor, 2000; Golden, 2000; Kitzinger, 2001; Wilchins, 1997).

When the naturalness of the duality of gender is called into question, the construction of heterosexuality is also questioned. The notion of two and only two genders that are opposite creates an unspoken presumption of the naturalness of the complementarity of heterosexuality (Fine and Gordon, 1991). Heterosexuality is the criterion by which intersexed infants are assigned to genders and genital surgery is evaluated. Sexual orientation depends on gender dualities—one is attracted to people of the opposite or same sex. If gendered bodies were not defined dualistically, then heterosexuality and sexual orientation more generally would become meaningless (Kessler, 1998).

The debate over the concepts of "sex" and/or "gender" has been an ongoing and often confusing one within feminist psychology. Early feminist attempts at making a sex/gender distinction were for the purpose of creating space for gender differences that were not biological (Marecek, 2001a; Scott, 1999). However, space for the cultural was created within psychology in at least two different ways. Rhoda Unger (1979) proposed that gender be used to refer to "nonphysiological components of sex that are culturally regarded as appropriate to males or to females" (p. 1086), and that it might serve to reduce or at least to make explicit parallels between the biological and the social. Implicit in this is the assumption that sex is to nature as gender is to culture. Suzanne Kessler and Wendy McKenna (1978), in a different construction, chose to collapse sex into gender, arguing that they wanted to emphasize the social construction of biological as well as cultural concepts. In their construction, everything relating to female and male, masculine and feminine, was gender. Sex was used only to describe reproductive and lovemaking activities (p. 7). Through the social construction of gender, "sex" (as in biology) disappeared (McKenna and Kessler, 2000).

However, both the distinction between sex and gender and the elimination of sex are difficult to maintain consistently. Suzanne Kessler (1998) acknowledges this in her work on intersexed people. In her system, "intergendered" would be the more accurate term, however, this is not the term that is used both in medical discourses and by the people concerned. So she uses "intersexed" rather than "intergendered" in her work. Several theorists have argued that the confusions over sex and gender are to be expected, and that feminists would be well advised to allow this confusion rather than to try to reduce the relationship between sex and gender to a single construction (Chanter, 2000; Connell, 1999; Scott, 1999). If both sex and gender are social constructs that vary in definition and use across situations and across time, then it is better to adopt a more flexible approach that assumes that the two concepts are neither partially or totally independent nor collapsible into one term. Bodies, as bodies, influence our conceptions of gender: "The *social* process of gender includes childbirth and child care, youth and aging, the pleasures of sport and sex, labor, injury, death from AIDS, and the struggle to live with AIDS" (Connell, 1999, p. 464, emphasis in original). And social processes create biology through, for example, the influence of social manipulations of hormone levels and surgical treatment of transsexual and intersexual people (Kessler, 1998; Kessler and McKenna, 1978; Unger, 1993).

The main strength of the theme of social construction of gender is that if gender is not natural, if it is the result of human linguistic and institutional processes, then it can be resisted and changed. What is constructed can be reconstructed. If gender is performance, then in each moment there is the possibility of change through a transgressive act or reading (Wilchins, 1997). By destabilizing the taken-for-granted world, new possibilities will emerge (Wilkinson, 2001). New questions can be asked, and new possibilities can be imagined. Understanding that all that seems natural is constructed, including physical categories, opens the way for more radical changes, for "the reality of other possibilities as well as the possibility of other realities" (Kessler and McKenna, 1978, p. 164).

The main weakness of this critique lies in the perceived naturalness of gender categories. Most people, including most psychologists, experience themselves most of the time within the natural categories of gender. The very notion of breaking down these categories, of deconstructing dualisms, is deeply disturbing to many, which will lead to resisting this kind of thinking and to violence against people who do not fit neatly into one of two gender categories (Wilchins, 1997). It will be very difficult, indeed has already proved very difficult, to use social constructionism to make inroads into traditional psychology. By defining gender and other identities as constructed through performances rather than stable, internal characteristics, political concerns arise that the basis of fighting oppressions will be lost. To some extent, this is a genuine risk, however, it can be overstated. The oppressions that identities arise out of have real and material consequences in peoples' lives. Identities can be questioned without denying oppressions (Wilchins, 1997). Gay identities formed around biological constructions have been often favored as a way of promoting gay rights, and social constructionism has been criticized as undermining gay liberation. However, biological research has rarely been used to support gay and lesbian liberation (Kitzinger, 2001).

CONCLUSION

As I argued in my introduction, all critiques of gender are partial, all are both useful and problematic, and all are necessary. All critiques must be evaluated in the contexts in which they are used, and even the most useful in a specific context will have limitations as well as strengths. One difference among the critiques discussed in this chapter is the relative impact that they have had on the discipline of psychology. The gender as variable critique has had the most impact because this critique shares important assumptions on which psychology has been constructed, whereas the "gender as social construction" has had the least impact because it seeks to deconstruct both the individual with stable identities and the possibility of a rational, disinterested observer.

My vision for psychology, as I would like it to become, needs all of these critiques. Quantitative research studies should routinely be required to include effect sizes and descriptions of non-normal distributions where they are found. The consideration of power and the influence of social institutions and dominance structures should be routinely considered, along with individual variables. Attention to context should not preclude generalizations, but it should routinely lead us to describe the limits of those generalizations. Identities should be approached as useful social constructions that are always multiple and open to change (Deaux and Stewart, 2001) and that can both strengthen political alliances and threaten individuality (Wilchins, 1997). Researchers should routinely evaluate their own and others' research in terms of both strengths and limitations (Kimball, 2001). The search for parsimony should not sacrifice important complexities. In thinking about similarities and difference, the quality of being "transminded" will help one be aware of differences as well as find commonalities (e.g., translations, transgendered; see Stimpson, 2000). The psychology toolbox needs to include not only multiple methodologies but also multiple critiques. Critiques that examine taken-for-granted concepts such as female and male are particularly important, as they open up visions of what might be, as well as what is (Kessler, 1998; Kessler and McKenna, 1978). An openness to the unexpected, to surprise, to the chance to think afresh, should be cultivated (Enloe, 2000). The whole range of critiques of gender is important for psychology as a discipline. Each provides a partial discourse though which psychology can become more inclusive and more supportive of social change.

NOTE

1. My preference throughout this chapter is to use "gender" rather than "sex." As I discuss under the subhead "Gender As Social Construct," the debate over the use of gender or sex has never been, and should not be, foreclosed. Both "sex" and "gender" are social constructions, however, given the tendency on the part of readers to more likely associate "gender" with social construction, it is my preferred usage here.

REFERENCES

APA Task Force on Women in Academe. (2000). *Women in Academe: Two steps forward, one step back.* American Psychological Association. Available: www.wpw.org/pi/wpo.

Aronson, J., Lustina, M. J., Good, C., & Keough, K. (1999). When white men can't do math: Necessary and sufficient factors in stereotype threat. *Journal of Experimental Social Psychology, 35,* 29–46.

Benbow, C. P., & Stanley, J. C. (1980). Sex differences in mathematical ability: Fact or artifact? *Science, 210,* 1262–1264.

Boatswain, S., Brown, N., Fiksenbaum, L., Goldstein, L., Greenglass, E., Nadler, E., & Pyke, S. (2001). Canadian feminist psychology: Where are we now? *Canadian Psychology, 42,* 276–285.

Bohan, J. S. (1993). Regarding gender: Essentialism, constructionism, and feminist psychology. *Psychology of Women Quarterly, 17,* 5–21.

Campbell, R., & Schram, P. J. (1995). Feminist research methods: A content analysis of psychology and social science textbooks. *Psychology of Women Quarterly, 19,* 85–106.

Canetto, S. S. (2001). Older adult women: Issues, resources, and challenges. In R. K. Unger (Ed.), *Handbook of the psychology of women and gender* (pp. 183–197). New York, NY: Wiley.

Chanter, T. (2000). Gender aporias. *Signs, 25,* 1237–1241.

Clayton, S. D., & Crosby, F. J. (1992). *Justice, gender, and affirmative action.* Ann Arbor, MI: University of Michigan Press.

Cole, E. R., Zucker, A. N., & Duncan, L. E. (2001). Changing society, changing women (and men). In R. K. Unger (Ed.), *Handbook of the psychology of women and gender* (pp. 410– 423). New York, NY: Wiley.

Connell, R. W. (1999). Making gendered people: bodies, identities, sexualities. In M. M. Ferree, J. Lorber, & B. B. Hess (Eds.), *Revisioning gender* (pp. 449–472). Thousand Oaks, CA: Sage.

Crawford, M., & Kimmel, E. (1999). Promoting methodological diversity in feminist research. *Psychology of Women Quarterly, 23,* 1–6.

Crawford, M., & Marecek, J. (1989). Psychology reconstructs the female: 1968–1988. *Psychology of Women Quarterly, 13,* 147–165.

Danziger, K. (1990). *Constructing the subject: Historical origins of psychological research.* Cambridge, UK: Cambridge University Press.

Deaux, K., & Stewart, A. (2001). Framing gendered identities. In R. K. Unger (Ed.), *Handbook of the psychology of women and gender* (pp. 84–97). New York, NY: Wiley.

Devor, H. (2000). Speaking subjects: Theory in the vernacular. *Feminism & Psychology, 10,* 41–45.

Dion, K. K., & Dion, K. L. (2001). Gender and Relationships. In R. K. Unger (Ed.), *Handbook of the psychology of women and gender* (pp. 256–271). New York, NY: Wiley.

Eagly, A. H. (1987). *Sex differences in social behavior: A social-role interpretation.* Hillsdale, NJ: Lawrence Erlbaum.

Enloe, C. (2000). The surprised feminist. *Signs, 25,* 1023–1026.

Favreau, O. (1997). Sex and gender comparisons: Does null-hypothesis testing create a false dichotomy? *Feminism and Psychology, 7,* 63–81.

Fidell, L. S. (1970). Empirical verification of sex discrimination in hiring practices in psychology. *American Psychologist, 25,* 1094–1098.

Fine, M., & Carney, S. (2001). Women, gender, and the law: Toward a feminist rethinking of responsibility. In R. K. Unger (Ed.), *Handbook of the psychology of women and gender* (pp. 388–409). New York, NY: Wiley.

Fine, M., & Gordon, S. M. (1991). Effacing the center and the margins: Life at the intersection of psychology and feminism. *Feminism & Psychology, 1,* 19–27.

Gerschick, T. J. (2000). Toward a theory of disability and gender. *Signs, 25,* 1263–1268.

Gilbert, L. A., & Rader, J. (2001). Current perspectives on women's adult roles: Work, family, and life. In R. K. Unger (Ed.), *Handbook of the psychology of women and gender* (pp. 156–169). New York, NY: Wiley.

Golden, C. R. (2000). Still seeing differently, after all these years. *Feminism and Psychology, 10,* 30–35.

Goodwin, S. A., & Fiske, S. T. (2001). Power and gender: The double-edged sword of ambivalence. In R. K. Unger (Ed.), *Handbook of the psychology of women and gender* (pp. 358–366). New York, NY: Wiley.

Gurevich, M. (2001). W(h)ither psychology of women?: Current trends and future directions for the Section on Women and Psychology. *Canadian Psychology 42,* 301–312.

Hare-Mustin, R. T., & Marecek, J. (1994). Asking the right questions: Feminist psychology and sex differences. *Feminism & Psychology, 4*, 531–537.

Henley, N. M. (1977). *Body politics: Power, sex, and nonverbal communication.* Englewood Cliffs, NJ: Prentice Hall.

Henley, N. M., Meng, K., O'Brien, D., McCarthy, W. J., & Sockloskie, R. J. (1998). Developing a scale to measure the diversity of feminist attitudes. *Psychology of Women Quarterly, 22*, 317–348.

Henwood, K., & Pidgeon, N. (1995). Remaking the link: Qualitative research and feminist standpoint theory. *Feminism & Psychology, 5*, 7–30.

Hogan, J. D., & Sexton, V. S. (1991). Women and the American Psychological Association. *Psychology of Women Quarterly, 15*, 623–634.

Hollingworth, L. S. (1914). Variability as related to sex differences in achievement: A critique. *American Journal of Sociology, 19*, 510–530.

Hollingworth, L. S. (1916a). Sex differences in mental traits. *Psychological Bulletin, 13*, 377–384.

Hollingworth, L. S. (1916b). Social devices for impelling women to bear and rear children. *American Journal of Sociology, 22*, 19–29.

Hollingworth, L. S. (1918). Sex differences in mental traits. *Psychological Bulletin, 15*, 427–432.

Hollingworth, L. S. (1919). Sex differences in mental traits. *Psychological Bulletin, 16*, 371–373.

Hull, H. R. (1917). The long handicap. *Psychoanalytic Review, 4*, 434–442.

Hyde, J. S. (1994). Can meta-analysis make feminist transformations in psychology? *Psychology of Women Quarterly, 18*, 451–462.

Hyde, J. S., Fennema, E., & Lamon, S. J. (1990). Gender differences in mathematics performance: A meta-analysis. *Psychological Bulletin, 107*, 139–155.

Jones, S. J. (1997). Reflexivity and feminist practice: Ethical dilemmas in negotiating meaning. *Feminism & Psychology, 7*, 348–353.

Kessler, S. J. (1998). *Lessons from the intersexed.* New Brunswick, NJ: Rutgers University Press.

Kessler, S. J., & McKenna, W. (1978). *Gender: An ethnomethodological approach.* New York, NY: Wiley.

Kimball, M. M. (1989). A new perspective on women's math achievement. *Psychological Bulletin, 105*, 198–214.

Kimball, M. M. (1995). *Feminist visions of gender similarities and differences.* Binghamton, NY: Haworth.

Kimball, M. M. (2001). Gender similarities and differences as feminist contradictions. In R. K. Unger (Ed.), *Handbook of the psychology of women and gender* (pp. 66–83). New York, NY: Wiley.

Kite, M. E. (2001). Changing times, changing gender roles: Who do we want women and men to be? In R. K. Unger (Ed.), *Handbook of the psychology of women and gender* (pp. 215–227). New York, NY: Wiley.

Kitzinger, C. (2001). Sexualities. In R. K. Unger (Ed.), *Handbook of the psychology of women and gender* (pp. 272–285). New York, NY: Wiley.

Kitzinger, C., & Wilkinson, S. (1997). Validating women's experience? Dilemmas in feminist research. *Feminism & Psychology, 7*, 566–574.

LaFrance, M. (2001). Gender and social interaction. In R. K. Unger (Ed.), *Handbook of the psychology of women and gender* (pp. 245–255). New York, NY: Wiley.

Lips, H. M. (1991). *Women, men, and power*. Mountain View, CA: Mayfield.

Marecek, J. (1995). Gender, politics, and psychology's ways of knowing. *American Psychologist, 50*, 162–163.

Marecek, J. (2001a). After the facts: Psychology and the study of gender. *Canadian Psychology, 42*, 254–267.

Marecek, J. (2001b). Disorderly constructs: Feminist frameworks for clinical psychology. In R. K. Unger (Ed.), *Handbook of the psychology of women and gender* (pp. 303–316). New York, NY: Wiley.

McKenna, W., & Kessler, S. J. (2000). Retrospective response. *Feminism & Psychology, 10*, 66–72.

Mednick, M. T., & Urbanski, L. L. (1991). The origins and activities of APA's Division of the Psychology of Women. *Psychology of Women Quarterly, 15*, 651–663.

O'Barr, J. F. (2000). My master list for the millennium. *Signs, 25*, 1205–1207.

Pyke, S. W. (2001). Feminist psychology in Canada: Early days. *Canadian Psychology, 42*, 268–275.

Rabinowitz, V. C., & Martin, D. (2001). Choices and consequences: Methodological issues in the study of gender. In R. K. Unger (Ed.), *Handbook of the psychology of women and gender* (pp. 29–52). New York, NY: Wiley.

Richie, B. E. (2000). A Black feminist reflection on the antiviolence movement. *Signs, 25*, 1133–1137.

Scott, J. W. (1999). Some reflection on gender and politics. In M. M. Ferree, J. Lorber, & B. B. Hess (Eds.), *Revisioning gender* (pp. 70–96). Thousand Oaks, CA: Sage.

Shields, S. A. (1975). Functionalism, Darwinism, and the psychology of women: A study in social myth. *American Psychologist, 30*, 739–754.

Shields, S. A. (1982). The variability hypothesis: The history of a biological model of sex differences of intelligence. *Signs, 7*, 769–797.

Shih, M., Pittinsky, T. L., & Ambady, N. (1999). Stereotype susceptibility: Identity salience and shifts in quantitative performance. *Psychological Science, 10*, 80–83.

Snodgrass, S. E. (1992). Further effects of role versus gender on interpersonal sensitivity. *Journal of Personality and Social psychology, 62*, 154–158.

Spencer, S. J., Steele, C. M., & Quinn, D. M. (1999). Stereotype threat and women's math performance. *Journal of Experimental Social Psychology, 35*, 4–28.

Steele, C. M. (1997). A threat in the air: How stereotypes shape intellectual identity and performance. *American Psychologist, 52*, 613–629.

Steele, C. M., & Aronson, J. (1995). Stereotype threat and the intellectual test performance of African Americans. *Journal of Personality and Social Psychology, 69*, 797–811.

Steinpreis, R. E., Anders, K. A., & Ritzke, D. (1999). The impact of gender on the review of the curricula vitae of job applicants and tenure candidates: A national empirical study. *Sex Roles, 41*, 509–528.

Stimpson, C. R. (2000). On being transminded. *Signs, 25*, 1007–1011.

Tiefer, L. (1991). A brief history of the Association for Women in Psychology. *Psychology of Women Quarterly, 15*, 635–649.

Tolman, D. L., & Brown, L. M. (2001). Adolescent girls' voices: Resonating resistance in body and soul. In R. K. Unger (Ed.), *Handbook of the psychology of women and gender* (pp. 133–155). New York: Wiley.

Unger, R. K. (1979). Toward a redefinition of sex and gender. *American Psychologist, 34*, 1085–1094.

Unger, R. K. (1992). Will the real sex difference please stand up? *Feminism & Psychology,* *2,* 231–238.

Unger, R. K. (1993). Alternative conceptions of sex (and sex differences). In M. Haug, R. Whelan, C. Aron, & K. L. Olsen (Eds.), *The development of sex differences and simi-larities in behavior* (pp. 457–476). Dordrecht, The Netherlands: Kluwer Academic.

Unger, R. K. (1998). *Resisting gender: Twenty-five years of feminist psychology.* London, UK: Sage.

Unger, R. K. (2001). Women as subjects, actors, and agents in the history of psychology. In R. K. Unger (Ed.), *Handbook of the psychology of women and gender* (pp. 3–16). New York, NY: Wiley.

Walsh, M., Hickey, C., & Duffy, J. (1999). Influence of item content and stereotype situation on gender differences in mathematical problem solving. *Sex Roles, 41,* 219–240.

White, J. W., Donat, P. L. N., & Bondurant, B. (2001). A developmental examination of violence against girls and women. In R. K. Unger (Ed.), *Handbook of the psychol-ogy of women and gender* (pp. 343–357). New York, NY: Wiley.

Wilchins, R. A. (1997). *Read my lips: Sexual subversion and the end of gender.* Ithaca, NY: Firebrand.

Wilkinson, S. (2001). Theoretical perspectives on women and gender. In R. K. Unger (Ed.), *Handbook of the psychology of women and gender* (pp. 17–28). New York, NY: Wiley.

Wintre, M. G., North, C., & Sugar, L. A. (2001). Psychologists' response to criticisms about research based on undergraduate participants: A developmental perspective. *Canadian Psychology, 42,* 216–225.

Woolley, H. T. (1910). A review of the recent literature on the psychology of sex. *Psychological Bulletin, 7,* 335–342.

Woolley, H. T. (1914). The psychology of sex. *Psychological Bulletin, 11,* 353–379.

Worell, J., & Johnson, D. (2001). Therapy with women: Feminist frameworks. In R. K. Unger (Ed.), *Handbook of the psychology of women and gender* (pp. 317–329). New York, NY: Wiley.

Wyche, K. F. (2001). Sociocultural issues in counseling for women of color. In R. K. Unger (Ed.), *Handbook of the psychology of women and gender* (pp. 330–340). New York, NY: Wiley.

Yamamoto, T. (2000). Millennial bodies. *Signs, 25,* 1243–1246.

CHAPTER NINE

RETRIEVING THE PAST FOR THE FUTURE
BOUNDARY MAINTENANCE IN HISTORICAL AND THEORETICAL PSYCHOLOGY

Henderikus J. Stam

History would be an excellent thing if only it were true.
— Tolstoy, as cited in *The Hedgehog and the Fox*
(Berlin, 1953/1997a)

THE HISTORY OF PSYCHOLOGY as a specialty within the discipline has undergone major changes over recent years, taking on broad intellectual considerations originally external to psychology and gradually infusing the very way in which some historians of psychology have come to write and speak of their subject. Such diverse influences include the rethinking that has come over the history of science and the influence of the question of "technology" on these histories, the profound reconstitution of history by feminist and postcolonial historians and the overall reconsideration of historiography itself by historians. The study of the history of the discipline of psychology, traditionally written by psychologists with an interest in the history of their discipline, is now more broadly conceived and has been enriched by the presence of historians not trained primarily as psychologists.

In this chapter I want to address a delimited question, albeit a central one, in the current historiography of psychology. This concerns the "proper" role of theory in history, a question raised in part by the influx of critical, poststructuralist, and narrative approaches introduced by contemporary philosophies of history and the strong counter-reaction it, in turn, has generated. I place "proper" in scare quotes only to emphasize that there are some historians who appear to believe that theory has no place in history proper, whereas others claim that history is simply theory of a certain kind. Hence, the notion that there is one "proper" way of engaging theoretical concerns in historical studies is already deeply dependent on the very understanding of theory that is contested. If theory is external to the core work of history, then it will always be an interloper. On the other hand, if theorizing the historical record is a requirement for doing history, then it behooves us to address how we can proceed to write histories of psychology.

I will take the stance that there is no escape from theory in historical writing, even in the most mundane and antiquarian of historical studies, since the very nature of the subject at hand requires some, if only commonly agreed upon, theoretical understanding. Obviously this is very much a matter of consensus and negotiation and may indeed be trivial if one is, for example, interested in some restricted aspect of local history. Nevertheless, as any reading of the postmoderns and their critics makes clear, history is hardly a question of establishing "matters of fact," even if such matters of fact are readily agreed upon. Current debates on whether there is indeed such a thing as "historical fact" are beside the point (e.g., Fox-Genovese and Lasch-Quinn, 1999). The language of "facts" is itself a language derived from particular views of science that are a product of 17th and 18th century natural philosophy and it is simply the wrong language for historical studies (Poovey, 1998).

After developing the idea of the inevitability of theory, I want to examine the relationship between this problem and the history of psychology. Historical studies of psychological topics range widely from descriptions of theories and the individuals who propounded them to institutional, social, and political influences on the development of disciplinary frameworks. Despite these dissimilarities, it is clear that there is a continuing tension between studies that treat history as a form of bookkeeping, clarification, and elucidation, as well as celebration versus those studies that rely on historical studies to rethink the very project of psychology. Often self-consciously "critical," these latter studies have focused on the way in which psychology has expressed itself in relation to such factors as institutional and social developments, gender, race, and so on. The distinction between these two "types" of history can be understood as a distinction between studies that take the disciplinary status of psychology as a fixed background versus those that see history as an occasion to question the very foundations of its disciplinary and institutional status.

THEORY DEBATES

Among recent debates concerning the place of interpretation in history, there has emerged a prolonged dispute about the force of narrative in constructing rather than reconstructing history. Certainly Mink, White, and Ricoeur have played predominant roles in this debate on their respective sides of the Atlantic and have fed into more broadly considered arguments concerning the place of history in a postmodernist context. The cognitive function of narrative form, on Mink's account, is not simply to relate a succession of events but to "body forth an ensemble of interrelationships of many different kinds as a single whole" (Mink, 1978). Historical narratives claim truth as a criterion of their coherence but, as Mink notes, they are always the product of imaginative construction, and they are "cognitive instruments." Evidence, wherever we might find it, does not dictate the form of the narrative.

Hayden White's narrative conception of history is less cognitive and more overtly formalist (his 1973 and 1978 works are foundational in this respect). His position is founded on a notion of the primacy of rhetoric over facticity, or the importance of the speculative, incomprehensible, and sublime in narrating events. History is not the outcome of an analytic and a systematic application of rules of evidence but has a kind of indeterminacy to it, an indeterminacy that allows it to remain open to utopian interests. Hence, historiography is never final and can never be reduced to the impulse of a science of history.[1]

Furthermore, White argues that to produce a history, the chronicle must be converted to a meaningful narrative and, hence, must be emplotted. But the past has no plot, thus the historian provides an account, a narrative that emplots or encodes the traces or evidence. History then becomes an inseparable combination of elements both found and invented. Furthermore, modes of emplotment are fundamentally dependent on tropes, since there is no other entry into the rhetorical structure of language. Hence, "all historical narratives . . . presuppose figurative characterizations of the events/ facts they purport to be representations of" (Jenkins, 1995, p. 168). In this respect, White is clear when he claims that "the ground is that of language itself, which, in areas of study such as history, can be said to operate *tropologically* in order to prefigure a field of perception in a particular modality of relationships" (White, 1978, p. 72, emphasis in origial). As a consequence, history must concern itself not just with fact but with meaning, and meaning is to be understood as dependent on tropological strategies.

As a conclusion to this triumvirate, it is important to note the role that Paul Ricoeur has played in attempting to downplay the one-sidedness of such debates as created by poststructuralism and its offshoots. In the first volume of *Time and Narrative*, Ricoeur (1984) attends to the necessity of narrative (through configuration and emplotment) for a historical under-standing. Indeed, history must be configured, brought into a meaningful relation with other events in time. Like White, Ricoeur argues that history is a combination of the found and made up, of the documented and the narrated. Without configuration and emplotment, there can be no history. Once narrated, history is appropriated as not only meaningful but it in turn becomes the ground for further configuration. Narratives extend the past into the present and make it possible to imagine a future (Ricoeur, 1988).

What binds these authors is their common commitment to a distinct division between what constitutes the past and its detritus over and against the written record that comes to constitute history. In White's analysis, tropes prefigure the written word, giving it shape and meaning. In addition, such factors as ideology and modes of emplotment (romance, tragedy, comedy) are active prior to the narration itself. In Ricoeur's case, the act of narration is dependent on mimesis, which in its original form simply prefigures our understanding. This mimetic process in turn is dependent on metaphor. History on these accounts is a project that comes into being from the inseparable relations of gathering, sifting, and weighing evidence, along with the telling of a tale to an audience whose sensibilities are themselves ad-dressed in the story line.

However disparate and unsettling such claims may seem, they are still not the postmodernist stuff that makes up some contemporary historiogra-phy. Indeed, they are more akin to the ongoing conversation on the nature of history that has spanned more than a century.[2] Much of this conceptuali-zation is already available in the work of Collingwood, particularly in his mature writing. It is important in this respect that Collingwood endorsed a realist program in his earlier works, such as *Speculum Mentis* (1924), even if this is only implicitly the case. By the time he comes to write the essays that make up *The Idea of History* (1946), he has worked out precisely why he is not a realist. For Collingwood, skepticism is a consequence of realism, "the discovery that the past as such is unknowable is the scepticism which is the permanent and necessary counterpart of the plain man's realism" (1965, p. 100). The search for a factual past is an illusion. His move away from a unknowable past-in-itself led Collingwood to the practices and activities of historians themselves (Goldstein, 1970). On this point, Collingwood is often considered a historian who wishes merely to relegate history to an act of imagination, although this is far too simple. In his important paper on the historical imagination appended to *The Idea of History*, he argues:

. . . neither the raw material of historical knowledge, the detail
of the here-and-now as given him in perception, nor the various
endowments that serve him as aids to interpreting this evidence,
can give the historian his criterion of historical truth. That criterion is the idea of history itself: the idea of an imaginary
picture of the past. That idea is, in Cartesian language, innate; in
Kantian language, *a priori*. It is not a chance product of psychological causes; it is an idea which every man possesses as part of
the furniture of his mind, and discovers himself to possess in so
far as he becomes conscious of what it is to have a mind. (p.
248).

What keeps the "self-dependent, self-determining, and self-justifying" (p.
249) historical imagination from falling into skepticism is the discipline of
history itself. Although Collingwood was not entirely clear about this, it is
the structure of the discipline, and what this discipline considers good research practices, reliable evidence, and the like, that prevents the individual
knower/historian from sliding off into the *mere* play of imagination. And
Collingwood defended the notion of the autonomy of history precisely to
preserve its status as a communal enterprise (Goldstein, 1970).

Collingwood's "furniture of the mind," Ricoeur's mimesis, and White's
tropes all are devices that prevent the slide of history into anarchy. Yet they
capture the problem of historical knowledge precisely in their acknowledgment of the impossibility of a history based on a factual, scientific, or
positivistic language capable of the kinds of epistemological checks and
balances available to the scientific community. This working out of the
relationship between the languages of science and history and their respective tasks and their practitioners cuts across the 20th century. Indeed, in
some respects, it marks the reaction against 19th century positivist historians,
and is already present in such diverse thinkers as Max Weber and Isaiah
Berlin. It was the latter who noted that the difference between "factual
knowledge" and "understanding" lay precisely in the point that understanding "makes intelligible that celebrated identity in difference . . . in virtue of
which we conceive of one and the same outlook as being expressed in
diverse manifestations" (1960/1997b, p. 53). The subject matter of history
"involves a 'thick' texture of criss-crossing, constantly changing and melting
conscious and unconscious beliefs and assumptions some of which it is
impossible and all of which it is difficult to formulate, on which, nevertheless, our rational views and rational acts are founded, and, indeed, which they
exhibit or articulate" (p. 55).

On these accounts, the historian can be likened to the technically
skilled violinist who finds herself confronted with a musical score that does
not contain all of the parts of a piece of music, nor all of the notes. Instead
she must take a few musical ideas and suggestions, partial movements, and

incomplete sections and improvise a performance. Obviously such playing requires not only creativity and flexibility but also a sufficient degree of technical skill, musicianship, and an appreciation of what the audience expects. Like the historian, there is indeed a standard of skill that is required before one deserves the label "musician." However, playing in ensembles of two or more now creates special problems for our string player, as would any occasion wherein the music must be coordinated. An orchestra would, by traditional standards, find the task impossible. It would be a fundamentally contested enterprise.

As appealing as the metaphor might be, it is not sufficiently radical. The generally modernist tenor of the preceding articulations of narrative versions of history constitutes a codification of insights already present in the work of Wilhelm Dilthey, who argued that lived experience is mediated through the imagination as well as the sociocultural practices of the historical world (Makkreel, 1992; Mos, 1996). They are located in the debates concerning the distinction between the *Geisteswissenschaften* and *Naturwisschenschaften* of the latter decades of the 20th century. On this account, it is particularly difficult to understand the attacks of historians such as Gertrude Himmelfarb on authors such as Hayden White, whom she (mistakenly, in my view) identifies as "the leading postmodernist philosopher of history" (1999, p. 76). According to Himmelfarb, White and others of the narrative persuasion construe all of history as "aesthetic and philosophical, its only meaning or 'reality' . . . being that which the historian chooses to give it in accord with his own sensibility and disposition" (p. 76). Lumping together all manner of historians who eschew the "facts" of history under the label "postmodernist," Himmelfarb eventually comes to console herself with the thought that "postmodernist history is of little importance in the profession at large" (p. 85), and that "one can foresee a desire to return to a more objective and integrated, less divisive and particularistic history" (p. 87).

As an example of the kinds of debates that continue to preoccupy (English-speaking) historians, this one is typical. Frequently falling into a division between an objectivist discourse and an array of possibilities that adhere to some or other version of narrative or postmodernist conceptions of history, these debates do not move either set of participants. Instead, they are often construed as boundary maintenance by historians, as Himmelfarb makes clear with her reference to the "profession at large." Even such sensitive and otherwise more careful critics such as Elizabeth Fox-Genovese admits that the postmodernist repudiation of authority is itself an outgrowth of the antiauthoritarian proclivities in liberal modernism (Fox-Genovese, 1999). As a recourse to this antiauthoritarianism, she argues for a need to protect the "standards of our craft, which include the *honest* use of evidence and the continuing attempt to reach *fair* and nonpartisan judgments" (1999, p. 54, emphasis added). Are postmodernists dishonest? Unfair?

It is interesting that the major preoccupation in these critiques of postmodernism concerns the need to protect the discipline of history, particularly as it depends on public support in the form of the financing of public education and the need to generate research grants from public agencies and, secondarily, a generally receptive public for historical works. Perhaps this only reflects the peculiar situation of post-secondary education in the United States. At the same time, however, theory (or perhaps *Theory*) has become the label by which all new forms of historiography are to be distinguished from the stolid suburban version of traditional history that now has such a phalanx of defenders. As Fox-Genovese and Lasch-Quinn have it, "the fashionable preoccupation with theory distracts historians from the intrinsic interest and significance of their work" (1999, p. 3). This is echoed by Alan Kors, who claims that "fields should be defined by subjects and questions, not by theoretical commitments" (1999, p. 16). Theory is thus anything that gets in the way of the analysis of primary sources and the "historical sensibility" that would recount the important events of the past. Indeed, Eugene Genovese (1999) claims that "contemporary academic history is being systematically gutted" (p. 6) and that the privileging of race, class, and gender in historical studies is nothing short of McCarthyism (p. 7).

Notwithstanding the rhetorical excesses of these debates, I maintain that there is no escape from theory for even the most modest of traditional historians. For what the recent debates have brought to the fore is that no historical account is ever innocent and free from the business of claims making. Histories require representations of action: no representation of action is free from the author's representational strategies (however conceived). Hence, no matter how much some historians wish to return to a less combative and more traditional form of historical narrative, it is inconceivable that such writing can be done without some explication of precisely what notion of history it is that is being defended. The metaphorical violinist must account for herself by indicating whether she intends to play classical or jazz violin and what kind of piece is on the program. Only the writing of popular history may be immune to such worries, but it is unlikely that within the academy that debates about the foundations of history will abate anytime soon.

HISTORIOGRAPHY IN AND OF PSYCHOLOGY

Disciplinary history is history of a rather specialized sort. Unlike most forms of political, military, social, and other forms of conventional history, the history of psychology sometimes fits under the rubric of intellectual history, or it is simply the history of a discipline strictly for consumption by those interested or engaged in the discipline (although, see Smith, 1997 for an exception). In addition, the history of psychology has served a pedagogical function for the latter half of the 20th century, inscribed as a standard course in many undergraduate curricula and included as a necessary component in most North American clinical training programs. The peculiar status of the undergraduate course in the history of psychology has been responsible, in part, for the development and maintenance of divisions and sections of the history of psychology in major psychological organizations. Many psychologists teach the course in history, but only a minority of those actually engages in historical research.

The history of psychology, as Danziger (1994) so clearly demonstrated, is no longer written by "insiders" to the discipline alone. Such insider histories tended to be largely celebratory rather than critical, and they have had the function of serving up appropriate questions for consumption by students. In addition, insider histories have made a science of history itself by denying the possibility of alternative histories. But Danziger (1994) noted that there was more than one way to be an "outsider." With the rapid disappearance of a central or core mission in the discipline, along with the global diffusion of psychology, the history of psychology no longer tells a single story. While one may be an outsider with respect to psychology's scientific identity, one can be an insider with respect to its professional identity. This, along with the impact of critical feminist studies of science, has led to considerable heterogeneity in the constitution of contemporary histories of psychology.

Critical or "outsider" histories have another function, however. Traditional accounts of the history of psychology have not only been criticized as "celebratory," but they mask the deeply contested nature of the discipline and its boundaries. What constitutes the subject matter of psychology in the first instance? The very diversity of the discipline and its history in the 20th century indicates that core questions remain unanswered. How to conceptualize behavior? Cognition? Emotion? The self? Social Interaction? Various historical accounts of research practices in the 20th century have told the story of a loosely related set of research practices often driven by pragmatic and social considerations (e.g., Danziger, 1990; Morawski, 1988; Richards, 1996). These histories have revised traditional accounts that emphasize the linear progression of ideas and research promulgated by uniquely inspired individuals.

By refusing to honor the parochial nature of the discipline, the historian can ask questions about which practices and concurrent theorizing made possible the claims for disciplinary singularity in the first place. Psychology has successfully created for itself a stage upon which to showcase various objects and events (such as cognition, behavior, and the like) whose constitution is carefully managed behind the scenes. Histories of psychology can critically articulate this stage management, or they can act as colorful props for the show itself. By refusing to do the latter, history is deeply engaged in theoretical work, namely, demonstrating how psychology's objects of investigation are rhetorical accomplishments as well as moments of great invention. This is not mere critical history or an engagement in deconstructing accounts created by psychologists. Instead, it is driven by alternative conceptions of psychological theory and subjectivity. The artificial separation of historical and theoretical moments in psychology serves to support the status quo and genuinely new and creative endeavors in the discipline always begin with a revision of a historical picture that has become otherwise problematic and contested. Historical accounts serve theoretical ends, just as theoretical accounts are reliant on a particular historical picture.

What recent critical histories make explicit is their reliance on alternative conceptions of psychology. They reject, for the most part, the picture of psychological reality that constitutes the framework of what gets called "the mainstream" of the discipline. In this sense, they are not only critical but remain marginal, for they question the manner in which the mainstream has built up the conceptions it has. Embedded in critical histories are alternative conceptions of psychological life, research, and disciplinary activity. But this is not always explicit, nor is it meant to be. Rather, alternative histories often leave its readers with a sense that the present need not be what it is, that the historical contingencies that led to, say, the adoption of particular research practices were not inevitable, that the development of certain ideas favored certain groups or individuals, and that other ways of proceeding were and are possible.

The most obvious recent example of this kind of history is seen in the impact of feminism on historical studies in general, as well as in psychology. Barbara Duden, who published an extended account of the way in which women spoke about their bodies to doctors over 250 years ago (Duden, 1991), can simultaneously bring such considerations to bear on contemporary conflicts concerning pregnancy and the unborn (Duden, 1993). Caroline Bynum's work has focused on the importance of flesh and gender in the high Middle Ages, examining how partition and putrefaction were related to notions of redemption (Bynum, 1991). Recasting various arguments about the Middle Ages, Bynum at the same time demonstrates the importance of gender and the body in spiritual matters. Equally forceful has been the impact of feminist histories in psychology, beginning initially with the important exercise of placing women's contributions to psychology on the agenda (e.g., Scarborough and Furumoto, 1987; Russo and Denmark, 1987). This presaged a range of contributions to histories of psychology that has had the effect of undermining the linear narrative of a progressive and cumulative generation of knowledge by great men. Indeed, as Morawski (1994) argued in her history of feminist efforts to refashion psychology, "by heeding their history, feminist psychologists can move to refashion both their sense-making narratives and their investigative practices. Self-reflection may well lead us to find ourselves not quite anywhere, yet en route to somewhere exciting" (p. 15).

Other examples of critical histories that have come to present alternative accounts of the origin and potential direction of psychological theory include histories of clinical psychology (e.g., Cushman, 1995), social psychology (Lubek, 2000), behaviorism (Mills, 1998), and developmental psychology (Bradley, 1989) among others. In the remainder of this chapter, I would like to concentrate on one of these, namely, the enduring dispute over the history of the "crisis" in social psychology, and how this is to be understood. The history of social psychology in particular demonstrates the manner in which historical accounts play an important role in defending the disciplinary status quo or in undermining it in favor of some other conception of the social.

HISTORICAL WOES OF SOCIAL PSYCHOLOGY

In the 1960s, a number of social psychologists in the United States began to wonder aloud if their field had not made some fundamental mistakes in its theoretical goals, the ethics of its research enterprises, or the way in which it was conducting research. Later these questions would raise more fundamental, epistemological concerns, but initially the first rumblings of the self-proclaimed "crisis" concerned methods and ethics. Orne (1962) noted that "demand characteristics" might account for some of the findings of human experimental research, and shortly thereafter Rosenthal (1966) published a major work on "experimenter effects." Both concepts emphasized the indirect influence of experimenter's expectations and situational demands on the outcome of research. Meanwhile, the questions that had been publicly raised by Milgram's obedience studies continued to bother some social psychologists, and in 1967, Kenneth Ring published a scathing critique of the "fun-and-games" approach to social psychological research. As a graduate student, Ring had participated in research with Festinger and others at Minnesota, and when he moved to a teaching post, his interactions with students led him to have serious doubts about high-impact experiments (Lubek and Stam, 1995). His paper was one of several crucial to the onset of the "crisis" in social psychology (see also Gergen, 1973; Sampson, 1977), although within ten to fifteen years, some of its participants and most social psychologists would, as Aronson did at an APA convention in the mid-1980s, declare the crisis over.

This period in North American social psychology's history has been the subject of many recent revisions and extensive discussions. Notable by their absence, however, is the inclusion of most practicing social psychologists except as commentators who regret that this episode ever occurred. For example, Jones (1985, 1998) dismissed worries articulated during the crisis as a "minor perturbation" (1985, p. 100) and a symptom of the "widespread need for self-flagellation" (1985, p. 99) among social psychologists. Other social psychologists, such as Zimbardo (1999), are equally dismissive. Of the high-impact experimental tradition in social psychology (what Ring criticized as the "fun and games" approach), he said, "that tradition is now dead and not mourned by those who hastened its demise, a cabal of some cognitive social psychologists, human subjects research committees, Protestants, and female social psychologists" (pp. 137–138). Even those sympathetic to a more nuanced historical account join in, such as Jay Jackson (1988), who said of the "crisis" that the "lack of agreement was almost total: in the targets of criticism, the perspectives, interests, and purposes of the critics, and in the interpretations of and responses to the crisis. It is problematic how much understanding was generated by this paroxysm of self-analysis" (p. 83). All of these authors note that the effect of the crisis was to change some institutional arrangements, but that it had no effect on the theories of social psychologists (see also Rodrigues and Levine, 1999).

Critical historians who revisit social psychology's recent past, however, have very different engagements with this period in social psychology's history. First, their history of social psychology begins with themes that indicate trouble from the outset. Social psychological experimentation is not taken for granted and instead has been contextualized and located in the history of 20th-century social science by a number of authors (e.g., Cherry, 1995; Danziger, 2000; Good, 2000; Stam, Radtke, and Lubek, 2000). One way, then, to account for the crisis is to locate "the troubles" as one moment in a discipline continually uncertain about its status as an experimental science, a science that at any moment threatens to become a carefully designed form of dramaturgy. Second, the radical divisions between social psychology in psychology and those related commitments in sociology are deeply problematized in critical histories. Whereas Jones (1985, 1998) attempted to downplay the relationship and argued that experimental social psychology was a uniquely psychological endeavor, Good (2000), for example, has argued that the boundaries of social psychology were historically seen as "fluid, contingent, local, and contestable, reflecting the thematic preoccupations, disciplinary origins, and meta-theoretical commitments of social psychologists, of the parent disciplines, and of those who represent disciplinary practices" (p. 383).

Most important, critical historians see the crisis as an opportunity rather than a nuisance or a temporary aberration. The break, however temporary, in the consensus of the majority in the field, far from representing a "lack of agreement" that was "almost total" (Jackson, 1988. p. 83), was a necessary reaction to the artificially created and unproductive hegemony of an experimental method in a field whose original ideals had been articulated by Lewin, but whose appeal to the "reality of social phenomena" (Lewin, 1949/1999, p. 29) had been repudiated. Indeed, there was agreement among the critics that (1) methods in social psychology led to problems understanding and interpreting the results of experiments, (2) ethical concerns needed to be taken more seriously by social psychologists, and (3) the results of social psychological experiments were often artificial if not artifactual and not applicable to complex social problems. The outcome of these critical moves gradually led to a realization among some critics in the 1980s and beyond that the foundations of social psychological experimentation are either false or nonexistent, and that the enterprise needs to start on some other epistemological foundations (e.g., Gergen, 1982).

Although I take responsibility for the above description, there are variations on these themes in many current historical accounts of post–World War II social psychology (e.g., Collier, Minton, and Reynolds, 1991; Danziger, 2000; Lubek, 1993; Parker, 1989; Stam, Radtke, and Lubek, 2000). Each of these accounts challenges the standard view of the discipline, its origin myths, its self-proclaimed areas of expertise, and each is at pains to contextualize the appearance of social psychology. Nonetheless, at the same time, this is not just a negative project. Aside from their obvious deconstruction of the boundaries of social psychology, these histories are also engaged in a form of "what if " narration. Implicit in their accounts is a version of the social that while not always clearly articulated works as an unspoken possibility for social psychology. Sometimes this possibility is obvious in the framework used to articulate the history. For example, MacMartin and Winston's (2000) account of the rhetoric of social psychological experimentation is derived from a discourse analysis perspective. This is an established alternative approach to social psychological questions that has produced a substantial literature and following, especially in the United Kingdom. Other historians speak out of a need to rearticulate social phenomena that are neither antithetical to an autonomous or emergent social world or a psychology of persons that is thoroughly embedded in that world. In revisiting the Milgram obedience research, for example, Stam, Lubek, and Radtke (1998) proposed that one way to understand this research is to understand both the laughter that erupts among participants in Milgram's original filmed version of the obedience research as well as the laughter that is now routinely heard in undergraduate showings of that film. The laughter is a display of both discomfort and an acknowledgment of the staged nature of the events. In that sense, it is more social than the world constructed by Milgram in his experiments, a world that in the end becomes a display of little more than the experimenter's cleverness and scientism.

While neither articulating a clear alternative to social psychology nor acceding to the hegemony of the mainstream, such histories continually remind us not just of what was done but also of what is important and what may yet be. Whatever is produced by the research community as new and relevant research will always define the limits and content of a field. If boundary maintenance serves political, social, and institutional purposes, then historical argument alone is unlikely to dislodge it. Nonetheless, the continual critical articulation of histories of research practices, ideational shifts, and productivity reminds the academy of the possibility of dialogues on the nature of the social that are far from settled.

CONCLUSION

The history of social psychology appears only remotely related to the questions of the philosophy of history with which this chapter began. I want to bring two points to bear on this question: first, histories of psychology, even as disciplinary histories, are not immune from any of the general conceptual issues raised in the first section of this chapter and, second, their articulation can only remind us that the problems of history and psychology are, foundationally, very similar.

Histories of psychology must, in some fundamental way, be narrated. They are dependent on the "trivia" of the discipline as a history of a military campaign is dependent on the remnants of the campaign. But this turns out to be nonfoundational for historiography itself. Every disciplinary history has a narrative structure, even if it is technical and obscure, for the artifacts of a discipline do not tell us how we should evaluate the discipline itself, its relationship to neighboring disciplines, its achievements, and so on. All of these are accomplishments of the historian who narrates with the tools of the trade: tropes (on White's account), mimesis (on Ricoeur's account), and so on. Contestation is, on this view, inevitable and to be welcomed. It refuses to take as given the historical record, even if that record is simply the written remains of the subject matter, for that record was the outcome of multiple and intersecting social agents, engaged in various institutional activities and subject to the mores and norms of the day, whose ambitions, hopes, and fears are not unlike those of other social agents in similar institutions.

Psychology is also not unlike history. It was Collingwood who believed, in his arguments with the psychology of his day, that the only true science of mind must be history. An ahistorical, scientific psychology can in the end only be a physiological science that studies sensations and feelings (Connelly and Costal, 2000). Not only are historical studies built up out of artifacts that do not speak, so is a psychology of mind dependent on artifacts that require a psychological narrative. Much of contemporary theory in human psychology is caught up in this dilemma. It informs not only postmodern, discursive, and feminist psychologies, to name only a few, but has implications for how psychology conceptualizes its very subject matter. History is inevitable on this account, and the history of the individual person is not unlike the history of the story that is used to tell that individual history. They are both subject to the reflexive properties of the tools used to tell the history, as well as the historian's situatedness in time and place.

Is the historian, then, still like our metaphorical violinist? Or is the violinist herself to be understood only with respect to the tradition in which she originates, carrying the tradition of her teachers and through them, her teachers' teachers. If, as I said above, the metaphor is not sufficiently radical, how might it be revised to suit our account of the historian? Our violinist plays both out of herself and out of her tradition. When our violinist performs, she must take the musical ideas and create a score as she proceeds. To satisfy her role as a metaphorical historian, she must discover, to her horror, perhaps, that the musical ideas are not only sketchy, but that there is no composer.

NOTES

1. See Jenkins (1995) for an extended discussion of the utopian character of Hayden White's work.
2. There are versions of postmodern historiography that are clearly more willing to break down the distinction between history and other fields than the narrative versions I discuss here, including some versions of the New Historicism (e.g., Veeser, 1989). The originator of the term "new historicism," Stephen Greenblatt (1989) prefers the term "poetics of culture" to describe a historiography that includes aspects of art and culture as part of an intelligible network of signs. And critics of postmodernist history frequently count Foucault among the worst offenders of historical good sense, although it is not always clear if they object to Foucault's historiography per se (which, after all, can be quite conventional) or to the genealogical analysis in which it is framed.

REFERENCES

Berlin, I. (1997a). The hedgehog and the fox. In H. Hardy & R. Hausheer (Eds.), *The proper study of mankind: An anthology of essays* (pp. 436–498). New York, NY: Farrar, Straus, and Giroux. (Original work published 1953)

Berlin, I. (1997b). The concept of scientific history. In H. Hardy & R. Hausheer (Eds.), *The proper study of mankind: An anthology of essays* (pp. 17–58). New York, NY: Farrar, Straus, and Giroux. (Original work published 1960)

Bradley, B. S. (1989). *Visions of infancy*. Cambridge, UK: Polity Press.

Bynum, C. W. (1991). *Fragmentation and redemption: Essays on gender and the human body in medieval religion*. New York, NY: Zone.

Cherry, F. (1995). *The "stubborn particulars" of social psychology*. London, UK: Routledge.

Collier, G., Minton, H., & Reynolds, G. (1991). *Currents of thought in American social psychology*. New York, NY: Oxford.

Collingwood, R. G. (1924). *Speculum mentis*. Oxford, UK: Clarendon.

Collingwood, R. G. (1946). *The idea of history*. Oxford, UK: Clarendon.

Collingwood, R. G. (1965). *Essays in the philosophy of history* (W. Debbins, Ed.). Austin, TX: University of Texas Press.

Connelly, J. & Costal, A. (2000). R. G. Collingwood and the idea of a historical psychology. *Theory & Psychology, 10*, 147–170.

Cushman, P. (1995). *Constructing the self, constructing America: A cultural history of psychotherapy*. Reading, MA: Addison-Wesley.

Danziger, K. (1990). *Constructing the subject: Historical origins of psychological research*. Cambridge, UK: Cambridge University Press.

Danziger, K. (1994). Does the history of psychology have a future? *Theory & Psychology,* *4,* 467–484.

Danziger, K. (2000). Making social psychology experimental: A conceptual history, 1920–1970. *Journal of the History of the Behavioral Sciences, 36,* 329–347.

Duden, B. (1991). *The woman beneath the skin: A doctor's patients in eighteenth-century Germany* (T. Dunlop, Trans). Cambridge, MA: Harvard University Press.

Duden, B. (1993). *Disembodying women: Perspectives on pregnancy and the unborn.* Cambridge, MA: Harvard University Press.

Fox-Genovese, E. (1999). History in a postmodern world. In E. Fox-Genovese & E. Lasch-Quinn (Eds.), *Reconstructing history* (pp. 40–55). New York, NY: Routledge.

Fox-Genovese, E., & Lasch-Quinn, E. (Eds.). (1999). *Reconstructing history.* New York, NY: Routledge.

Genovese, E. D. (1999). A new departure. In E. Fox-Genovese & E. Lasch-Quinn (Eds.), *Reconstructing history* (pp. 6–8). New York, NY: Routledge.

Gergen, K. (1973). Social psychology as history. *Journal of Personality and Social Psychology, 26,* 309–320.

Gergen, K. (1982). *Toward transformation in social knowledge.* New York, NY: Springer-Verlag.

Goldstein, L. J. (1970). Collingwood's theory of historical knowing. *History and Theory, 9,* 3–36.

Good, J. M. M. (2000). Disciplining social psychology: A case study of boundary relations in the history of the human sciences. *Journal of the History of the Behavioral Sciences, 36,* 383–403.

Greenblatt, S. (1989). Towards a poetics of culture. In H. A. Veeser (Ed.), *The new historicism* (pp. 1–14). New York, NY: Routledge.

Himmelfarb, G. (1999). Postmodernist history. In E. Fox-Genovese & E. Lasch-Quinn (Eds.), *Reconstructing history* (pp. 71–93). New York, NY: Routledge.

Jackson, J. (1988). *Social psychology, past and present: An integrative orientation.* Hillsdale, NJ: Erlbaum.

Jenkins, K. (1995). *On "What is history?": From Carr and Elton to Rorty and White.* London, UK: Routledge.

Jones, E. E. (1985). Major developments in social psychology during the past five decades. In G. Lindzey & E. Aronson (Eds.), *The handbook of social psychology* (3rd Ed., Vol. 1, pp. 47–108). New York, NY: Random House/Erlbaum.

Jones, E. E. (1998). Major developments in five decades of social psychology. In D. T. Gilbert, S. T. Fiske, & G. Lindzey (Eds.), *The handbook of social psychology* (4th Ed., Vol. 1, pp. 3–57). New York, NY: Oxford University Press.

Kors, A. C. (1999). The future of history in an increasingly unified world. In E. Fox-Genovese & E. Lasch-Quinn (Eds.), *Reconstructing history* (pp. 12–17). New York, NY: Routledge.

Lewin, K. (1999). Cassirer's philosophy of science and the social sciences. In M. Gold (Ed.), *The complete social scientist: A Kurt Lewin reader* (pp. 23–36). Washington, DC: American Psychological Association. (Original work published 1949)

Lubek, I. (1993). Social psychology textbooks: An historical and social psychological analysis of conceptual filtering, consensus formation, career gatekeeping and conservatism in science. In H. J. Stam, L. P. Mos, W. Thorngate, & B. Kaplan (Eds.), *Recent trends in theoretical psychology* (Vol. 3, pp. 359–378). New York, NY: Springer-Verlag.

Lubek, I. (Ed.). (2000). Special Issue: Re-engaging the history of social psychology. *Journal of the History of the Behavioral Sciences, 36,* 319–528.

Lubek, I., & Stam, H. J. (1995). Ludicro-experimentation in social psychology: Sober scientific versus playful prescriptions. In I. Lubek, R. van Hezewijk, G. Pheterson, & C. Tolman (Eds.), *Trends and issues in theoretical psychology* (pp. 171–180). New York, NY: Springer.

MacMartin, C., & Winston, A. S. (2000). The rhetoric of experimental social psychology, 1930–1960: From caution to enthusiasm. *Journal of the History of the Behavioral Sciences, 36,* 349–364.

Makkreel, R. A. (1992). *Dilthey: Philosopher of the human studies.* Princeton, NJ: Princeton University Press.

Mills, J. A. (1998). *Control: A history of behavioral psychology.* New York, NY: New York University Press.

Mink, L. O. (1978). Narrative form as a cognitive instrument. In R. H. Canary & H. Kozicki (Eds.), *The writing of history: Literary from and historical understanding* (pp. 129–149). Madison, WI.: University of Wisconsin Press.

Morawski, J. G. (1994). *Practicing feminisms, reconstructing psychology: Notes on a liminal science.* Ann Arbor, MI.: University of Michigan Press.

Morawski, J. G. (Ed.). (1988). *The rise of experimentation in American psychology.* New Haven, CT: Yale University Press.

Mos, L. P. (1996). Immanent critique of experience: Dilthey's hermeneutics. In C. Tolman, F. Cherry, R. van Hezewijk, & I. Lubek (Eds.), *Problems of theoretical psychology* (pp. 368–377). Toronto, ON: Captus.

Orne, M. T. (1962). On the social psychology of the psychological experiment: With particular reference to demand characteristics and their implications. *American Psychologist, 17,* 776–783.

Parker, I. (1989). *The crisis in modern social psychology, and how to end it.* London, UK: Routledge.

Poovey, M. (1998). *A history of the modern fact: Problems of knowledge in the sciences of wealth and society.* Chicago, IL: University of Chicago Press.

Richards, G. (1996). *Putting psychology in its place: An introduction from a critical historical perspective.* London, UK: Routledge.

Ricoeur, P. (1984). *Time and narrative* (Vol. 1., K. McLaughlin & D. Pellauer, Trans.). Chicago, IL: University of Chicago Press.

Ricoeur, P. (1988). *Time and narrative* (Vol. 3., K. Blamey & D. Pellauer, Trans.). Chicago, IL: University of Chicago Press.

Ring, K. (1967). Experimental social psychology: Some sober questions about some frivolous values. *Journal of Experimental Social Psychology, 3,* 113–123.

Rodrigues, A., & Levine, R. V. (Eds.). (1999). *Reflections on 100 years of experimental social psychology.* New York, NY: Basic.

Rosenthal, R. (1966). *Experimenter effects in behavioral research.* New York, NY: Appleton-Century-Crofts.

Russo, N. F., & Denmark, F. L. (1987). Contributions of women to psychology. *Annual Review of Psychology, 38,* 279–98.

Sampson, E. (1977). Psychology and the American ideal. *Journal of Personality and Social Psychology, 35,* 767–782.

Scarborough, E., & Furumoto, L. (1987). *Untold lives: The first generation of American women psychologists.* New York, NY: Columbia University Press.

Smith, R. (1997). *The Norton history of the human sciences.* New York, NY: Norton.

Stam, H. J., Lubek, I., & Radtke, H. L. (1998). Repopulating social psychology texts: Disembodied "subjects" and embodied subjectivity. In B. M Bayer & J. Shotter (Eds.), *Reconstructing the psychological subject: Bodies, practices and technologies* (pp. 153–186). London, UK: Sage.

Stam, H. J., Radtke, H. L., & Lubek, I. (2000). Strains in experimental social psychology: A textual analysis of the development of experimentation in social psychology. *Journal of the History of the Behavioral Sciences, 36,* 365–382.

Veeser, H. A. (Ed.). (1989). *The new historicism.* New York, NY: Routledge.

White, H. (1973). *Metahistory.* Baltimore, MD: John Hopkins University Press.

White, H. (1978). *Tropics of discourse.* Baltimore, MD: John Hopkins University Press.

Zimbardo, P. G. (1999). Experimental social psychology: Behaviorism with minds and matters. In A. Rodrigues & R. V. Levine (Eds.) *Reflections on 100 years of experimental social psychology.* (pp. 135–157). New York, NY: Basic.

CONTRIBUTORS

Colin M. Burchfield is a graduate student at Brigham Young University. He teaches courses in clinical and personality psychology.

Kurt Danziger, is Professor Emeritus of Psychology at York University. Author of numerous articles and books including *Naming the Mind: How Psychology Found Its Language* and *Constructing the Subject: Historical Origins of Psychological Research.*

Amy Fisher Smith is Assistant Professor of Psychology at University of Dallas. Her training is in clinical psychology, and she has a wide background and experience with several therapeutic modalities and populations including inpatient psychiatric, sexual abuse offender, substance abuse, and domestic violence. Currently, she is Member-at-Large of the Division of Theoretical and Philosophical Psychology of the American Psychological Association. Her publications have focused on the area of psychotherapy and values.

Scott Greer is Assistant Professor of Psychology at University of Prince Edward Island. Recent publications include "Freud's 'Bad Conscience': The Case of Nietzsche's Genealogy" in the *Journal of the History of the Behavioral Sciences.* Dr. Greer is also "Chair-elect" (2000–03) for the Section on History and Philosophy of Psychology, Canadian Psychological Association.

Darryl B. Hill is Assistant Professor of Psychology at Concordia University. He is interested in macrosocial influences on self and identity, especially gender and sex identities in the postmodern context, and has published on the connections between theory and practice in social psychology in the *Journal of Theoretical and Philosophical Psychology.* He is past Assistant Editor of the *History and Philosophy of Psychology Bulletin* of the Section on History and Philosophy of Psychology, Canadian Psychological Association.

Meredith M. Kimball is Professor of Women's Studies and Psychology at Simon Fraser University. Her teaching interests include adult development and aging, theories of gender, and history of feminisms. She has published in the areas of gender similarities and differences in achievement, gender and math, and theories of gender similarities and differences. Her current project is a study of women in the history of psychology and psychoanalysis. She has published a paper on Bertha Pappenheim and is just beginning work on a study of the work of Mary Whiton Calkins.

Michael J. Kral is Associate Professor of Psychology, University of Windsor, where he is a past Director of Clinical Psychology Training. His interests include cultural psychology, kinship and social change, theory and method, and well-being among Inuit and First Nations. He is co-editor of *Handbook for Psychologists and Psychological Service Providers* and *Suicide in Canada,* and past editor of *History and Philosophy of Psychology Bulletin* of the Section on History and Philosophy of Psychology, Canadian Psychological Association.

Jack Martin is the Burnaby Mountain Endowed Professor at Simon Fraser University. He is author of articles in *American Psychologist, Theory and Psychology,* and the *Journal of Theoretical and Philosophical Psychology,* and author of *Psychology and The Question of Agency* (with J. Sugarman and J. Thompson), and *The Psychology of Human Possibility and Constraint* (with J. Sugarman).

Karen M. Seeley is Adjunct Lecturer in Anthropology at Columbia University and Adjunct Assistant Professor of Psychology at Barnard College. She teaches courses in interdisciplinary psychology and anthropology, and with special interest in culture & mental health. She is author of *Cultural Psychotherapy: Working With Culture in the Clinical Encounter.*

Brent D. Slife is Professor of Psychology at Brigham Young University. As a Fellow of several organizations, including the American Psychological Association, he recently served as the President of the Division of Theoretical and Philosophical Psychology and the Editor of the *Journal of Theoretical and Philosophical Psychology* for almost a decade. He has authored over 100 articles and books, with three new books: *Critical Issues in Psychotherapy: Translating New Ideas into Practice* (2001), *Psychotherapists as Crypto-Missionaries: Managing Values in "Post" Modern Era* (due 2003), and *Developing Critical Thinking in Psychology* (in press).

Henderikus J. Stam is a Professor in the Theory Program in the Department of Psychology at the University of Calgary. His research is focused on the history of early twentieth-century North American psychology and the history of the brief flourishing of Phenomenological Psychology in Europe. In addition, he has published on foundational problems in psychology. He is the founding and current editor of the journal "Theory and Psychology."

Jeff Sugarman is Assistant Professor of Education at Simon Fraser University. He is co-author (with J. Martin) of *The Psychology of Human Possibility and Constraint* (SUNY, 1999) and (with J. Martin and J. Thompson) *Psychology and the Question of Agency.* He is a Fellow of the American Psychological Association and co-recipient (with J. Martin) of the American Psychological Association George Miller Award for an Outstanding Recent Article in General Psychology (2001).

Charles W. Tolman is Emeritus Fellow in the Centre for Studies in Religion and Society at the University of Victoria. He is author of *Psychology, Society, and Subjectivity: An Introduction to German Critical Psychology,* editor of *Positivism in Psychology: Historical and Contemporary Problems* and *Critical Psychology: Contributions to An Historical Science of the Subject,* co-editor of *Problems of Theoretical Psychology* (with F. Cherry and I. Lubek). He is past Chair of the Section on History and Philosophy of Psychology, Canadian Psychological Association.

CONTRIBUTORS